P9-BJU-108

BLACKS WHO
STOLE THEMSELVES

BLACKS WHO STOLE THEMSELVES

Advertisements for Runaways

in the *Pennsylvania Gazette*,

1728–1790

Billy G. Smith and
Richard Wojtowicz

uPP

UNIVERSITY OF PENNSYLVANIA PRESS

Philadelphia

Library of Congress Cataloging-in-Publication Data

Blacks who stole themselves: advertisements for runaways in the
Pennsylvania gazette, 1728–1790/[compiled by] Billy G. Smith and
Richard Wojtowicz.
     p.   cm.
   Bibliography: p.
   Includes indexes.
   ISBN 0-8122-8145-4.
     1. Fugitive slaves—United States—History—18th century—Sources.
   2. Slavery—United States—History—18th century—Sources.
   3. United States—History—Colonial period, ca. 1600–1775—Sources.
   4. Afro-Americans—History—To 1863—Sources. I. Smith, Billy
   Gordon. II. Wojtowicz, Richard. III. Pennsylvania gazette.
   E443.B525   1989
   973'.0496—dc19   88-32636
                                                              CIP

To my mother, Betty Smith, and to the
memory of my father, Jack G. Smith
and
To my parents, Lottie and Joseph,
and to my wife, Dianna Wojtowicz

Contents

Acknowledgments

This collection of documents treats an extraordinary group of people who struggled to maintain their dignity under extremely difficult conditions. From Moses Grimes, who ran away repeatedly, from Shadwell, who was identified and apprehended for his fondness for walking on his hands, and from Caesar, who escaped even though both his legs were cut off at the knee, we can learn a great deal about the best of what it means to be human. It is those men, women, and children who fought for their self-respect that we want to acknowledge by this volume. In more practical terms, Jean R. Soderlund and Gary B. Nash offered valuable comments, Ronald Schultz generously lent us dozens of microfilm reels, Adrienne Mayor drew several illustrations, and Peter Wood first used the title of this book to describe runaways in South Carolina. Financial support from Montanans on a New Trac for Science and from the Research/Creativity program at Montana State University enabled us to hire several research assistants: Patrick Caufield and Stacy Dimaggio located and transcribed hundreds of advertisements. Finally, we especially appreciate our wives, Michelle Maskiell and Dianna Wojtowicz, for their unfailing assistance, understanding, and support while we were engaged with this study.

Introduction

MONTAIGNE WROTE THAT HISTORIANS RUIN history because "they chew our meat for us." While the analysis of scholars does not necessarily destroy history, non-specialists can greatly benefit by interpreting historical sources on their own. This collection of newspaper advertisements for runaway slaves should enable readers to chew primary sources themselves and, thus, to taste more fully the varied flavors of eighteenth-century American slavery and those who fled it. These valuable notices, all taken from the Philadelphia newspaper owned for decades by Benjamin Franklin, present a firsthand view of history, portraying the characteristics of escapees as well as the attitudes of their masters, supplying details about everyday life, and creating a human dimension for the monumental historical events of the period.[1] The documents focus on a group of black Americans who declared their personal independence in a direct and forceful manner even as white Americans initially rebelled against the threat posed to their own liberties by the English government and subsequently struggled to define their rights during the Constitutional era.

Despite the great quantity and high quality of scholarly studies, slavery remains one of the most enigmatic aspects of our past. Most of us have difficulty imagining what it was like to be a slave or a master, understanding how owners viewed their human property, or realizing the ways many blacks resisted. Of course, no simple answer exists for these and the myriad of related questions about the lives of millions of people enmeshed in the institution of unfree labor. As always, human experience varied tremendously from person to person. Even where those experiences can be grouped into categories, many of them are best understood on a case-by-case basis. These published notices, mostly written by masters offering rewards for the apprehension and return of their property, chronicle the stories of hundreds of blacks who attempted to escape their bondage.[2]

Besides noting individual differences, we must recognize that slavery varied over time and space.[3] The great majority of historical studies of the "peculiar institution" have concentrated on the southern states during the nineteenth century. But to comprehend fully the heterogeneous nature of racial bondage, we also need to consider the areas outside that time and that place. Slaves and masters lived and interacted quite differently in the eighteenth century from in the nineteenth century, while conditions in the northern colonies and states, the Chesapeake Bay, the Lower South, and the West Indies contrasted markedly with one another.[4] These advertisements focus primarily on fugitives and owners in the Mid-Atlantic region: three of every four runaways escaped from sites in Pennsylvania, New Jersey, or Delaware, while one in five fled Maryland masters.[5]

Designed to identify as precisely as possible the men, women, and children who had escaped, the published notices contain considerable information about a group of people who left behind few other personal records. A number of advertisements offer extensive vignettes of individual runaways, sketching their fortunes, revealing their perceived idiosyncrasies, and suggesting the complexity of their relationships with other slaves, white servants, and their owners. Nearly all the advertisements delineate a host of particulars about the slaves who fled; taken as a group, the notices lend themselves to a systematic analysis of many of those traits. For example, the physical aspects of runaways—including their age, sex, height, color, scars, and bodily markings—as well as the type of clothing they wore are exquisitely detailed. Various features of their daily lives, from the kind of work they performed to the type of chains in which some were shackled, often are reported along with their place of birth, musical and linguistic talents, speech difficulties, number of previous owners, and frequency of escape attempts. The runaway's name, primary language, ritualistic African markings, religion, literacy, and connections to friends and family offer clues to the culture and values of many slaves.

Masters likewise provided subjective assessments of their human chattel that suggest much about both slaves and owners. Testifying to their own limited views of their bondspeople, whites employed a great

FIGURE 1: Slave apparel. William Moore of Chester County, Pennsylvania, described his fugitive slave, Jack, to be wearing "a new ozenburg Shirt, a pair of strip'd home-spun Breeches, a strip'd ticking Wastecoat, an old dimity Coat of his Master's with Buttons of Horse-teeth set in Brass, and Cloth Sleeves, a Felt Hat almost new." From the *Pennsylvania Gazette*, August 13, 1730. *Drawing by Adrienne Mayor.*

many adjectives to classify runaways into three elementary personality types: "surly," "sour," "impudent," and "bold" described one category; "shy," "complaisant," and of "meek countenance" designated another; "cunning," "artful," "sensible," "ingenious," and "smooth tongued" denoted a third. The advertisements also offered clues to the owners' beliefs about the motivations and escape strategies of runaways, their fears about the people who aided that flight, and the monetary value they placed on their slaves by the rewards they offered. The subject index should help readers locate descriptions of specific characteristics contained in individual notices.

Constables and jailers published newspaper announcements designating where and when suspected fugitives had been apprehended and identifying whom, if anyone, the imprisoned blacks had specified as their owner. Thus a number of slaves can be traced from their escape to their capture. The name index should be of particular value for such a project; Abel, for example, absconded from his owner in Cumberland County, Maryland, on July 26, 1770, but was arrested six weeks later in Chester County, Pennsylvania. While most black prisoners undoubtedly were returned to their masters, sheriffs sold unclaimed ones (some of whom were not slaves) into servitude for a period of months or years to pay for the costs of their advertising and maintenance while detained in jail.[6]

These advertisements, like all historical records, exhibit a peculiar set of biases and limitations that must be considered when using them to interpret the past. Most important, they reflect the perspective of the masters rather than the slaves who are described. Although we may generally trust the portrayal of such objective traits of fugitives as their sex, height, and occupation, we must be considerably more wary of the depiction of personality types or the motivations for escape. The latter characteristics may reflect the perceived reality of the owners more than the actual nature of the slaves. Many masters, for example, were predisposed to envision their bondspeople in certain ways: docility might justify their enslavement and deviousness explain their attempted escape. And some slaves undoubtedly found it personally advantageous to play on the misconceptions of whites, to behave outwardly in ways which reinforced those images. Still, in the Mid-Atlantic region where most masters worked side by side with their slaves on farms or in shops, whites usually knew their slaves well. The detailed descriptions contained in the advertisements from these areas, for example, distinguish them from the more sketchy accounts provided in contemporary newspapers in South Carolina where owners of large plantations sometimes had little contact and limited acquaintance with their bondspeople.[7]

The notices included in this volume by no means indicate *all* of the escape attempts by blacks living in the middle colonies. Many fugitives went unadvertised for a number of reasons. Owners sometimes expected, quite correctly, that their bondspeople would voluntarily return after taking a "holiday" for a few days; the difference between the time a slave disappeared and the submission date of the advertisement suggests that belief. The low value of some older or less-skilled slaves who absconded did not justify the expense of advertising them. That hardly any escapees older than fifty appear in the announcements may in part reflect the unwillingness of their masters to spend much money to track them down.[8] In addition, notices placed in newspapers other than the *Pennsylvania Gazette* are not included in these selections. Franklin's newspaper enjoyed the widest circulation and was the only one published during the entire period, but at least a dozen other Philadelphia newspapers appeared intermittently during these decades, and most contained advertisements for runaways that were not always duplicated in the *Gazette*.[9]

We have included 300 advertisements for 364 runaway slaves that appeared in the *Pennsylvania Gazette* between 1728 and 1790. During those years masters published announcements for 1,324 black escapees in that newspaper. We selected notices that offered the most varied, interesting, and extensive descriptions. Although not drawn randomly, this sample accurately reflects the information contained in all of the advertisements. The statistical breakdown of nearly all variables—including the age, sex, height, race, place of birth, language skills, occupation, site of escape, and supposed objectives—is almost identical for the sample of 364 Afro-Americans and for all the 1,324 advertised fugitives.[10] To provide a comparative perspective about the characteristics, motivations, and escape strategies of black runaways, we have included 26 announcements from the same newspaper for white indentured servants who fled their masters.

Except for occasional silent alterations of punctuation and expansions of abbreviations to facilitate comprehension, the advertisements are reproduced exactly as they appeared in the *Pennsylvania Gazette*. The date at the top of each notice indicates the day of the newspaper issue; any other date at the top or bottom of the advertisement is that of the submission to the newspaper. The subject and name indexes refer to the case numbers at the beginning of each advertisement. A glossary defines the meanings of many terms that the advertisements commonly include.

★   ★   ★

The remainder of the introduction is devoted to providing the background necessary to enable readers to interpret these advertisements more effectively. Thus, it will sketch the number and distribution of slaves in the Mid-Atlantic region, the type of work they performed, various aspects of their cultural and family lives, the laws regarding fugitives and slavery, and a profile of the terrain through which escapees had to make their way. A quantitative analysis of the characteristics of the runaways and a statistical comparison with their counterparts in the Upper and Lower South will provide a fuller context within which to understand individual advertisements.

The number of blacks enslaved in the Mid-Atlantic region during the eighteenth-century is impossible to chart with certainty. In 1790 the first federal census-takers counted 16,422 slaves in Pennsylvania, Delaware, and the southern counties of New Jersey, from which most fugitives advertised in the *Pennsylvania Gazette* had escaped. But many slaves had gained their liberty during the previous fifteen years. Pennsylvania's gradual emancipation law of 1780, the rash of manumissions granted by individual owners, the achievement of freedom by blacks who fought in the war, and the successful escapes of many bondspeople meant that slaves probably were more numerous in the region at the end of the colonial period than in 1790. Pennsylvanians, for example, owned nearly 6,000 bondspeople in 1770 but fewer than 3,800 two decades later.[11] Afro-Americans multiplied by natural increase and forced immigration during most of the century; their population in the three colonies may have quadrupled from nearly 5,000 to more than 21,000 between 1730 and 1780.

Still, slaves never accounted for the substantial segment of the work force in the middle colonies that they comprised in the southern ones. The best estimate is that blacks formed between 4 and 5 percent of the inhabitants of Pennsylvania, New Jersey, and Delaware during the half century preceding the Revolution.[12] Yet these aggregate statistics disguise the importance of slave labor in particular locales. For example, blacks counted for one of every six residents in certain New Jersey towns in 1790. And the proportion of slaves in Philadelphia ranged widely over time, varying from a high of 28 percent in the early years of the century (making its racial configuration comparable to some southern areas) to a low of 7 percent during the decade before the Revolution.[13]

Slavery was not a homogeneous institution throughout the Delaware Valley. The nature of bondage and the lives of bondspeople differed significantly from the countryside to the region's dominant city, Philadelphia. Like whites, the vast majority of blacks lived in farm communities and engaged in the myriad of tasks associated with raising cereals and livestock, the area's primary products. Black males spent much of their time laboring in the fields of wheat and corn as well as cutting firewood, mending fences, repairing buildings, and hauling goods to and from small towns and the larger urban centers of New York and Philadelphia. As owners sought employment for their slaves during the slack winter months on the farm, many blacks must have operated as craftsmen, making everything from bricks and chairs to shoes and wheels. While they helped plant and harvest crops, slave women generally performed different, gender-specific tasks, from tending gardens, chickens, pigs, and cows to carrying out the plethora of domestic chores encompassing cleaning, cooking, preserving food, washing clothes, and caring for both their own and their masters' children. A minority of rural slaves worked in skilled and unskilled capacities for millers, tanners, and iron masters (especially in Pennsylvania and New Jersey), as well as personal servants for the wealthiest members of the community.[14]

Philadelphia's slaves worked in a great variety of jobs in nearly every sector of the city's economy. Domestic duties defined the work world of most black women, although their owners sometimes hired them out to wash clothes, wait tables, and help out in taverns and inns. Males likewise toiled around their masters' homes as cooks, coachmen, and personal attendants, but a great many also sailed on ships as common sailors, hauled cargoes on and off boats, cleaned chimneys, and labored daily digging ditches, wells, and foundations for buildings. Artisans owned a considerable portion of black bondsmen, so that many slaves not only assisted in fashioning furniture, barrels, houses, and boots, but also mastered the complete art and mystery of a particular craft.[15]

Even while they served important economic functions, slaves in both rural and urban settings frequently acted as status symbols for their owners. Black bondspeople cost considerably more than either white indentured servants or hired casual laborers, and the seasonal demands of cereal farming meant that enslaved workers could not always be easily employed profitably for the entire year, making the necessary heavy capital investment questionable. Most residents of the Mid-Atlantic region strongly preferred to buy the labor of whites, whether bound or free. Still, the wealthiest residents of rural areas oftentimes owned slaves, in part to define their social standing in the community. That their wills and inventories sometimes grouped their human chattel with luxury items rather than with practical agricultural implements or livestock is telling evidence. The most prominent Philadelphians—merchants, professionals, proprietary officeholders—likewise kept retinues of black footmen, coachmen, and personal servants to help solidify their elite status.[16]

As in all slave-holding areas, the needs of masters shaped black life, setting the parameters within which bondspeople existed and thereby greatly influencing the nature of their culture and families. Most slaves were held singly or in groups of two or three. Only a few in Pennsylvania and New Jersey regularly worked with large numbers of their own race, primarily in iron foundries or tanneries. Slaves in Delaware and in the northern and eastern counties of Maryland, from which a large minority of fugitives advertised in the *Pennsylvania Gazette* escaped, were more likely to live and work in larger groups on tobacco plantations. But wheat farming was important even in those areas, meaning that most black bondspeople throughout the Delaware Valley worked side by side with their white masters on small farms and often lived in their owner's home. In the more cramped quarters of Philadelphia, slaves not only occupied back rooms and closets in their master's house but they associated with white laboring people at a host of daily events and holidays.

Blacks consequently found it necessary to learn the rudiments of Anglo-American culture quickly. Although slaves did socialize with one another, especially in the urban setting, their physical isolation from each other in the countryside undermined their ability to maintain distinct African languages, religions, or traditions. Moreover, before 1740 owners had purchased most of their slaves from the mainland South or the West Indies, blacks who had previously been forced to cope with European customs. At mid-century, when masters increasingly began to purchase slaves directly from their homeland, African culture was reinvigorated in the Delaware Valley. Even though the shift in forced immigration was a short-lived phenomenon, as slave importation into the region's major port declined dramatically after the mid-1760s, the lingering cultural effects were significant.[17] During the next few decades, for example, the City of Brotherly Love provided a setting within which blacks could define their own Afro-American community and institutions. The hundred or so free blacks who lived in Philadelphia on the eve of the Revolution mushroomed to nearly two thousand by 1790, as manumitted and escaped slaves sought not only refuge but also a chance to create viable lives with others of their own race.[18]

Bondspeople in the middle colonies and states enjoyed less success in establishing and maintaining families than did slaves in the Upper and Lower South. Afro-Americans in Philadelphia usually led fragmented family lives, bearing relatively few children, living together infrequently, and forming short-term relationships at best.[19] Birth rates were much lower among urban slaves than among rural ones in the Mid-Atlantic region or the southern colonies. Although farmers may have valued slave children because of their potential productive capacity, most urban owners viewed them as an extra expense and an added burden. Philadelphia masters thus actively discouraged their human property from reproducing. As one newspaper contributor commented, "in this city, negroes just born, are considered as an incumbrance only, and if humanity did not forbid it, they would be instantly given away." Confirming this observation, advertisements offered slave children for sale at a very tender age, and many notices indicated that women were sold "for no Fault but breeding."[20] Since most masters found it difficult profitably to employ or shelter more than one or two slaves, the great majority of Philadelphia's bondspeople could not cohabit with their loved ones. Those who formed intimate relationships must have visited one another frequently, but the ties among them were extremely fragile. The brisk market in slaves and the high mortality in the city meant that black families frequently were torn asunder by sale or by the death of a master. Even though Philadelphia blacks struggled hard to establish viable families, circumstances beyond their control doomed most of their efforts.

Slaves in the Mid-Atlantic countryside were more capable than their Philadelphia counterparts in creating families and having children. Their familiarity with white society and close contact with their masters afforded some blacks the opportunity to manipulate both their situation and their owners, enabling them to establish loving relationships with others of their own race. Still, the physical distance between slaves must have caused considerable problems. Most bondspeople were held in small groups on farms scattered across Pennsylvania, New Jersey, and parts of Delaware and Maryland, thus limiting the degree to which blacks could define their intimate interpersonal relations. Consequently, black birth rates were slightly lower in the rural Delaware Valley than in the southern counties of Maryland and Virginia, while fewer slaves resided together in family groups in the former than in the latter region.[21]

All the British-American colonies established elaborate regulations to restrain the black population. While slave codes in the northern colonies generally were not as harsh nor as strictly enforced as those in the South, they nevertheless defined a brutal network of repression. Officials in the Mid-Atlantic region restricted the mobility of blacks, prevented them from gathering together in groups, forbade them access to liquor and guns, and established curfews and patrols to enforce them. Legislatures passed laws which denied blacks the right to testify against whites in court, provided separate systems of justice for the two races, assumed the guilt rather than the innocence of blacks, and inflicted more severe punishments on Afro-Americans.[22]

The codes devoted a great deal of attention to one of the most difficult problems of slave control—running away. The Delaware Valley colonies mandated that slaves must carry a pass when away from home. If caught without a written permit more than five miles from their owners in New Jersey or ten miles from their Pennsylvania masters, a bondsperson, according to the law, "shall be whipped by order of any justice of the peace on the bare back at the owner's charge not exceeding ten lashes." People who harbored fugitives particularly concerned officials, and such activities drew stiff penalties. Free blacks who aided a runaway in Pennsylvania were fined five shillings for the first hour and one shilling for each succeeding hour; those unable to pay the fine were liable to be sold into servitude themselves. The law assessed whites thirty shillings for each day they abetted a runaway, to discourage them from hiring or enslaving escapees for their own use. Constables could jail, without a warrant, any black suspected of being a runaway. If no owner claimed them after advertisements appeared in the newspapers, sheriffs generally sold suspects as a servant for weeks or months to pay the cost of their detention.[23] Under such conditions, even free blacks, once arrested, encountered considerable difficulty regaining their freedom.[24]

The antislavery movement enjoyed notable successes and affected in important ways the lives of blacks in the Mid-Atlantic region during the second half of the eighteenth century.[25] Led initially by Quakers, the movement received considerable inspiration from Christian idealism, the intellectual ferment of the Enlightenment, and the libertarian principles of the American Revolution. The abolitionists achieved their greatest victories in the northern colonies, where slavery was less well entrenched and least profitable. Moved by the arguments against slavery, thousands of masters in the Delaware Valley manumitted their slaves. More important, in 1780 Pennsylvania became the first state to abolish Negro slavery by legislative act. Reflecting on their own continuing struggle for independence from Britain, the state assembly, desiring "to extend a portion of that freedom to others, which hath been extended to us, and a release from that state of thraldom, to which we ourselves were tyrannically doomed," abolished slavery. But the institution of racial bondage was to be brought to a gradual rather than an abrupt end: all children born to slaves after the law took effect were to be freed once they had served their mother's master as an indentured servant until their twenty-eighth birthday.[26]

The law against slavery was not designed, however, to "give any relief or shelter to any absconding or runaway negro."[27] Masters retained the right to pursue and claim their human property, and the legal rewards and penalties for seizing fugitives or aiding their escape remained unchanged. Still, the gradual emancipation of slaves after 1780 encouraged the growth of a sizable free black community in Pennsylvania, especially in Philadelphia, and thus provided a place where runaways might blend into the population. The news about emancipation also must have circulated widely among the people held in bondage in surrounding states and even further afield. As one Virginia master commented in his advertisement for an escaped black, "the slaves in this state generally supposing they may obtain their freedom by going into Pennsylvania makes it highly probable that he is in some part of that state."[28]

By 1784 nearly all states from Pennsylvania northward had passed emancipation laws, most of which freed blacks through a gradual process. New York took fifteen more years and New Jersey two more decades to abolish slavery officially, but by the early nineteenth century racial bondage seemed to be withering away in the North. Delaware and Maryland, the other two states comprising the Delaware Valley, also hotly debated ending slavery during the years following the Revolution, but the emancipationists failed in their efforts. Although a number of owners in both areas released their bondspeople, slavery did not end in those areas until the Civil War.[29]

Runaways confronted an environment blending a montage of obstacles and opportunities. The weather, access to food and shelter, and the physical landscape numbered among the major challenges, and they help explain the seasonal nature of escape attempts since most runaways left during the warmer months.[30] The "rigour" of winters in the Mid-Atlantic region astonished English travelers, a few of whom noted that "the navigation of the Delaware is almost every winter stopt by ice for two or three months," and that the early spring thaw made "the rivers totally impassable . . . for several days." When icejams no longer presented a problem, "the thickest fogs, attracting the moisture on the rivers and coasts" reduced visibility until the sun burned the mists away.[31] Snows and heavy rains turned the dirt roads into quagmires. Even in pleasant weather, escapees confronted a confusing, poorly marked transportation system, with "so many Cross Roads" that it was "exceedingly difficult to keep [to] the Right one." The limited number of primary routes linking villages to one another and to Philadelphia attracted frequent traffic and exposed runaways to significant risks of detection and recapture.[32]

Winter accorded fugitives little opportunity to harvest the bounties of nature, although spring, summer, and autumn brought a rebirth of plenty in forest and field. By contemporary accounts, small animals such as opossums and raccoons were relatively easy to catch by hand, while clouds of passenger pigeons and rivers of "Roach, Pearch, and Trouts" further assured that runaways would not starve. Supplementing their diet "with many sorts of Fruits and Roots" from the wilds, fugitives might survive entirely on nature's yield for a short time. As the Delaware Valley filled with farms "surrounded with great Numbers of Gardens and Orchards" during the eighteenth century, runaways may have encountered simultaneously the problem posed by increased population density and the greater possibilities to pilfer from crops and gardens.[33] Farm animals provided another potential source of food, although owners would likely note their absence. Of course, many escapees raided their own master's larder or saved food in preparation for their flight. Water presented less of a problem in the moist Mid-Atlantic region since a ready supply flowed in the numerous rivers and streams, which often also served as conduits for escape.

Runaways undoubtedly found temporary shelter in various forms. Forests, abundant in the area even in the late eighteenth century, furnished concealment from pursuit, a haven from the elements, and the warmth of a cautiously maintained fire. Abandoned cabins, barns, and other structures allowed escapees greater comfort and protection. In addition, as one sojourner noted, caves were abundant and "convenient."[34]

The topography of the region eased the runaway's journey but provided few areas in which to take permanent refuge. "Generally level, but woody" terrain and gently rolling hills with "but few mountainous Parts" characterized southeastern Pennsylvania and northern Delaware. Southern Delaware and the eastern shore of Maryland were quite flat, though "well cultivated."[35] Between Philadelphia and New York City, New Jersey was "broken only by some hills." Sandy, sterile soils "producing red cedar and black pine" typified the eastern New Jersey coasts from Sandy Hook to Cape May. Besides the Pennsylvania back country, which rapidly filled with Scots-Irish and German immigrants during the century, the pine barrens of New Jersey offered practically the only area in which blacks might partially escape from white communities.[36]

A brief statistical overview of select characteristics of slaves who fled in the Mid-Atlantic region should provide a context within which to interpret individual advertisements. Between 1728 and 1790 the *Pennsylvania Gazette* carried announcements for approximately twenty-one fugitives or captured blacks each year. But the average annual number of advertised runaways changed dramatically over time, increasing from eight per year between 1728 and 1750, to thirty during the third quarter of the century, and then declining slightly to twenty-six annually between 1776 and 1790. The vast majority of blacks escaped from the Mid-Atlantic region: 46 percent ran from Pennsylvania, 10 percent from Delaware, 17 percent from the southern counties of New Jersey, and 19 percent from the northern and eastern areas of Maryland. Masters seeking their slaves paid for three of every four notices, while constables who had detained blacks suspected of being runaways published the other advertisements.

A quantitative comparison of runaways publicized in the *Pennsylvania*

Gazette with those in the newspapers of Virginia and South Carolina suggests some of the similarities and differences among black fugitives in North America. Young men typified escapees in all three areas. Males accounted for about nine of every ten runaways in the Mid-Atlantic region and Virginia, although females absconded in higher proportions in the Lower South (see Table 1). That the burden of child care gener-

TABLE I: RUNAWAYS IN THE MID-ATLANTIC REGION, VIRGINIA, AND SOUTH CAROLINA

Characteristic of Runaways	Mid-Atlantic %	Virginia %	South Carolina %
SEX			
Males	91%	88%	77%
Females	9	12	23
AGE			
1–19	14	17	26
20–29	54	46	43
30–39	23	26	20
40–49	8	10	9
50+	1	2	1
BIRTHPLACE			
American Continent	55	62	38
Africa	13	*	*
West Indies	12	*	*
Not American Continent	20	38	62
PHYSICAL TRAITS			
Smallpox-pitted	6	6	1
Whip Scars	2	3	1
"African Marks"	2	*	*
Branded	1	2	3
ITEMS STOLEN			
None noted	72	70	88
Extra clothes	20	26	8
Horse	2	3	1
Cash	3	1	0
Gun	3	1	0
NUMBER OF CASES	1,323	1,276	2,424

* Data not available

Source: Information on runaways from the Mid-Atlantic Region was tabulated from advertisements in the *Pennsylvania Gazette*. Lathan Algerna Windley compiled data on fugitives advertised in newspapers in Virginia and South Carolina in "A Profile of Runaway Slaves in Virginia and South Carolina from 1730 through 1787" (Ph.D. diss., University of Iowa, 1974).

ally fell to black women undoubtedly limited their escape opportunities, since few may have been willing to flee without their offspring. Slaves between the ages of twenty and forty comprised between two-thirds and three-quarters of escapees in all three areas. Children would have encountered great difficulty making their way as fugitives in a white world, while older slaves previously may have made the choice to remain because of ties to their family, the partial security available to many elder bondspeople, and the likely physical tribulations of life on the run.[37]

Masters indicated the birthplace of only 29 percent of the runaways; based on the available data, 55 percent in the Delaware Valley, 62 percent in Virginia, and 38 percent in South Carolina were native to the mainland of North America. These figures generally reflect the nature of the slave population in those areas. Masters in Pennsylvania, New Jersey, and Deleware purchased many of their slaves from the South, bondspeople multiplied by natural increase in the Chesapeake Bay area, while South Carolina depended heavily on imports from Africa and the West Indies. The physical descriptions of fugitives indicate that relatively few runaways in any area suffered disfigurement from smallpox, scars from whippings, marks from tribal rituals, or brands inflicted by masters. Finally, many slaves undoubtedly pilfered food from their owners to sustain them during their flight, but most did not steal other items of note. The greatest proportion—20 percent in the Mid-Atlantic, 26 percent in Virginia, and 8 percent in South Carolina—carried along extra clothing, but only a handful left with cash, a horse, or a gun. Their limited access to these items and the increased possibility of recognition of their runaway status may have discouraged such activities.

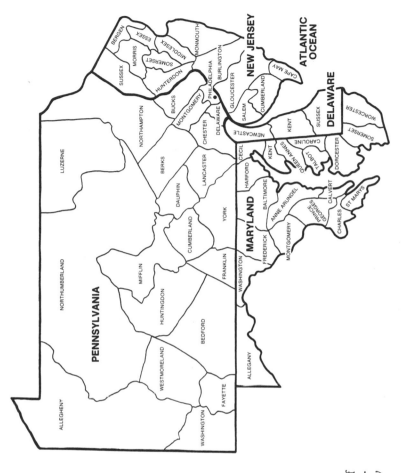

FIGURE 2: Map of the counties of Pennsylvania, New Jersey, Delaware, and Maryland. *Drawn by Adrienne Mayor.*

Advertisements for Runaway Blacks

1. March 11, 1731

RUN away the 27th of *February* from *John England* and Company, at *Principle* Iron Works, a Negro Man named *Jack,* formerly belonging to Sir *William Keith,* Bart at his Works in *New-Castle* County: He is an elderly Man, speaks thick, and generally pretty Sawcy; is a Carpenter by Trade, and has a Wife in *New-Castle* County. Whoever secures him, so as his Master may have him again, shall have *Five Pounds* Reward, and reasonable Charges paid, by   John England.

2. October 11, 1733

RUN *away from Justice* Farmer's *of Whitemarsh* a Negroe Man named *Gloster,* from *John Petty,* Indian Trader, a Negroe Man and Woman, from *John Baily* of *Philadelphia* Shoemaker, a Negroe Man named *Corke,* from the Widow *Bird* of *Philadelphia,* a Negroe Man, and from *John Noble* of *Philadelphia,* a Negroe Man called *Bristor.* They all went away last Saturday, and took Guns with them, and have been seen going up *Perkiomy* Road last Monday Night. Whoever takes up the said Negroe's or any of them so that they may be had again, shall have from Justice *Farmer's* Five Pound, from the Widow *Bird's* Three Pounds, and from the others Two Pounds, and reasonable Charges paid by, Justice *Farmer, John Petty, John Baily,* Widow *Bird,* and *John Noble.*
October 11, 1733.

3. *June 27, 1734*

RUN away on Thursday last from the House of John Richardson, Shoemaker, a new Negroe Girl about 16 or 18 Years of Age, short Stature, branded upon the Breast N R mark'd round the Neck with three Rows like Beads, suppos'd to be a Whedaw Negroe; had on a check'd Cotten Petticoat and a Seersucker Jacket. Her Name is Rose.

Whosoever takes up the said Negroe, and brings her to John Richardson aforesaid, or B. Franklin Printer, shall have Twenty Shillings Reward and reasonable Charges paid by   John Richardson.

4. *September 21, 1738*

RUN away on Saturday the 15th of July last, from Mr. Humphrey Brooke, in King William County in Virginia, a Servant Man named John Harris, a Welshman. He had on a light colour'd Kersey Coat, nicanees Wastecoat, Duroy Breeches, brown linnen Shirt, and worsted Cap.

A Negro Man named Abraham, belonging to Col. Geo. Braxton, of King and Queen County in Virginia. He is a lusty young Fellow about 25 Years of Age, bow legg'd. Had with him a cloth-colour'd Coat, and several other Sorts of wearing Apparel. He is a Shoemaker by Trade.

A Negro Man named Windsor, belonging to the Subscriber of the same County. He is about 5 foot and half high, very square & strong made, about 20 Years of Age. He has a black cloth Coat full trim'd, and some other wearing Apparel. The Negroes are both Virginia born, and are sensible Fellows. They went away by Water. It is probable, the Whiteman will offer the Negroes to Sale.

Whoever will secure the said Runaways so that I may get them again, or will bring them to me, shall have Two Pistoles Reward for each, and also a reasonable Allowance for the Charge of bringing them, in Case they should be taken at any great Distance, besides what the Law allows; paid by   George Braxton, jun.

5. *June 7, 1739*

STOLEN, on the 15th Instant, from on Board the Snow Drake, James White, Master, at Philadelphia, a Negro Man named Jack, aged about 21 Years, very black, with large Lips, wide Mouth, speaks good English, can read and figure a little, formerly belonging to the Estate of Joseph England, taken at the Suit of Thomas Stretch for a Debt of said England's Widow.

Whoever will inform Messrs. Edward Bradley and Company, Owners of said Snow, where said Negro is, shall have Forty Shillings Reward and reasonable Charges paid by   Edward Bradley,
    Philad. May 31, 1739.

6. *October 11, 1739*

RUN away on the 20th of Aug. past, from the Subscriber near the Head of Bush River in Baltimore County, Maryland, an Indian Man, named Pompey, aged about 24 Years, of middle Stature, well set, speaks nothing but English, very much scarrified on the Body with whipping in Barbadoes; he had on his Neck when he went away an Iron Collar, but its suppos'd he has got it off. Also a lusty Negro Woman named Pegg, aged about 22 Years, this Country born and speaks plain English; They carried away with them a striped Duffle Blanket, an old Ticken Jacket and Breeches with black Buttonholes, a Felt Hat near new, a coarse linnen Bag, a new white Linsey woolsey Petticoat and other coarse Negro Apparel. Whoever secures the said Indian and Negro so that their Master may have them again, shall have Five Pounds Reward and reasonable Charges paid by   Richard Ruff.
    October 11, 1739.

7. *April 10, 1740*

RUN away the 8th Instant from *George Smith*, in *Arch-Street, Philadelphia*, a Negroe Fellow of about 22 Years of Age, of middle Stature, born in *Bermuda*, and speaks good English; named *Jo*. Had on a wollen Jacket. It's suppos'd he will endeavour to get off in some *Bermudas* Vessel. Whoever secures or brings him to the said *Smith* shall be reasonably rewarded.

8. *September 11, 1740*

RUN away on the 23d past, from *James Leonard*, of *Kingston*, in *Middlesex* County, *East-New-Jersey*, a Negro Man named *Simon*, aged about 40

Years, is a well-set Fellow, about 5 Feet 10 Inches high, has large Eyes, and a Foot 12 Inches long; he was bred and born in this Country, talks good *English,* can read and write, is very slow in his Speech, can bleed and draw Teeth, pretending to be a great Doctor and very religious, and says he is a Churchman. Had on a dark grey Broadcloth Coat, with other good Apparel, and peeked toe'd Shoes. He took with him a black Horse, about 13 Hands and an half high, a Star in his Forehead, branded with 2 on the near Thigh or Shoulder, and trots; also a black hunting Saddle, about half worn.

   Whoever takes up and secures the said Negro, so that his Master may have him again, shall have *Three Pounds* Reward and reasonable Charges, paid by   James Leonard.

9. September 18, 1740

STOLEN, Stray'd, or Run-away, on the 12th from Dr. *John Finney* in *New-Castle,* a Negro Woman, named *Betty,* aged about 18 Years, of small Stature, round Face, has been about a Month in this country, speaks very little *English,* has had one Child: Had on, the Body of an old Gingham Gown, and an ozenbrigs Petticoat. She is supposed to have been taken from hence by an Oyster-Shallop, *Benj. Taylor* Master, bound for *Philadelphia,* and may be sold on some Part of the River.

   Whoever brings her to the Subscriber in *New-Castle,* and discovers the Person who carried her off, shall have *Forty Shillings* Reward, and reasonable Charges, paid by   John Finney
   New-Castle, Septemb. 15, 1740.

10. September 10, 1741

RUN away the 21st of August, from the Subscribers, of Kingsess, Philadelphia County, a White Man and a Negro, it is supposed they are gone together; the White Man's Name is Abraham Josep, a Yorkshire Man, a Shoemaker by Trade, aged about 24 Years, of middle Stature: Had on, a ratteen Jacket and Breeches of a light colour, a castor Hat pretty much worn, a check Shirt with white patches on the Back, two pair of yarn Stockings, one pair of a grey colour and t'other pair blue, a pair of thin Shoes round toed, and a pair of Boots.

   The Negroe's Name is Tom, of a yellowish colour, pretty much pitted with the Small Pox, thick set: Had on, a light coloured cloth Coat, a linnen Jacket and Breeches, a pair of check Trowsers, good Shoes sharp toed.

Two Nights before there were several things Stolen, and it's supposed they have them, a List whereof follows, viz. a suit of Drugget of a snuff colour half trim'd, a light coloured cloth Coat, two linnen Jackets, a pair of leather Breeches, two pair of check Trowsers, two Hats, a drab coloured broad cloth Coat pretty much worn, a Jacket of the same colour of the first mentioned Suit, a dark brown Wig, two napt Caps, a Gun, and a Pocket Book with two Bonds in it, one of Ten Pounds, the other of Eight Pounds, with a Note written at the end for Sixteen Shillings, with several other small things.

Any Person or Persons that will take up and secure the said Men, so that they may be had again, shall have for the White Three Pounds, and for the Negro Five Pounds Reward, and reasonable Charges, paid by

James Hunt,
Peter Elliot.

N.B. They took a Cedar Canoe with them, broken at the Stern and split at the Head.

11. October 28, 1742

RUN away from the Subscriber, living at Elk-Ridge in Anne-Arundel County, Maryland, the 26th of September, 1742, the following Servants, viz. John Simms, a Convict Servant Man, well set, about 30 Years of Age, and is of a pale Complexion; he is without his Hair, and had on when he went away, a Castor Hat, a ruffled Holland Shirt, a Flower'd Vest, a Pair of new Pumps, and blue ribb'd Stockings. Also, Thomas Handfield, a Convict Servant; he is a young raw Youth, about 18 or 20 Years of Age, fresh coloured and somewhat pitted with the small Pox, wears his own yellow, curl'd Hair, had on a Castor Hat with a Gold Button and Loop, his other Cloaths unknown. Likewise, a Negro Woman named Jenny, supposed to be dressed in Man's Cloaths; if so, she has on a Felt Hat, an Oznabriggs Jacket, a Pair of check'd Trowsers, and an old Pair of Mens Pumps. If she is in Woman's Apparel, she has on a Country Cloth Habit, a Hempen Roll Petticoat, she is a slim young Wench, looks smooth, with large Eyes. Whoever apprehends the said Servants and brings them to the Subscriber shall have Ten Pounds Reward for the Three; or Three Pounds each for the Men, besides what the Law allows, and Four Pounds Reward for the Woman.

John Howard.

12. *July 14, 1743*

RUN away on Friday the 1st of July, from John Pennington, Innholder, in Frederickstown-Cecil County Maryland, a Negro Man named Minto, upwards of 20 Years old, of middle Stature, speaks good English, and understands Plantation Business: Had on when he went away an ozcnbrigs Shirt and short coarse Breeches, an old felt Hat and white linen Cap.

Run away on Tuesday the fifth, from Thomas Hynson, jun. near Sassafrax, a Negro Man named Adam, of middle Stature, left handed, bowlegg'd, and a yellow Complexion; has a Negro Mark or Scar, from the back of his Neck down his Back, speaks but poor English, is about 22 Years old: Had on a white Shirt, coarse striped ticken Jacket, and took with him a seersucker Jacket and two pair of Trowsers, coarse felt Hat and a white Cap. Whoever takes and secures the said Slaves, and gives Notice to their said Masters, so that they may be had again, shall have Twenty Shillings Reward for each, and reasonable Charges, paid by   John Pennington, and Thomas Hynson, jun.

N.B. 'Tis supposed they are in Company together.

13. *August 4, 1743*

Maryland, Baltimore County, July 25, 1743.

RUN away from the Subscriber, a Negro Man, named *Squallo,* of middle Stature, well-set, aged about 26 Years, Country-born: Had on an old light colour'd cloth Coat, a red Jacket, a pair of red pimstone Breeches, Hat, Stockings, and Shoes with Buckles in them, one of Brass and one of Iron. He was bought from one Dr. *Radman,* who lives near *Burlington,* and it is supposed he will go that Way, or towards the back Parts of *Pennsylvania.* Whoever takes up and secures the said Negroe, so that he may be had again, shall receive *Forty Shillings* Currency of the Province where taken, as a Reward, and if taken in *Pennsylvania,* and brought to the Subscriber, shall receive *Four Pounds* Reward of that Currency, from   Stephen Onion.

N.B. 'Tis supposed he is gone in Company with a Molatto Man belonging to Mr. *Charleson Waters,* and that they have taken Horses.

14. April 26, 1744

RUN away on the 20th of April from George and Valentine Robinson, of Brandywine Hundred, New-Castle County, two Mulatto Men, named George and William Hugill, two Brothers, this Country born; one a lusty able Fellow, and the other a slender long-limb'd, spare thin fac'd Fellow; their Cloathing made of home-spun gray Cloth, leather Breeches, check Trowsers, linnen Shirts, gray yarn Stockings, and Thread ones, with Country-made Shoes and Pumps, felt Hats; they wore their own Hair; it's suppos'd they took with them two Periwigs, of different Colours, and each of them a Gun.

Whoever secures the said Servants, and what Things they have with them, committing them to the first Goal, and there well secur'd, and sending Account to their Masters, shall have Three Pounds Reward, for each Man, paid by us,   George Robinson, Valentine Robinson.

15. November 1, 1744

RUN away about the 18th of September last, from the subscriber, then in Annapolis, a Negro Man, named Joseph Paterson, he is a square Fellow, pitted with the small Pox: Had on when he went away, a grey Coat, with flat Pewter or white metal Buttons, he is a Cook by Trade, and formerly lived with Samuel Ogle, Esq; late Governor of Maryland, as such he has procured a Writing, from under the Hand of the Rev. Mr. Jacob Henderson, which has prevailed with one or two of the Justices of Ann Arundle County, to subscribe a Pass for him. Whoever apprehends the said Negro, and delivers him to me at my House, in St. Marys County, in Maryland, shall receive Ten Pounds Reward, more than the Law allows, if taken up out of this Province, and Six Pounds, if taken within the same, besides reasonable travelling Charges, which shall be paid by   Philip Key.

16. April 4, 1745
Maberrin, in Bertie County, North-Carolina, March 13, 1745.

RUN away from the Subscriber, in *Bertie* County, *North-Carolina*, a likely Negroe Slave, named *Tony, Virginia* born, about Thirty Years of

Age, middle sized, well set, short Neck, and somewhat round Shoulder'd, yellow Complexion, and scarr'd on his Shoulders by Correction. He pretends to making and burning Bricks, and is a good Sawyer. He ran away the 18th of *June, 1743,* and has been heard of in *Pennsylvania* Government. Whoever takes him up, and brings him to the Subscriber, in *North-Carolina*, shall be Paid Ten Pistoles, or if delivered to Mr. *Hugh Parker*, in *Philadelphia*, shall receive Five Pistoles. *Benjamin Hill.*

17. June 20, 1745

Philadelphia, June 17, 1745.

RUN away from the Sloop Sparrow, lately arrived from Barbados, Joseph Perry Commander, a Negro Man, named John; he was born in Dominica, and speaks French, but very little English; he is a very ill featured Fellow, and has been much cut in his Back, by often Whipping; his Cloathing was only a Frock and Trowsers. Whoever brings him to John Yeats, Merchant in Philadelphia, shall have Twenty Shillings Reward, and reasonable Charges, paid by John Yeats.

18. October 31, 1745

RUN away on Saturday the 26th of October, from Thomas Cadwalader, of Trenton, a Negro Man, named Sam, a likely Fellow, about 26 Years of Age, speaks very good English: Had on when he went away, a good Duroy Coat, a fine Hat, almost new, a Pair of good Leather Breeches with Trowsers over them; but as he has other Clothes with him, he may have changed them since. He was enticed away by one Isaac Randall, an Apprentice of Thomas Marriot, jun. They took with them a likely bay Gelding, six Years old, thirteen Hands and a Half high, paces well, and is shod before: And they are supposed to have gone with a Design to enter on board a Privateer, either at New-York or Philadelphia. Whoever takes them up, and secures the Negro and Gelding, shall be well rewarded, by THOMAS CADWALADER.

19. October 31, 1745

WHEREAS Negroe Jo (who formerly liv'd with Samuel Ogle, Esq; then Governor of Maryland, as his Cook) about 13 Months ago run away from the Subscriber, who was then at Annapolis, and has since been out a Voyage in one of the Privateers belonging to Philadelphia, and is returned there: These are to desire any Person to apprehend the said Negroe, so that he may be had again, for which, on their acquainting me therewith, they shall be rewarded with the Sum of Five Pounds, current Money: Or if the said Negro will return to me, at my House in St. Mary's County, he shall be kindly received, and escape all Punishment for his Offence. PHILIP KEY.

20. *July 31, 1746*

Philadelphia, July 31, 1746.

RUN away the 2d of July from Richard Colegate, of Kent County on Delaware, a Molatto Man, named James Wenyam, of middle Stature, about 37 Years of Age, has a red Beard, a Scar on one Knee: Had on when he went away, a Kersey Jacket, a Pair of plain Breeches, a Tow Shirt, and a Felt Hat. He swore when he went away to a Negro Man, whom he wanted to go with him, that he had often been in the back Woods with his Master, and that he would go to the French and Indians, and fight for them. Whoever secures the said Molatto Man, and gives Notice thereof to his Master, or to Abraham Gooding, Esq; or to the High Sheriff of Newcastle County, so that his Master may have him again, shall have Three Pounds Reward, and reasonable Charges, paid by RICHARD COLEGATE.

21. *September 4, 1746*

Philadelphia, September 4, 1746.

RUN away the 17th of August, from Thomas Mayburry, at Hereford Furnace, in the County of Philadelphia, a Spanish Negro Man, named Mona, of about 28 or 30 Years of Age, of middle Stature, thin Visage, very full of Flattery, apt to laugh, and talks broken English: Had on when he went away, an Oznabrigs Shirt, check'd Linnen Trowsers, old Hat, old double Worsted Cap, no Shoes nor Stockings; had some Money, suppos'd to be given him by the Papist Priest. Whoever takes up and secures said Negro Man, so that his Master may have him again, shall have Forty Shillings Reward, and reasonable Charges, paid by THOMAS MAYBURRY.

N.B. All Masters of Vessels are desired not to harbour him on board, or carry him off.

22. September 4, 1746

Philadelphia, September 4, 1746.

RUN away on the 16th of July, from Thomas Rutter, of this City, a Negro Man, named Dick, commonly call'd Preaching Dick, aged about 27 Years: Had on when he went away, a Bearskin Jacket, and a light Duroy Jacket, without Sleeves, Oznabrigs Shirt and Trowsers, and one Pair of brown Linnen Trowsers, blue Stockings, new Shoes, a new Castor Hat, and blue Worsted Cap. Whoever takes up and secures the said Negro, so that his Master may have him again, shall have Thirty Shillings Reward, and reasonable Charges, paid by

THOMAS RUTTER.

23. October 1, 1747

Philadelphia, October 1, 1747.

RUN away, on the 20th of September last, from Cohansie Bridge, a very big Negroe man, named Sampson, about 50 years of age, has some Indian blood in him, is hip-shot, and goes very lame; he has taken his son with him, a boy about 12 or 14 years of age, named Sam; he was born of an Indian woman, and looks much like an Indian, except in his hair; both belonging to Silas Parvin of Philadelphia, and are both well clothed, only the boy is barefoot; they have taken with them a gun and ammunition, and two rugs; can both talk Indian very well, and it is likely they have dressed themselves in Indian dress, and gone towards Carolina. Whoever secures said slaves, so that their master may have them again, shall have Five Pounds reward, and all reasonable charges, paid by   SILAS PARVIN.

24. October 8, 1747

Philadelphia, October 8, 1747.

RUN away from Francis Mines, in Appoquinimy, Newcastle county, a servant woman named Ann Wainrite: She is short; well-set, fresh-colour'd, of a brown complexion, round visage, was brought up in Virginia, speaks good English and bold. Had on when she went away, a blue linsey-wolsey gown, a dark-brown petticoat, and a Bath bonnet. She hath taken with her a striped cotton shirt, and some white ones, a drab-colour'd great coat, a silver-hilted sword, with a broad belt, and a cane; with a considerable parcel of other goods: Also a large bay pacing

horse, roughly trimm'd, shod before, and branded on the near buttock S R. There went away with her a Negroe woman belonging to Jannet Balvaird, named Beck; she is lusty, strong, and pretty much pock-broken; had on when she went away, a brown linnen gown, a striped red and white linsey-wolsey petticoat, the red very dull, a coarse tow petticoat, and callicoe one, with a great piece tore at the bottom, and stole a black crape gown: Also a bay horse, with three white feet, a blaze down his face, and a new russet hunting saddle. Whoever takes up the above-mentioned women and horses, and secures them, so as they may be had again, shall have Four Pounds reward, and reasonable charges, paid by
Francis Mines [and] Jannet Balvaird.

25. October 29, 1747

Philadelphia, October 29, 1747.

TAKEN up and committed to Newtown-goal in Bucks county, on suspicion of running away, a Negroe man nam'd John Cuffee, aged about Twenty-six years, has a blemish in the right eye, mark'd very much with scars on each side his face, and all over his forehead, has a light colour'd broadcloth surtout coat, with mohair buttons. He says he did belong to one John Harding, master of a ship from Madeira to Patapsco in Maryland, and that his master was shot in the voyage by a Spanish Privateer. Any person that can claim a property to the said Negroe, is hereby desir'd to come and pay the charges, and take him away.   AMOS STRICKLAND, sheriff.

26. May 5, 1748

Philadelphia, May 5, 1748.

RUN away, last Thursday, from Philip Syng, of this city, silversmith, a Negroe man, named *Cato*, about 20 years old, a short, well-set fellow, and speaks good *English:* Had on when he went away two jackets, the uppermost a dark blue halfthick, lined with red flannel, the other a light blue homespun flannel, without lining, ozenbrigs shirt, old leather breeches, yarn stockings, old shoes, and an old beaver hat. When he went away he had irons on his legs, and about his neck, but probably has cut them off, as he has done several times before on the like occasion; he generally skulks about this City. Whoever brings him home, shall have *Twenty Shillings* reward, and reasonable charges, paid by
PHILIP SYNG.

27. *June 23, 1748*

Philadelphia, June 23, 1748.

RUN away from John Potts, of Colebrook-dale, Philadelphia county, Esq; about the 10th instant, a Spanish Negroe fellow, named John, of middle stature, about 30 years of age: Had on when he went away, only a shirt and trowsers, a cotton cap, and a pair of old shoes; he is a cunning fellow, and subject to make game at the ceremonial part of all religious worship, except that of the Papists; he is proud, and dislikes to be called a Negroe, has formerly been a privateering, and talks much (with seeming pleasure) of the cruelties he then committed. Whoever takes up said Negroe, and take him to his master at Colebrook-dale aforesaid, or secures him in any goal, shall have *Thirty Shillings* reward, and reasonable charges, paid by said JOHN POTTS, or THOMAS YORKE.

28. *July 28, 1748*

Philadelphia, July 28, 1748.

RUN away from the subscriber, on the 17th instant, a Negroe lad, called Ned, about 18 years of age, 5 feet 7 inches high, speaks pretty good English, but thick, has very thick lips, and is much pitted with the small-pox; Had on when he went away an ozenbrigs shirt, tow trowsers, striped woollen cap, and new shoes.

Also run away the 20th instant, from the subscriber, a Spanish Negroe man, called Mona, about 28 or 30 years of age, 4 feet 8 inches high, speaks broken English, a very bragging fellow, given much to flattery, is very well set, something of a stoop in his shoulders, which are very round, and has a down, designing look: Had on when he went away, an ozenbrigs shirt, tow trowsers, felt hat, and old woollen cap; he carried off a blanket, a pair of buckskin breeches, and some other things; and is the same Negroe which the subscriber's late husband, Thomas Maybury deceased, advertized about a year ago.

Whoever takes up said Negroes, or either of them, and apprizes the subscriber thereof, who lives at Green Lane Forge, Philadelphia county, or Michael Hillegas, merchant in Second-street, a little above Arch-street, Philadelphia, shall have *Twenty Shillings* reward for each, and reasonable charges, paid by said HILLEGAS, or SOPHIA MAYBURY.

N.B. As the subscriber is certain there are people that encourage her Negroes, by giving them liquor, and harbouring them in their houses, to her great detriment and loss; and as she hath forewarned them of such

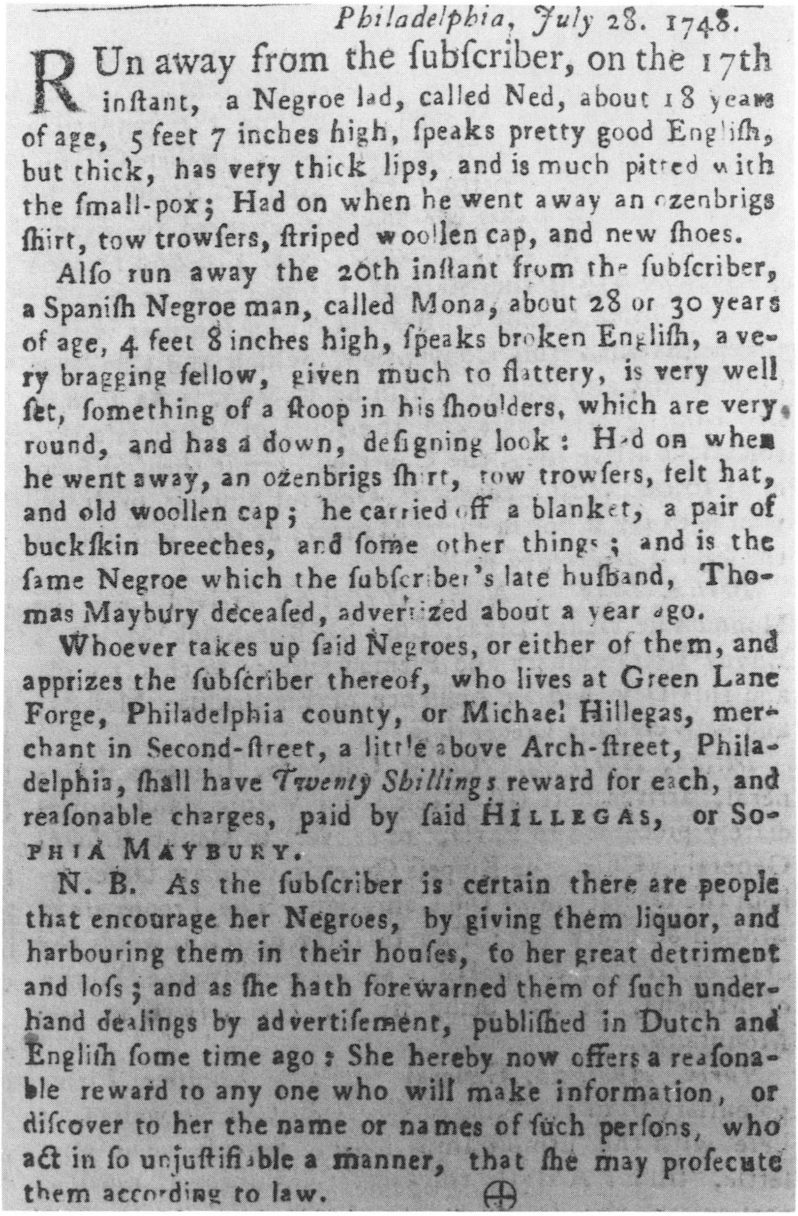

Philadelphia, July 28. 1748.

RUn away from the subscriber, on the 17th instant, a Negroe lad, called Ned, about 18 years of age, 5 feet 7 inches high, speaks pretty good English, but thick, has very thick lips, and is much pitted with the small-pox; Had on when he went away an ozenbrigs shirt, tow trowsers, striped woollen cap, and new shoes.

Also run away the 20th instant from the subscriber, a Spanish Negroe man, called Mona, about 28 or 30 years of age, 4 feet 8 inches high, speaks broken English, a very bragging fellow, given much to flattery, is very well set, something of a stoop in his shoulders, which are very round, and has a down, designing look: Had on when he went away, an ozenbrigs shirt, tow trowsers, felt hat, and old woollen cap; he carried off a blanket, a pair of buckskin breeches, and some other things; and is the same Negroe which the subscriber's late husband, Thomas Maybury deceased, advertized about a year ago.

Whoever takes up said Negroes, or either of them, and apprizes the subscriber thereof, who lives at Green Lane Forge, Philadelphia county, or Michael Hillegas, merchant in Second-street, a little above Arch-street, Philadelphia, shall have *Twenty Shillings* reward for each, and reasonable charges, paid by said HILLEGAS, or SOPHIA MAYBURY.

N. B. As the subscriber is certain there are people that encourage her Negroes, by giving them liquor, and harbouring them in their houses, to her great detriment and loss; and as she hath forewarned them of such underhand dealings by advertisement, published in Dutch and English some time ago: She hereby now offers a reasonable reward to any one who will make information, or discover to her the name or names of such persons, who act in so unjustifiable a manner, that she may prosecute them according to law. ⊕

FIGURE 3: Advertisement from the *Pennsylvania Gazette*, July 28, 1748. *Courtesy of The Historical Society of Pennsylvania.* (See case 28.)

underhand dealings by advertisement, published in Dutch and English some time ago: She hereby now offers a reasonable reward to any one who will make information, or discover to her the name or names of such persons, who act in so unjustifiable a manner, that she may prosecute them according to law.

29. *September 22, 1748*

Philadelphia, September 22, 1748.

RUN away, on Tuesday last from James Coultas, at the Middle Ferry on Schuylkill, a Negroe man, call'd Tom, about 40 years of age, five feet ten inches high, and square sett, a surly ill natured fellow, hath some scars in his face, customary to Guinea Negroes; he formerly belonged to Samuel Swift, of Smithfield; had on a striped jacket, fustian breeches, with tow trousers, limps a little, having lately had a sore foot. Who ever takes up the said Negroe, and secures him in any goal, so that his master may have him again, shall have *Twenty Shillings* reward, and reasonable charges, paid by   James Coultas.

30. *June 1, 1749*

RUN away, the 2d of last month, from the subscriber, living at the old town Potomack, Frederick county, Maryland, a mulattoe servant man, named Isaac Cromwell, about 40 years of age, a tall, slim fellow, very smooth tongued, by which some people may perhaps be imposed upon: Had on when he went away, a blanket coat, leather breeches, worsted stockings, new shoes, with brass buckles in them.

   Run away at the same time, an English servant woman, named Anne Green, about 45 years of age, short, and well-set, one of her legs much shorter than the other, much pock-marked: Had on when she went away, a white jacket, striped linsey petticoat. They took with them the following goods, viz. blankets, a striped cotton gown and petticoat, several shirts and shifts, with other clothing, too tedious here to mention; also a small bay horse, not branded, a large bay pacing horse, his hind feet both white, about 7 years old, branded on the near buttock with a heart, and a T through it; and a small old black horse, his brand not known, with some white spots on his back. Whoever takes up the said servants, and secures them, so as their master may have them again, shall have Five Pounds reward, if taken in Maryland, and if in Pennsylvania or the Jerseys, Ten Pounds, and reasonable charges, paid by *Thomas Cresap*, or *James Whitehead*, Work-house-keeper in *Philadelphia*.

31. *June 8, 1749*

RUN away, the second of this instant from the subscriber hereof, living in Hatsborough, Philadelphia county, a molattoe slave, named John Poole, commonly call'd Molattoe Jack; he had on when he went away a brown coat, and check shirt, trowsers of country linnen, those he may change, having several negroes about the city of Philadelphia, and the county also, that he was acquainted with; he is a well set fellow, and has a great cut under his left knee, which was cured last winter; he knows the country well, and will pretend that he is about his masters business, &c. Whoever takes him up in this county, five miles from home, without my note, or some others, that will be ordered by me to take care of him, shall have *Twenty Shillings* reward, if taken in this province; if in Maryland or Virginia, *Forty Shillings* of that country currency; or if aboard of any ship or vessel, same as aforesaid, paid by me   HUGH MATHEWS.

32. *June 29, 1749*

Philadelphia, June 29, 1749.

RUN away, on the 20th instant from George Marpole, of Goshen Neck, in Burlington county, a Spanish mulattoe servant man, named George, is short, thick, and well-set, with thick curl'd hair: Had on when he went away, a green cloth jacket, half worn beaver hat, check shirt and trowsers, new shoes, with brass buckles, and 'tis thought he has taken other clothes with him. Whoever takes up and secures said servant, so as his master may have him again, shall have *Thirty Shillings* reward, and reasonable charges, paid by   GEORGE MARPOLE.

N.B. Said fellow formerly ran away from Charles Read, of Burlington, and went a privateering, and may attempt to get on board same vessel; therefore all masters of vessels, and others, are warned not to take him on board, or harbour him, at their peril.

33. August 31, 1749

Westmoreland County, Virginia, August 17, 1749.

RUN away from the subscriber, on Monday last, a convict servant, named Thomas Winey; he is a middle siz'd fellow, about five foot, seven inches high, of a swarthy complexion, has had a piece cut out of one side of the end of his nose, which is very remarkable; he says it was done by the kick of a horse; he professes farming; was imported lately in the Litchfield, Capt. Johnson, and came from Maidstone goal, in the county of Kent, Great-Britain; his dress, when he went off, was a brown cloath coat, with a small cape, a pair of sailor's trowsers, a brown wig, check shirt, and dark coloured worsted stockings.

The above mentioned servant took with him a Molattoe slave, nam'd James, a well set fellow, 21 years old, about five foot seven inches high, is very apt to stutter when closely examin'd, having a stoppage in his speech; he has on his back a large white scar: His dress was a dowlas shirt, and a brown linnen coat and breeches, and has been us'd to drive a chariot for several years. I have been inform'd by their confederates, since they went off, that they intend to Pennsylvania, and from thence to New-England, unless they can on their way get a passage in some vessel to Great Britain, where the Molattoe slave pretends to have an uncle, who escap'd from his master in this colony near 20 years ago, and is said to keep a coffee-house in London. Whoever apprehends the said runaways, and secures them, so that they may be had again, if taken in Maryland or Pennsylvania, shall have Ten Pounds sterling reward, besides what the law allows, or Five Pounds for either of them: and if taken in any government to the northward of Maryland and Pennsylvania, the reward shall be Twenty Pounds sterling for both, or Ten Pounds sterling for either, which shall be paid on demand, by

WILLIAM FITZHUGH.

34. November 2, 1749

Philadelphia, November 2, 1749.

RUN away three weeks ago, from Marcus Kuhl, of Philadelphia, baker, a Negro man, named Scipio, wears a blue broad cloth coat, or a black ditto, old shoes, and stockings, of a short stature, plays on the banjou, and sings with it, speaks but indifferent English. Whoever takes up and secures said slave, so that his master may have him again, shall have Fifteen Shillings reward, and reasonable charges, paid by

MARCUS KUHL.

35. *February 13, 1750*

LATELY absented from his master's service, and is lurking about this city, a Negroe man, named Jack, but calls himself John Powell; he is by trade a cooper, of a yellow complexion, and a sour dogged look; he is generally known amongst the Coopers, having worked with several of them; but they are hereby forewarned employing him without agreeing with the subscriber; and all persons from entertaining or dealing with him, as they may be sure to answer it at their peril; any person that will secure him, or carry him to the city work-house, shall receive Ten Shillings of William Whitehead, the keeper of the said house; and if taken 20 miles from the city Twenty Shillings, and reasonable charges, paid by   MORDECAI MOORE.

36. *May 31, 1750*

RUN away, on the 26th of this instant May, in the night, from John Gilleylen, of the township of Southampton, in Bucks county, a Negroe woman, named Lilly, 35 years of age, born in Bermudas, about 5 feet 6 inches high, a little pitted with the small pox: Had on when she went away, a good homespun striped peticoat, a new green serge ditto, a linnen ditto, 3 jackets of the same sort of cloth; she took with her several other good clothes, and some cash; she formerly belonged to Mr. Bailey of Lewistown, Pilot, and is supposed to be secreted some-where in Philadelphia. Whoever takes up said Negroe woman, and brings her to Mr. Francis Manny, Sale-maker in Chestnut-street, shall have *Thirty Shillings* reward, and reasonable charges, paid by

JOHN GILLEYLEN.

N.B. As it is supposed she intends to go to Bermudas or Lewistown, all masters of vessels and others are desired not to carry her off.

37. *February 19, 1751*

New York, February 7, 1751.

Run away last Sunday night, from Judah Hays, a Negroe wench, named Sarah, aged about 30 years; she is a likely wench, of a Mulatto complexion, was brought up at Amboy, in Col. Hamilton's family, and has had several Masters in the Jerseys: She dresses very well, has a good parcel of cloaths, and speaks good English. Whoever takes up the said wench, and brings her to her said master, or secures her in any county goal, so that he may have her again, shall receive Forty Shillings reward, and reasonable charges. Whoever entertains said wench, shall be prosecuted with the utmost rigour of the law. All masters of vessels, boat-men, &c. are forewarned of conveying said wench away, as they shall answer the same.   JUDAH HAYS.

N.B. Said wench has robb'd her said master, in apparel, &c. upwards of Fifty Pounds.

38. May 9, 1751

Run away in July last, from Nicholas Everson, living in East-New-Jersey, two miles from Perth-Amboy ferry, a mulatto Negroe, named Tom, about 37 years of age, short, well-set, thick lips, flat nose, black curled hair, and can play well upon the fiddle: Had on when he went away, a red colored watch-coat, without a cape, a brown coloured leather jacket, a hat, blue and white twisted yarn leggins; speaks good English, and Low Dutch, and is a good Shoemaker; his said master has been informed that he intends to cut his watchcoat, to make him Indian stockings, and to cut off his hair, and get a blanket, to pass for an Indian; that he enquired for one John and Thomas Nutus, Indians at Susquehanna, and about the Moravians, and the way there. Whoever secures him in the nearest goal or otherwise, so that his master may have him again, shall have Forty Shillings reward, and reasonable charges, paid by   NICHOLAS EVERSON.

39. May 23, 1751

Whereas the subscriber hereof, has great reason to apprehend that his Negroe wench Sarah, formerly advertised in this paper, has been and is now harboured and concealed by some white person in this town; this is to give publick notice, that whoever brings said wench to me, or has her confined in goal, shall immediately receive from me Five Pounds as a reward: And farther, that whoever will give information upon oath, who it is that harbours and detains said Negroe wench, shall have Ten Pounds reward.

N.B. All masters of vessels, boatmen and others, are cautioned against taking said wench on board, as she has lately been seen in sailors dress.   JUDAH HAYS.

40. *October 3, 1751*

Run away from the subscriber, on the 4th of May last, a Negroe man named Sampson, about 40 years of age, a short well-set fellow, much pitted with the small pox, has a very old look: Had on when he went away, a blue fearnothing jacket, ozenbrigs shirt and trowsers, and old felt hat; makes a practice of running away, and skulk in woods near plantations, was taken up last year and put into Amboy goal. Whoever takes up said Negroe, or secures him in any prison, so that his master may come to the knowledge of him, shall have Forty Shillings reward, and reasonable charges, paid by his master, JOHN PHILLIPS, of Philadelphia.

41. *October 12, 1752*

Run away from doctor Thomas Graeme's plantation, in Horsham township, Philadelphia county, a Molatto slave, named Will, about 29 years of age, approaching very near the Negroe complexion, being of a Negroe father, and Indian mother, about five feet eight inches high, of an open bold countenance, somewhat pitted with the small-pox, speaks both English and Dutch, and is a very cunning sensible fellow. There went with him, a labouring man, that work'd by the day or month, called Thomas Stillwell, a tall smooth fac'd fair complexion'd fellow, with pale strait hair, and may be farther known by a sore not quite heal'd on one of his shins; he has been at sea, and pretends to be a sailor. The said Stillwell is supposed to countenance the escape of the Molatto, by assuming the character of his master, or some such false pretence.

Whoever apprehends said Molatto, either with or without Stillwell, and secures him in any goal, or brings him to Philadelphia, shall have Five Pounds reward, and reasonable charges, paid by his master,
THOMAS GRAEME.

N.B. It is supposed he is gone towards New-York: All masters of vessels are forbid to carry him off at their peril.

42. *June 21, 1753*

Philadelphia, June 21, 1753.

RUN away the 14th instant from the subscriber, living in Germantown, a Negroe woman, named Phillis, about 25 years of age, of middle

stature, well-set, much marked about the neck and back with large whales or lumps, which she received in Barbados: Had on when she went away, an ozenbrigs jacket and petticoat, with a stripped ditto over it, new black grain'd shoes, has a shrill voice, and when in good humour very talkative; much inclined to company. Whoever takes up said Negroe, and brings her to my house, or to the work-house, in Philadelphia, shall, if taken up within ten miles, have Ten Shillings reward, and if upwards, Twenty Shillings, with reasonable charges, paid by
JOHN JONES.

43. July 5, 1753

Philadelphia, July 5, 1753.

RUN away on Monday, the 27th of June last, from the Brigantine Warren, at Clark's wharff, below the Draw-bridge, Francis Butterfield master, a Negroe man, named Sam, about five feet ten inches high, 27 years of age, a slim fellow, speaks pretty good English, has had the small-pox, and is an ill looking fellow: Had on a frock and trowsers, and straw hat; has a wife, a Negroe, who belongs to the widow Conyers, but now lives with Capt. Condy, who it is thought secrets him. Whoever takes up and secures said Negroe, or brings him to Henry Elwes, shall have Forty Shillings reward, and reasonable charges, paid by
HENRY ELWES.

44. December 6, 1753

RUN away from Mr. Stephen Onion's Iron-works, in Baltimore county, about the middle of June last, a Negroe fellow, called Jemmy, about five feet six inches high, of a yellow complexion, pretty much pock-fretten, has been in the country about 16 months, talks very little English, and has been most part of the said time cutting cord-wood: I am doubtful whether he can explain or even express his master's name. Whoever takes up said Negroe, and secures him, so that the subscriber may have him again, shall receive Two Pistoles reward, besides the allowance by law, and if brought to said works, any reasonable charges.
BENJAMIN WELSH.

N.B. I am suspicious that the said fellow is (by some ill disposed person or other) stolen and carried into the back woods.

45. August 8, 1754

RUN away on the 28th of July last, from Derrick Aten, of Readens town, Hunterdon county, in New-Jersey, a Negroe man, named Jack, about 30 years of age, near five feet high, has a flat nose, much pock marked, a lover of white women, and a great smoaker: Had on when he went away, a red strait bodied coat, striped homespun jacket, and another whitish ditto. Whoever takes up and secures said Negroe, so that his master may have him again, shall have Three Pounds reward, and reasonable charges, paid by   DERRICK ATEN.

46. March 25, 1755

Chestertown, Maryland, March 12, 1755.
TEN PISTOLES Reward.

RAN away last night, from James Ringgold, of Eastern Neck, in Kent county, in the province of Maryland, the two following servant men; one named James Francis, an indented servant for five years, a middle siz'd young fellow, about 26 years of age, of a smooth fair complexion, his hair cut off, is an Englishman, and speaks a little in the west country dialect; was brought up to farming and husbandry: Had on, a country kersey jacket and breeches, blue fearnought jacket, and an old dark colour'd coat. The other a lusty young Mulatto fellow, named Toby, a slave about the same age, he is a well-set, clean limb'd, stout fellow, neither a very bright or very dark Mulatto, has large nostrils, is a likely fellow, and when he talks drawls his words out in a very slow manner, is no other way very remarkable; he had on the same sort of clothes with the other servant, and one of them has a check or striped green and red everlasting jacket on or with them; and perhaps the Mulatto may set up for a cooper or carpenter, having work'd at both those businesses, and also under-stands plantation affairs. Whoever takes up and secures the above persons, and gives notice, so as their master gets them again, shall have Four Pistoles reward for the white servant, and Six Pistoles for the Mulatto; and if brought back either to their master or to the subscriber, shall be paid reasonable charges for their trouble of bringing them, either by their master or the subscriber. That this slave should runaway, and attempt getting his liberty, is very alarming, as he has always been too kindly used, if any thing, by his master, and on in whom his master has put great confidence, and depended on him to overlook the rest of his slaves, and he had no kind of provocation to go off. It seems to be the interest at least of every gentleman that has slaves, to be active in the beginning of these attempts, or whilst we have the French such near neighbours we shall not have the least security in that kind of property. I should be greatly obliged to any gentlemen that shall hear of these fellows, to endeavour to get certain intelligence which way they have taken, and to inform me of it by express, and also to employ some active person or persons immediately to take their tract and pursue and secure them, and I will thankfully acknowledge the favour, and immediately answer all expences attending it.   THOMAS RINGGOLD.

47. February 19, 1756

RUN away on the 6th instant from Joseph Phipps, miller, living in Uarbland township, Chester county, a Mulatto slave, named Guy, alias James, about 30 years of age, about five feet six inches high, a well set fellow, of a sour countenance, with deep wrinkles in his forehead, short hair, pretty complaisant, and speaks very good English: Had on when he went away, an old felt hat, brown colour'd cloth jacket and breeches, homespun shirt, white homespun yarn stockings, and half-worn shoes, tied with thongs. His former masters lived in Maryland; he is an old runaway, and has been in New Castle, Chester and Philadelphia goals within this twelvemonth. 'Tis thought he may follow the recruits. Whoever takes up and secures said slave, so as his master may have him again, shall have Forty Shillings reward, and reasonable charges, paid by   JOSEPH PHIPPS.

48. April 15, 1756

RUN away from the subscriber, living at Middletown, in East New-Jersey, the 9th of January last, a Negro man, named Cato, alias Toby, aged about 30 years, a lusty well set fellow, full faced: Had on when he went away, a plain made bearskin coat, with flat metal buttons, a white woollen vest, wool hat and cap, a brown tow shirt, buckskin breeches, wool stockings, a pair of pumps with large brass buckles; he was branded when a boy, in Jamaica in the West Indies, with B (and I think) C on his left shoulder blade; he is a sly artful fellow, and deceives the credulous, by pretending to tell fortunes, and pretends to be free, speaks English as well as if country born, and plays on the fiddle; it is thought he is gone towards the cedar swamps, and that some base person has given him a pass. Whoever apprehends the said slave, and secures him, so that his master may have him again, shall receive Forty Shillings reward, and reasonable charges, paid by RICHARD STILLWELL.

49. August 12, 1756

Philadelphia, August 9, 1756.

THIS day absented himself from his master's service, a Mulattoe slave, named Harry, about five feet six inches high, a broad well set fellow, speaks good English, and Dutch: had on when he went away, a blue cloth coat, with flat metal buttons, old check shirt, white tow trowsers, good shoes, and an old hat; chews Tobacco much, is a nimble lively fellow, about 25 years of age. He formerly belonged to George Johnson, in Frederick county, in Virginia; from thence assigned to one John Lindsay; from thence to John Clark, of Lancaster; from thence to one Cookson, and from thence to the subscriber. Whoever secures said Harry, in any goal, or brings him to his master, if taken in or near Philadelphia, shall have Four Dollars reward, if more than 20 miles, shall have Ten Dollars, and reasonable charges, paid by

THOMAS BARTHOLOMEW.

N.B. he pretends to be a free man, and to have great friends in Maryland and Virginia. All masters of Vessels, and others, are forbid to carry him off at their peril.

50. September 9, 1756

New-Castle county, August 28, 1756.
FIFTEEN POUNDS Reward.

WHEREAS Godfrey Brown, late of Christiana Hundred, and county aforesaid, a German, but talks tolerable English, nigh sixty years of age, about five feet three inches high, slender in body, has short brown frizley hair, small face, and little hollow eyes, his chin stands remarkably out, and his mouth far in, so that his chin and nose almost meet, seems to lisp when he speaks, from his want of teeth, and is of a swarthy complexion, is absconded from his usual place of abode, and is strongly suspected to have murdered a certain Mary Reel, and her son, whose bodies are found on his plantation. These are to give notice, that whoever will apprehend said Godfrey Brown, and secures him, so that he may be brought to justice, shall have Fifteen Pounds reward, which reward is offered by

Col. William Armstrong, David Bush, and Richard M'William, Esquires, three of his majesty's justices for said county.

N.B. There are in the goal of this county, a white man, named Arthur M'Claskin, and a Negroe man, named James Hoburn, they both say they are free; M'Claskin is a short well-set fellow, wears his own black hair, is of a black complexion; has on, a coarse shirt and trowsers. The Negroe is slender in body, about 40 years of age, and says he was set free by Henry Rennalds, of Chester County. Any person having any demands against said persons, are desired to come in four weeks after this date, and take them out, otherwise they will be sold for their charges, by

JOHN THOMPSON, Sub-Sheriff.

51. October 21, 1756

RUN away on the fifth day of September last, from the subscriber, living in Red-lion Hundred, New-Castle county, a Mulattoe man, named Ned, 23 years of age, about 5 feet 8 inches high, of a pretty dark colour, is this country born, and talks good English, and is a very smart, active, cunning fellow: Had on when he went away, a coarse tow shirt and trowsers, and a new 20 Shilling hat, but the rest of his apparel not known. As he has several times expressed a desire of going to sea, it is probable he may endeaveur to get on board some privateer, or other vessel, and for that end may pretend to be a free man, and no doubt will produce some counterfeit pass or certificate; therefore all masters of vessels are requested not to carry him off. Whoever apprehends the said slave, and brings him to his master, or secures him in any county goal, so that his master may have him again, shall have Three Pounds reward, paid by VALENTINE DUSHANE.

N.B. It is probable he will change both his name and apparel.

52. November 11, 1756

New-Castle, October 20, 1756.

THERE are now in the goal of this county three Negroe men, committed some days ago as runaways. One, who calls himself Ben, says he belongs to Mr. Rhody Neil in Virginia. Another, who calls himself Jem, says he belongs to Mr. Spencer Smith in Virginia. They seem both to be new Negroes, and can read. The other calls himself James, and says he belongs to Samuel Blunt, captain of a company of foot living in Kent

Island, Maryland. The owners of said Negroes are hereby desired to come in six weeks from this date, and take them out of goal, otherwise they will be sold for their fees, by   JOHN THOMPSON, Goaler.

53. March 17, 1757

Philadelphia, March 17, 1757.

NOW in the Goal of this City one *Timothy Jeffries*, a Mulattoe Fellow, committed as a Runaway Servant, and says, that he lived with one *Gideon Pierce*, in *George-Town, Kent County*, in *Maryland:* These are therefore to desire said *Pierce*, or any other Person that claims a Right to him, to come or send for him, otherwise he will be sold for his Fees, in three Weeks after the above date, by   THOMAS JAMES, Goaler.

54. March 31, 1757

Run away the 29th instant March, from the Subscribers, living in Philadelphia, a Mulatto Fellow, about 40 Years of Age, 5 feet, 10 inches high, has round Shoulders, stoops when he walks, and calls himself Timothy Jeffreys; has been in Philadelphia Goal for some Time past, and was sold out for his Fees: Had on when he went away, an old light coloured coat, a new blue double breasted Jacket, with Slash Sleeves without Lining, old Breeches, white Yarn Stockings, good Shoes, a new Ozenbrigs Shirt, Woollen Cap, and an old Hat: He stole and took with him about ten Yards of Ozenbrigs, and it is supposed he is gone to Kent County, in Maryland. Whoever secures said Fellow, so that the Subscribers may have him again, or brings him to us, shall have Forty Shillings Reward, and reasonable Charges, paid by

THOMAS and GEORGE WELLS.

55. August 11, 1757

Middletown, Monmouth County, East New Jersey, August 1, 1757.

RUN away from the Subscriber the first of January, twelve Months past, a Negroe Man, named Cato, who has since his Elopment changed his Name several times: Had on when he went away, a Pair of Buckskin Breeches, fine brown Linen Shirt, a plain made whitish Camblet Coat, dark Yarn Stockings, new Shoes, and a Wool Hat. He is a stout well set Fellow, understands Husbandry in all its parts, an excellent Hand with

Scythe in Grass or Grain, speaks English as well as if Country born, and pretends to be free. Underneath his Right-shoulder blade he was branded in Jamaica when a Boy with the letters BC, which are plain to be seen. He plays poorly on the Fiddle, and pretends to tell Fortunes. It is supposed he has a forged Pass. Whoever secures the said Negroe, so that his Master may have him again, shall receive a Reward of FIVE POUNDS and reasonable Charges, paid by

RICHARD STILLWELL.

56. October 13, 1757

RUN away from the Subscribers, living in Kent County, Maryland, the following servant and Slave, viz. One Thomas Rogers, an English Convict, about 25 years old, or less, about 5 feet 8 Inches high, a well-set Fellow, smooth faced, his Hair black, well featured, and as yellow as an Indian or Mulatto: Had on when he went away, an old Kersey Jacket, and an old purple Coat, and a Pair of old Leather Breeches cut without a Seam in the Inside, and both Ends of the Pocket flaps sewed to the Waistband. Also, Anne Sawyer, an Englishwoman, well-set, but of low Stature, very homely faced, of a swarthy Complexion, and with Child. Likewise a Negroe, called Tom, about twenty Years old, pretty tall, and a Scar on the right Side of his Lip; was sold by one Henry Batuer, at the Head of the Bay, about two Years ago. Their Cloathing is uncertain, and will change them, as they have Money, and a Silver Watch. The Woman stole her Indentures, and it is likely the Man has forged a Pass or Discharge, and a Bill of Sale for the Negroe. Whoever secures the said Servants, or Slave, so as the Owners may have them, shall have Two Pistoles for each of the Men, and one for the Woman, paid by JAMES BLEAKE, and ANNE MILTON.   October 4, 1757.

57. November 17, 1757

RUN away from the Subscriber, living in Chester Town, Kent County, Maryland, some time in July last, a Negroe Man, called Scipio, formerly the Property of Mr. Marcus Kuhl, of the City of Philadelphia, and it is very probable is gone that Way; he is a little short thick Fellow, speaks broken English, pretends to be a Hatter by Trade, and says, he is intitled to his Freedom, and plays well on the Banjoe. Whoever secures the said Fellow, so that the Subscriber may have him again, shall have *Two Pistoles* Reward, if taken out of the Province, and *One Pistole,* besides what the Law allows, if taken in Maryland, and reasonable Charges, paid by   JOSEPH NICHOLSON.

58. April 6, 1758

Philadelphia, March 28, 1758.
SIX PISTOLES Reward.

RUN away from Wharton and Story, on the 18th of last Month, a Mulattoe Fellow, who calls himself Joe Leek, abut 5 feet 9 inches high, round shoulder'd, and is remarkably well set: Had on when he went away, a coarse brown Kersey Coat, with flat white Metal Buttons, light Kersey Jacket, and old Leather Breeches, with Brass Buttons, coarse brown Yarn Stockings, new Shoes, and white Metal Buckles. Said Fellow is the Property of Mr. George Rock, late of Cecil County, Maryland. 'Tis imagined he has, or will endeavour to inlist himself with some of the Recruiting Parties in this or the neighbouring Provinces, as he has attempted it before. Whoever apprehends said Fellow, and will give Information thereof to Wharton and Story, or Mr. Robert Cummings, near Charlestown, Maryland, shall receive the above Reward, and reasonable Charges, if brought to any of the above Persons.

59. April 20, 1758

RUN away from the Subscriber's Plantation, in Halifax County, Virginia, on the First of February last, a likely Molattoe Fellow named Will; he is well set and strong, about 5 feet 9 or 10 Inches high, speaks good English, understands something of the Carpenter's Trade, is a good Sawyer, 36 or 37 Years Of Age. Whoever takes up said Molattoe, and secures him, so that his Master, now living in West-Nottingham, Chester County, may have him again, shall have Five Pounds Reward, and reasonable Charges, paid by   JAMES HUNT.

N.B. He is supposed to have been conveyed away by a white Man, who was heard to make him Proposals of Freedom, and to carry him where his Master should never hear of him again, if he would serve him twelve Months.

60. *September 14, 1758*

SIX PISTOLES Reward.

RUN away, last Summer, from the Subscriber, in St. Mary's County, Maryland, a likely Negroe Fellow, named Frederick, about 21 Years of Age, is tall and thin, the Calves of his Legs grow remarkably high, was always used to work about House, is inclinable to use his Left Hand more than his Right, and plays on the Violin; he took with him a small sorrel Gelding, with a Star in his Forehead, and branded on the near Buttock IC joined in one. Whoever brings the said Negroe to the Subscriber, in the County aforesaid, shall have Five Pistoles Reward, and one Pistole for the Gelding, and reasonable Charges, paid by

JOHN CHESHEY.

N.B. He was supposed to be inveigled away by one James Seager, who frequents the Back Parts of Virginia.

61. *October 26, 1758*

Philadelphia, October 24, 1758.

RUN away, on the 21st Instant, from Robert Wakely, of this City, a Negro Woman, named Anne, about 18 or 20 Years of Age, is short and well set, and had on a blue Jacket and Petticoat, Ozenbrigs Apron, and an old Cap, but no Shoes or Stockings. Also run away, at the same Time, a Negroe Man, named Frank, belonging to Alexander Collay, of Whitemarsh, about 30 or 35 Years of Age, is a slender middle sixed Fellow, and had on a new Wool Hat, Bearskin light coloured Coat, a Snuff coloured Jacket, without Sleeves, a striped Shirt, Leather Breeches, blue Stockings and good Shoes. They are Man and Wife, and supposed to be gone together. Whoever takes up said Negroes, and brings them to either of the Subscribers, shall have Fifty Shillings Reward for both, or if put into the next Goal where taken up Forty Shillings, paid by

ROBERT WAKELY, or ALEXANDER COLLAY.

62. *June 14, 1759*

RUN away from John Lloyd, of Stanford, in the Colony of Connecticut, on the 26th of May last, A Negroe Man Servant, named Cyrus, about Five Feet Nine Inches high, well built, but rather slim waisted, Legs and Feet somewhat large, has lost one or more of his fore Teeth, about 28 or 30 Years of Age, long visaged, very black, active and ingenious in all Sorts of Country Business, and is a good Butcher; bred in the Country, speaks good English, and a little French, but stammers when frighted or confused: Carried off with him a brown Irish Camblet Coat, a brown Fustian Vest, one of white Flannel, and one of Calicoe; one Pair of blue Cloth Breeches, one of brown Thickset, one of good Buckskin, and about 30 or 40 Dollars in Money: 'Tis imagined he went off with some Soldiers who deserted from the 48th Regiment, just before they embarked at Boston, as some of them have lately been discovered lurking in these Parts, and are possibly gone to the Westward or Northward. Whoever secures said Negroe in any of His Majesty's Goals, and sends me Word, so that I may have him again, or brings him to me, shall have FIVE POUNDS New-York Money Reward, and all reasonable Charges, paid by JOHN LLOYD, or RICHARD SMITH, in Philadelphia.

N.B. Whoever takes up said Negroe is desired to put him in Irons, and not to trust him out of Sight, unless in a strong Goal; and all Masters of Vessels and others, are cautioned against harbouring or carrying him off, as they will answer it at their Peril.

It is supposed said Negroe has a Counterfeit Pass with him.

63. June 14, 1759

RUN away from Dumfries, on Potomack River, in March last, a Mulattoe Man Slave, named Dick, Country born, about 35 Years of Age, a well made slim Fellow, very active, is much addicted to Liquor, and when drunk stammers in his Speech. He is by Trade a Wheel wright, and so much of a Smith as to shoe the Wheels he makes; he is also a good Cooper, House carpenter and Sawyer; he has likewise been employed frequently by Water, and is therefore a tollerable Sailor. Since he has run away he has been seen on board several Ships in Rappahannock River, and was once apprehended, but made his Escape by swimming on Shore from the Vessel.—He has been out-law'd. Whoever secures him in some Goal, so as he may be delivered to me at Dumfries, shall have Forty Shillings Reward of   ALLAN MACRAE.

64. June 21, 1759

Forty-five Pounds, Proclamation Money, Reward

RUN away last night from the subscribers, living in Hopewell, in New-Jersey, one Mulatto, and three Negroe men, viz.

The Mulatto, named Bood, and a Negroe, named Bristol, the property of William Hunt, is about five feet ten inches high, and pretty well set; each had a dark coloured coat, several shirts and pairs of shoes, stockings and breeches, for taking up and bringing back to their Master, Twenty Pounds reward will be given for Bood, and Ten Pounds for Bristol.

A Negroe man, named Jack, thick and well set, the property of John Hart; took with him, a cloth coloured kersey coat, several shirts, and pairs of breeches, shoes and stockings, Ten Pounds will be given for taking up and bringing him back to his Master.

Also a Negro man, named Tom, short and well set, the property of Joseph Golder, took with him a dark coloured coat, several shirts, pairs of breeches, shoes and stockings, Five Pounds reward will be given for taking him up, and bringing him back to his said Master.

It is supposed they all went away and will travel together, and that they are gone to some of the Indian towns upon Sasquehannah, the Molatto, Bood, having been entertained by the Indians there several months, some years ago; they took two guns, two or three hatchets, and several blankets with them.

WILLIAM HUNT, JOHN HART, JOSEPH GOLDER.

65. *July 5, 1759*

RUN away on the 9th ultimo from Richard Britton, in Middletown Township, Bucks County, A Negroe Man, named Jemmy, 6 Feet high, strait limbed, small legs, sticks forward, a Scar in each Temple, a Hole in each Ear, and Scars cut on each Arm: Had on a pale blue homespun Cloth Coat, red Flannel Jacket and Breeches, and old Beaver Hat. He speaks broken English; he understands making of Corn Baskets, and it is supposed he will go about to sell them. Whoever takes up and secures the said Negroe, so as his Master may have him again, shall have Three Pounds Reward, and reasonable Charges, paid by me

RICHARD BRITTON.

66. *July 12, 1759*

RUN away from Henry Brooks, living in Kent County, Maryland, on the 3d of July instant, a Negroe Woman, named Jane, about 25 Years of

Age, of a middle Size, born in Maryland: Had on when she went away, an old blue quilted Petticoat, old Jacket, two coarse Tow Linen Shifts, and an old green Bath Bonnet; it is supposed she was taken away by a Woman that lived some time in the Neighbourhood, who absconded at the Time the Wench was missing; the Woman calls herself Catherine M'Claughlin, is a large fat Pock marked Woman. They are certainly gone together, as M'Claughlin has several times threatened to take her away. Whoever takes up and brings said Negroe to John Hughes, Merchant, in Water street, Philadelphia, or secures her so as her Master may have her again, shall have Thirty Shillings Reward, paid by JOHN HUGHES or HENRY BROOKS.

67. August 2, 1759

RUN away from the subscriber, in Kent County, Maryland, on the 9th of this Instant July, a Molattoe Servant Man, named Thomas Williams, about 5 feet 8 or 10 Inches high, is a strong, able, well made man, his Cloaths uncertain; he had about Thirty Pounds Cash with him, and also his Wife, who is of his own Colour, and has a great Impediment in her Speech. It is supposed they went to Virginia in a Shallop. Whoever takes up the said Runaway and secures him so that his Master gets him again, shall have Fifteen Pistoles Reward, and Eight Pistoles for discovering the Person that carried him away, so that he may be convicted thereof according to Law.   JOHN BORDLEY.

68. September 20, 1759
Kingstows, Queen Ann's County, September 10, 1759.
RUN away the 8th of this Instant, a Negroe Man, named Caesar, he has both his Legs cut off, and walks on his Knees, may pretend that he was Cook of a Vessel, as he has been much used on board of Ships; he was seen by New-Castle on Saturday last. Whoever secures the said Negroe in any Goal or Work-house, shall receive Twenty Shillings Reward, paid by me SARAH MASSEY.
N.B. He has been a Ferry man at Chester Town, Queen Ann's County, for many Years.

69. May 29, 1760

RUN away from William Bird, Esq; a Negroe Man, named Hercules, about 26 Years of Age, has a Blemish in one Eye, and a remarkable Eye Lid. Whoever brings the said Negroe to Jacob Kern, in Reading, shall have Forty Shillings Reward. It is thought he is secreted, in Lancaster County, among the Germans, as he speaks that Language well.

JACOB KERN.

70. July 24, 1760

New-York, July 10, 1760.

RUN away from DENNIS HICKS, of Philipsburgh, in Westchester County, and Province of New-York, A Mulatto Man Slave, named Bill, about 20 Years of Age, has a long sharp Nose, with a black Mole on the right Side of his Face, near his Nose, has very large Ears, speaks good English, and pretends to be free, and can read and write well; says he has a White Mother, and was born in New-England: He is of a middle Size, and has a thin Visage, with his Hair cut off. All Persons are forbid to harbour him, and all Masters of Vessels are forbid to carry him off, as they will answer it at their Peril. TWENTY-FIVE POUNDS Reward for securing him in any Goal, or bringing him to me, so that I may have him again, and reasonable Charges, paid by DENNIS HICKS.

N.B. This Fellow was advertised in the New-York Papers the 5th of June, and in New-Haven the 11th of June, 1759; was afterwards taken up in Waterbury, and was put into Litchfield Goal, from thence he was brought to Bedford, and there made his Escape from his Master again. Those who apprehend him, are desired to secure him in Irons. He was taken up by Moses Foot, of North-Waterbury, in New-England. It is likely he will change his Cloaths, as he did before. The Mole above mentioned is something long.

*By Information he was in Morris County, in the Jerseys all the Winter, and said he would enter into the Provincial Service.

71. August 28, 1760

TWENTY POUNDS Reward.

RUN away on Tuesday, the 12th Day of this instant August, from the County of Kent, upon Delaware, a certain Robert Caten, born in the said County; he is a short well built Fellow, his upper Teeth before ride over each other; he had on, when he went away, a blue Coat, a cock'd Hat, and ties his Hair behind; he took with him four Negroes, three of which he stole, they being taken in Execution by me the Subscriber; these three are, a Wench about 40 Years of Age, named Cate; a Girl about nine or ten Years old, named Sue; and a Boy about two and a Half Years old, named Tony; the other was a young Child, in the Wench's Arms. He is supposed to have gone to the Back Woods, somewhere near Potomack, he being acquainted there, and has a Brother living there, named Thomas Caten; he rode a roan Mare. Any Person, who may have the Opportunity of apprehending him, and the said Negroes, are desired to take very good Care of them, as he will perhaps make fair Promises, and thereby deceive them. I would likewise inform the Public, that the Debt for which the Execution arose was, That the said Robert Caten took, some time ago, a free born Mulattoe Woman, and sold her for a Slave; which villainous Affair he was obliged to compound, by giving a Judgment Bond, upon which the above mentioned Execution issued; therefore People may judge what sort of a Person he is. The above Reward shall be paid on the Delivery of the aforsesaid three Negroes, Cate, Sue and Tony, at Dover, in the County aforesaid, or in Proportion for any of them, and reasonable Charges, by

THOMAS PARKE, Sheriff.

August 16, 1760.

N.B. All persons are forbid buying them.

72. November 13, 1760

Philadelphia, November 13, 1760.

Run away from JOHN LEACOCK, Goldsmith, on Monday Night last, A Negroe Fellow, named CUFF, about Twenty or Twenty-one Years of Age: Had on when he went away, A Bearskin Jacket, and another under it, black Stockings, brown Broadcloth Breeches, and a Hat: He may possibly change his Clothes, as he has taken them all with him. It is thought he is secreted in some Gentleman's House by Negroes, unknown to their Master, or by some free Negroes, or somewhere in the Skirts of the Town. Whoever will bring in the said Fellow to his Master, shall receive TWENTY SHILLINGS Reward.

All Persons are forbid to harbour or conceal said Negroe at their Peril; and all Ferry-men are desired not to put him over.

73. *May 21, 1761*

FIVE POUNDS Reward.

Run away from the Subscribers, living at Little-Elk, Caecil County, Maryland, a Servant Woman named Margaret Sliter (but probably will change her Name) about 28 Years old, fresh coloured, darkish brown Hair, born in England; had on when she ran away, two Bed-Gowns, one blue and white, the other dark Ground, both Callicoe, new Linsey Petticoat, and one of coarse Tow Cloth, new blue worsted Stockings, with white Clocks, good Shoes, two striped Linen Handkerchiefs, and one Silk one changing Colour, five Yards of about 700 Linen; and has stolen some Mens white Shirts.

Also a Negroe Man, named Charles, a lusty able Fellow, about 29 Years of Age, pitted with the Small-Pox, speaks good English, talks fast, is apt to get drunk, and pretends to be married to the aforesaid Margaret Sliter; had on when he ran away, a Pair of Thickset Breeches, a Pair of blue Yarn Stockings, old Shoes, with round Steel Buckles, a light coloured Jacket, an old brown Body-coat, a great Coat of a greyish Colour, and has a Pair of Breeches of the same (the great Coat has Metal Buttons on) some coarse Shirts, and one fine one, but may have more, two Pair of Trowsers, and two Pair of brown Yarn Stockings. Stole one white Gown of about 1200 Linen, one red and white striped Silk Handkerchief, some Womens Caps, a Ribbon, and a small Gun: Likewise a white Horse of about twelve Years old, branded on the near Shoulder R. and a bay Mare five Years old, bob tailed, some of her Feet white, a white Spot in her Face, a Man's Saddle with blue Housing, a Woman's old Saddle, the Seat of which is brownish, with Leather Skirts. Whoever takes up and secures said Woman and Negroe, with the Horse and Mare, and other Things, shall have the abovementioned Reward of Five Pounds, and all reasonable Charges, or Fifty Shillings for either the Woman or Negroe, and Fifteen Shillings for the Horse or Mare, with reasonable Charges, paid by   DAVID ELDER, ANN HOLY.

N.B. The Negroe had two Felt Hats with him.

74. *May 28, 1761*

Run away from the Subscriber, living in Baltimore County, Maryland, on the Fifth Day of April last, a Country born Negroe Man, named Shadwell, a well made Fellow, about 5 Feet 5 or 6 Inches high, about 40 Years of Age, he is bald upon the Head, has lost his upper fore Teeth, has a Scar on one of his Eyelids; had on when he went away, an old grey

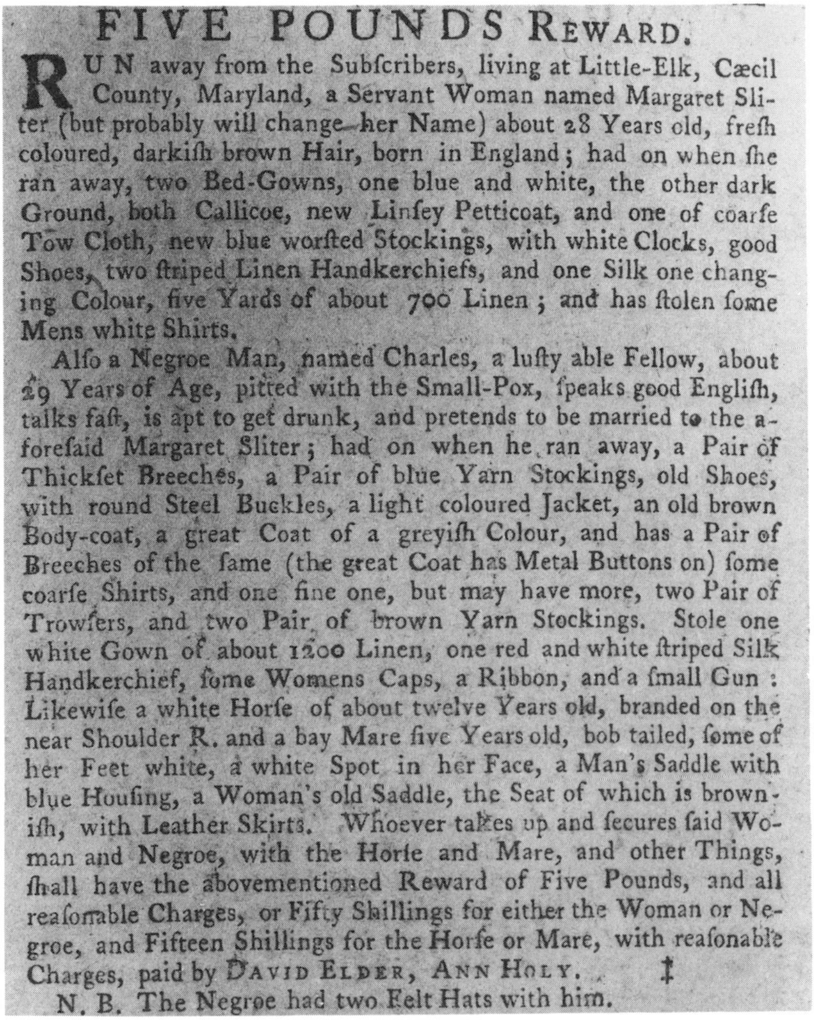

FIVE POUNDS Reward.

RUN away from the Subfcribers, living at Little-Elk, Cæcil County, Maryland, a Servant Woman named Margaret Sliter (but probably will change her Name) about 28 Years old, frefh coloured, darkifh brown Hair, born in England; had on when fhe ran away, two Bed-Gowns, one blue and white, the other dark Ground, both Callicoe, new Linfey Petticoat, and one of coarfe Tow Cloth, new blue worfted Stockings, with white Clocks, good Shoes, two ftriped Linen Handkerchiefs, and one Silk one changing Colour, five Yards of about 700 Linen; and has ftolen fome Mens white Shirts.

Alfo a Negroe Man, named Charles, a lufty able Fellow, about 29 Years of Age, pitted with the Small-Pox, fpeaks good Englifh, talks faft, is apt to get drunk, and pretends to be married to the aforefaid Margaret Sliter; had on when he ran away, a Pair of Thickfet Breeches, a Pair of blue Yarn Stockings, old Shoes, with round Steel Buckles, a light coloured Jacket, an old brown Body-coat, a great Coat of a greyifh Colour, and has a Pair of Breeches of the fame (the great Coat has Metal Buttons on) fome coarfe Shirts, and one fine one, but may have more, two Pair of Trowfers, and two Pair of brown Yarn Stockings. Stole one white Gown of about 1200 Linen, one red and white ftriped Silk Handkerchief, fome Womens Caps, a Ribbon, and a fmall Gun : Likewife a white Horfe of about twelve Years old, branded on the near Shoulder R. and a bay Mare five Years old, bob tailed, fome of her Feet white, a white Spot in her Face, a Man's Saddle with blue Houfing, a Woman's old Saddle, the Seat of which is brownifh, with Leather Skirts. Whoever takes up and fecures faid Woman and Negroe, with the Horfe and Mare, and other Things, fhall have the abovementioned Reward of Five Pounds, and all reafonable Charges, or Fifty Shillings for either the Woman or Negroe, and Fifteen Shillings for the Horfe or Mare, with reafonable Charges, paid by DAVID ELDER, ANN HOLY.   ‡
     N. B. The Negroe had two Felt Hats with him.

FIGURE 4: Advertisement from the *Pennsylvania Gazette*, May 21, 1761. *Courtesy of The Historical Society of Pennsylvania.* (See case 73.)

fearnothing Jacket, without Sleeves, a Cotton Jacket, and Breeches, and coarse Yarn Stockings, all of them dyed yellow, a felt Hat about Half worn, a coarse Shirt, and old Shoes, but it is likely he may steal other Clothes. It is supposed he will, or has made for the back Parts of Pennsylvania, or for the Ohio, or the upper Parts of Virginia, he has run away before, and has been at Conegocheague, at Chambers's Fort.

Whoever apprehends the said Negroe Man, and brings him Home, shall have Forty Shillings Reward, if taken in this Province, and if out of the Province, and within the South Mountain, Three Pounds; if over the South Mountain Four Pounds; and if over the North Mountain, or in Virginia, Five Pounds Reward, and reasonable Charges allowed; or if secured in any Goal out of the Province, so as he may be had again, Forty Shillings, paid by   THOMAS COCKEY.

N.B. He has run away several times before, and almost always changes his Name, and denies his Master.

75. August 27, 1761

FOUR PISTOLES Reward.

Run away from Cornwall (alias Grubb's Iron-Works) August 24, a Negroe Man, named Sam, about 35 Years of Age, speaks good English, is Pock-marked pretty thick, full-faced, smoaks much, about 5 Feet 7 Inches high: Had on when he went away, an Ozenbrigs Shirt and Trowsers, Felt Hat; and with great Probability is supposed to make for Philadelphia, as he was bought there last Summer. Whoever takes up and secures said Negroe, and brings him to said Works, or sends Word, shall have the above Premium, paid by me   NATHANIEL GILES.

76. September 10, 1761

Run away on the First of this instant September, from the Subscriber, living in Amwell Township, West New-Jersey, a Negroe Man, named Peter, about Twenty-five Years of Age, five Feet nine Inches high, walks very upright, and speaks good English: Had on when he went away, a lightish coloured Kersey Jacket, considerably too large for him, a Pair of brownish Fustian Breeches, blue Worsted Stockings, half worn Shoes, with Brass Buckles, Ozenbrigs Shirt and Trowsers, with a Tow Frock, Felt Hat, and wears a white Cap. He was seen within a few Miles of Philadelphia, enquiring whether there were any Privateers fitting out, and it is very probable he will endeavour to get on board some Vessel, as he has sailed some Time in small Craft. He is a cunning Fellow, and perhaps may change his Apparel. Whoever apprehends said Negroe, so that his Master may have him again, shall have Forty Shillings Reward, and reasonable Charges, paid by   JOHN WOOD.

All Masters of Vessels are forbid to harbour him at their Peril.

77. October 22, 1761

Stamford, October 6, 1761.

Run away on the 5th Instant from John Lloyd, of Stamford, in the Colony of Connecticut, A Negroe Man Servant, named Cyrus, about 5 Feet 9 Inches high, well-built, but rather slim waisted, Legs and Feet somewhat large, has lost one or more of his fore Teeth, about 30 or 32 Years of Age, long Visage, very black, he is active and ingenious in all Sorts of Country Business, and is a good Butcher; bred in the Country, speaks good English, and a little French, but stammers when frightened or confused: Had on when he went off, an Iron Collar riveted round his Neck, and an Ox Chain fastened to it. Carried with him a red Cloth Jacket, and another of brown Frize, both considerably worn, black Everlasting Breeches, almost new, Tow Trowsers, white Stockings, Cotton or Linen, and coarse Tow Shirt; it is not unlikely he may consort with any Deserter, or other stragling Fellow he may meet with, as about 2 Years ago he run off with two Deserters, and was taken up at Philadelphia. Whoever takes up said Negroe, is desired not to trust him a Moment till he is put in Irons, and secured in some of His Majesty's Goals, otherwise (his Crime being great) he will certainly give them the slip, and upon sending me Word, so that I may have him again, such Person shall have Five Pounds, New-York Money, Reward, and all reasonable Charges, paid by RICHARD SMITH, in Philadelphia, or JOHN LLOYD.

N.B. As inserting the Advertisement in the several News-Papers is judged the most expeditious Method of spreading them far and near, if any Gentlemen will be so kind, when they have read their Papers, to cut out the Advertisement, and set it up in the most publick Place, it will be esteemed a Favour; and all Masters of Vessels, and others, are cautioned against harbouring or carrying him off, as they will answer it at their Peril.

78. February 18, 1762

FIVE POUNDS Reward.

Philadelphia, Feb. 12, 1762.

Run away, on Saturday Night, between the 12th and 13th of December past, from John Comes, of Jamaica, on Long-Island, a Negroe Fellow, named York (but goes, as I am informed, by the Name of Rodman's James) about 30 Years of age, very likely, a mannerly fellow, full-faced and eyed, well set, smooth skin'd, his knees a little bending in, a small pitt or two on the left side of his nose, and one on his forehead; he pretends to know something of the sadler's business. Had on when he went away, a red great coat, made of coating, a red waistcoat, and leather breeches. The said Negroe produces a pass, signed by justice Hall, of Bristol, and justice Rodgers, of Allen-Town. It is said he worked some time with Lewis Jones, near Schuylkill, and has been seen travelling with a white man. Whoever takes up the said Negroe, and secures him, so that his master may have him again, shall have the above reward, and all charges, paid by me   JOHN COMES.

N.B. All masters of vessels are forbid to carry him off.

79. March 25, 1762

New Castle County, March 13, 1762.

COMMITTED to the Goal of this County, a Negroe Fellow, named York, who says he belongs to John Comes, of Jamaica, on Long-Island; he is full faced, has large Eyes, well set, his Knees bending a little in; says he is a Sadler. His Master is desired to come or send for him, in four Weeks after this Date, and pay his Charges, otherwise he will be sold for the same by   SWEN COLESBERRY, Goaler.

80. April 29, 1762

New-York, Printing-Office, in Beaver-Street, April 17, 1762.

Run away, on Monday the 12th Instant, from the Subscriber, a Mulattoe Servant Man, named CHARLES, and known by the Name of CHARLES ROBERTS, or GERMAN. He is a likely well set Fellow, 28 or 30 Years of Age, about 5 Feet 6 Inches high, and has had the Small-Pox. He has a Variety of Clothes, some of them very good, affects to dress very neat and genteel, and generally wears a Wig. He took with him two or three Coats or Suits, viz. A dark brown, or Chocolate coloured Cloth Coat, pretty much worn; a dun, or Dove coloured Cloth, or fine Frize, but little worn; and a light blue grey Summer Coat, of Grogram, Camblet, or some such Stuff; a Straw coloured Waistcoat, edged with a Silver Cord, almost new; and several other Waistcoats, Breeches, and Pairs of Stockings; a blue Great Coat, and a Fiddle. His Behaviour is excessively complaisant, obsequious and insinuating; he speaks good English, smoothly and plausibly, and generally with a Cringe and a Smile; he is extremely artful, and ready at inventing specious Pretences to conceal villainous Actions or Designs. He plays on the Fiddle, can read and write tolerably well, and understands a little of Arithmetick and Accounts. I have Reason to believe some evil minded Persons in Town have encouraged, and been Accomplices with him in villainous Designs; and it is probable he will contrive the most specious Forgeries to give him the Appearance of being a Free Man: I have already been informed of a Writing he has shewn for that Purpose, by which he has imposed upon many People; who may all be easily satisfied that he has no legal Claim to Freedom, even from Slavery, nor any Pretence to it but by the very Law by which he is my Servant for 40 Years, as the Records of the Superior Court at New Haven will Witness. At that Place, where the former Owner of the said Slave lived, he was guilty of a Variety of Crimes and Felonies, for which he was several Times publickly whipped, and only escaped the Gallows by want of Prosecution. When he became my Servant, I intended to have shipped him to the West Indies, and sold him there; and kept him in Prison till I should get an Opportunity; but on his earnest Request, solemn Promises of his good Behaviour, and seeming Penitence, I took him into my Family upon Trial, where for some Time he behaved well, and was very serviceable to me. Deceived by his seeming Reformation, I placed some Confidence in him, which he has villainously abused; having embezzled Money sent by him to pay for Goods, borrowed Money, and taken up Goods in my Name unknown to me, and also on his own Account, pretending to be a Freeman. By this villainous Proceeding I suppose he has collected a considerable Sum of Money, and am also apprehensive that he has been an Accomplice in some of the late Robberies committed in and near this City. Whoever will take up the said Servant, and bring him to me, or secure him in some of His Majesty's Goals, so that I may get him again, if taken up in the City of New-York, shall have Five Pounds Reward, and a greater, if taken up at a greater Distance. Any Persons who take him up, are desired to be careful to carry him before the next Magistrate, and have him well searched, leaving all the Money and Goods found upon him, except the necessary Clothes he has on, in the Hands of the said Magistrate; and to be very watchful against an Escape, or being deceived by him, for he is one of the most artful of Villains.   JOHN HOLT.

81. July 8, 1762

RUN away from the Subscriber, living in Baltimore County, Maryland, on the 14th Day of this Instant June, a Country-born Negroeman, named Shadwell, he has run away several Times before, has been in Carlisle and York Goals, and in Frederick County Goal, in Maryland. He always Changes his Name, and denies his Master, and wants to pass for a Free-man; he is a well made Fellow, about 40 Years of Age, about 5 Feet 5 or 6 Inches high; he is bald upon the Head, has lost his upper Fore-Teeth, has a Scar upon one of his Eye-lids, knows a great many People both in Ann Arundel County and Baltimore, and in Frederick County, in Maryland, and also in the Back Parts of Pennsylvania: Had on, when he went away, an Iron Collar about his Neck, and a Pair of Iron Fetters double riveted; it is likely he has got them off, as he has done several Times; he had likewise on, a Cotton Jacket, with a Piece of striped Linsey-woolsey put upon the Back of it, a Pair of new coarse Trowsers, a coarse Shirt; it is likely he will Change his Cloaths, as he is Rogue enough to steal any that he comes across; it is supposed he will make for the back Parts of Pennsylvania, or for the Ohio; he was taken up last Year 30 Miles above Carlisle. Whoever apprehends the said Negroe Man, and brings him Home, shall have Forty Shillings Reward, if taken in this County, if out of the County Three Pounds, and if out of the Province, Five Pounds; or if secured in any Goal, out of the Province, Forty Shillings, paid by   THOMAS COCKEY.

N.B. He can walk upon his Hands with his Feet up in the Air.

82. July 22, 1762

RUN-AWAY from Capt. Richard Todd, Commander of the Sloop Henry, about the First of this instant July, A likely Negroe Fellow, about 5 Feet 6 Inches high, born in Coracoa, about 22 Years of Age, called Jack, but carried with him a Negroe's free Pass, who was called Ben, and it is supposed he goes by that Name. The said Pass was signed by William Poppell, Esq; Whoever apprehends him, and delivers him to the Subscriber, or to Mr. Emanuel Josiah, opposite the London Coffee-House, or secures him in any Goal, shall have Three Pounds Reward, and reasonable Charges, paid by   GEORGE LUSHER.

83. August 26, 1762

Philadelphia, August 24, 1762.

RUN away from the Subscriber Yesterday, a Mulattoe Man Slave, named Joe, alias Joseph Boudron, a middle-sized Man, a brisk lively Fellow, about 23 Years of Age, was born at Guadaloupe, has lived some

Time in New-York, and Charles-Town, in South-Carolina, speaks good English, French, Spanish, and Portuguese: Had on when he went away, an old whitish coloured Broadcloth Coat, faced with Plush, and Metal Buttons, a Calicoe Jacket, black knit Breeches, blue Worsted Stockings, new Shoes, with large Brass Buckles, Check Shirt, an old laced Hat, and has other Things not known; he is a good Cook, and much used to the Seas, where it is thought he intends, or for New-York. Any Person that takes up said Runaway, and brings him to me, or secures him in any Goal in this Province, shall have Two Pistoles Reward, and if in any other Province, Four Pistoles, and reasonable Charges, paid by me

THOMAS BARTHOLOMEW, junior.

N.B. All Masters of Vessels and others are desired not to carry him off, or harbour him, on any Account.

84. August 26, 1762

THREE POUNDS Reward.

RUN away from Hugh Bowes, of Philadelphia, a Negroe Man, named JOHN, a slim middle-sized Fellow, about 35 Years of Age, speaks good English, but when surprized or talks fast, stutters very much: Had on when he went away, an old Check Shirt, a blue Pea Jacket, with Pieces stitched on the Elbows, such as Sailors wear, a Pair of brown Thickset Breeches, old Shoes, with large carved white Metal Buckles; generally carries a Piece of Rope with him, pretending to look for a strayed bay Horse; says his Master's Name is Denny, which is the Person that sold him to the Subscriber; supposed either to have gone over Schuylkill or towards New-York, as he was up the Road near the Robin Hood Tavern two Weeks, but has not been seen there since Friday last. Whoever takes up and secures the said Negroe Man, so that his Master may have him again, shall have the above Reward, paid by   HUGH BOWES.

N.B. All Masters of Vessels, and all Ferry-men, are forbid to carry him off.

85. August 26, 1762

SIX POUNDS Reward.

RUN-AWAY from the Subscriber, near the Town of Joppa, in Baltimore County, in May last, a lusty, well-set Mulattoe Slave, named Mike, but very likely he may alter his Name; he is about 24 Years of Age, has a large Face, flat Nose, a very wide Mouth, and much resembles an Indian in Colour; he can read, and suppose write a little; his Apparel cannot be well described, as he had many Confederates in the Neighbourhood. Whoever takes up the said Run-away, if in the County, and brings him home, shall have Four Pounds Reward, and if further off, and secured in Goal, so as his Master may get him again, Six Pounds, paid by

PETER CARROLL.

N.B. All Masters of Vessels and others are forbid to take him away at their Peril.

86. September 2, 1762

RUN away from the Subscriber, at the Sign of the Mermaid, in Kingston, a Negroe Man, named Joe; had on, when he went away, a green Jacket, without Sleeves, a Tow Shirt, and Trowsers of the same, pretty much worn, a Pair of new Pumps, and old Felt Hat; no Stockings. He is about six Feet high, very talkative, and about Thirty Years of Age; pretends great Knowledge in Farming and Horses. Whoever takes up and secures said Negroe, so that his Master may have him again, shall have Forty Shillings Reward, and reasonable Charges, paid by

WILLIAM CALLENDER.

N.B. The said Negroe can read and write, and may perhaps forge a Pass.

87. September 2, 1762

Virginia, August 2, 1762.

RUN away last Night, from the Subscriber living in Westmoreland County, a Servant Man, named John Grocott, an Englishman, near 40 Years old, about 5 Feet 9 Inches high, well set, full faced, wears his Hair, which is of a brown or sandy Colour, strait and newly shaved on the Top of the Head, talks much, and is a Bricklayer and Plaisterer by Trade, he has worked in a Garden at Times whilst with me, so that he may pretend to that Business: He took with him a dark Kersey Coat with large Metal Buttons, and Breeches of the same almost new, an old light Duffel Coat, a blue jump Jacket, double-breasted, with small Metal Buttons, white and coloured Stockings, several Shirts, white, brown and checked Linen, Several Pair of Trowsers, and other Things I know not of. I am told he has an Indenture that he has got from some Person for this Purpose, with a Discharge on it, and suppose he may change his Name to answer that.

Also a Negroe Woman Slave, called Betty, of a middle Stature, and a yellowish or dingy black Complexion, her Face rather thin than otherwise, proud in her Carriage, of a tolerable good Shape, Country born, and about 24 Years old: Carried with her a white Linen Jacket, ruffle cuffed, a Peticoat of the same, and blue and white striped Cotton Gown, a black and Striped Petticoat, and several other Cloaths of different Kinds.

It is supposed they were persuaded away by one William Wood (who is with them) who has formerly been a Sailor, and has been hired a small Time by me: He is, I believe, an Englishman, about 5 Feet 7 Inches high, of a tawny Complexion, thin Visage, and his Hair is off, the Toe next his great Toe turns under at the End, and his little Toe is lost, supposed to be from the right Foot.

They stole sundry Bedcloaths, and went off in a Schooner Boat, 18 Feet Keel, decked to the Main-mast, Sails and Main-mast new, Fore-sail not tabled, and daubed in several Places with Turkey-Point Paint, no Bow-sprit; they took with them a large Pine Canoe, a Locker in her Stern, an Iron Chain in her Head, fixed for two Oars. Whoever apprehends the said Runaways, so that I get them again, shall receive a Reward of Eight Pounds for John Grocott, Forty Shillings for the Negroe Woman, and Twenty Shillings for William Wood, Current Money; and if taken in Pennsylvania, Ten Pounds for the Bricklayer, Four Pounds for the Negroe, and Forty Shillings for William Wood, paid by   JO[HN] NEWTON.

N.B. When taken be careful of the Indenture and let me have it.

88. September 2, 1762

RUN away from the Subscribers, at the Globe Mill, in the Northern Liberties of Philadelphia, the Night of the 24th ultimo, a likely well set Negroe Man, named Friday, about 22 Years of Age, and 5 Feet 7 or 8 Inches high, has a Scar on his left Cheek, very near his Mouth, and some large ones on his Arms, which he said he received when taken in Guiney; has been in this Country 3 Years, yet speaks but poor English: Had on, and took with him, a good brown Thickset Coat, a good white Shirt, almost new, and old Ozenbrigs ditto, a good white Linen Jacket, white Linen Breeches, with a Patch on one Knee; also one Pair of old fine black Plush Breeches, good white Thread Stockings, and Shoes, almost new. Whoever takes up and secures the said Negroe, or gives such Information of him, that he may be had again, shall receive Twenty Shillings

Reward, and reasonable Charges, paid by JACKSON and COMPANY, at the Glove Mill aforesaid, or at their Mustard and Chocolate Store in Letitia Court, Philadelphia.

N.B. He is supposed to be gone with a white Woman, as it is not the first Time he has done so; therefore whoever harbours him, may depend on being prosecuted to the Extremity of the Law.

89. December 23, 1762

RUN-away on the 16th of November last, from the Subscriber, living on Sassafras River, Cecil County, Maryland, A Negroe Man, named Caesar, of a middle Stature: Had on, and took with him, A Felt hat, a blue Broadcloth lappelled Coat, with Metal Buttons, a green Cloth Vest, brown Cloth Breeches, white Linen Shirt, white Yarn Hose, and new Shoes, tied with Strings, and small Nails drove round the Heels and Soals. He pretends to understand something of the tight Cooper's Business. Whoever takes up said Negroe, and gives Notice thereof to his Master, or secures him, so as he may be had again, shall have a Reward of Six Dollars, and reasonable Charges paid, if brought Home, by

JOHN HALL.

90. December 23, 1762

New-Castle, December 2, 1762.

NOW in the Goal of this County, A Negroe Fellow, calls himself Caesar, says he belongs to John Hall, Esq; in Caecil County, Maryland; his Master is hereby desired to come, in four Weeks after this Date, pay Charges, and take him away, otherwise he will be sold for the same, by

ALEXANDER HARVEY, Goaler.

N.B. He is a Cooper by Trade.

91. December 30, 1762

RUN away, on the 22d of December instant from Samuel Parr, of Waterford Township, Gloucester County, West New-Jersey, three Miles from the new Bridge on Cooper's Creek, a Negroe Man, named Moses, about five Feet three or four Inches high: Had on when he went away, a new Cloth upper Jacket, an old red under Jacket, and old Leather Breeches. Took with him a Wherry, with Oars and Sail, and a

Gun. He is Country born, about 23 Years of Age, formerly belonged to Standish Ford, and afterwards to George Keen, who sold him out of the Workhouse for running away. Whoever takes up said Negroe, and brings him to his Master, shall have Three Pounds Reward, paid by
SAMUEL PARR.
All Masters of Vessels are forbid to carry him off.

92. December 30, 1762
Philadelphia, December 13, 1762.

RUN away last Saturday Night, from the Sloop Nabby, Josiah Godfrey Master, a Spanish Negroe Man, named Peter, a stout lusty Fellow, about 35 Years of Age, and well made: Had on when he went away, a blue Jacket and Breeches, a Hat and Cap, and took sundry other Cloaths with him. It is supposed he is concealed by some of the free Negroes about Town, as he speaks both English and Spanish very well, and will no Doubt pretend that he is free. Whoever will take up and secure the said Negroe, or bring him to Alexander Lunan, at Mr. Hamilton's Wharff, shall receive Forty Shillings Reward, and reasonable Charges.

N.B. All Masters of Vessels, and others, are desired not to carry him away, at their Peril.

93. January 20, 1763
New Castle, Jan. 15, 1763.

COMMITTED to the Goal of this County, a Negroe Man, who calls himself Tom, says he is a free Man, and a Tenant to Mr. Thomas Riche, Merchant, in Philadelphia; he is about five Feet ten Inches high, wears a good blue Coat, with Metal Buttons, Great Coat, Leather Breeches, good Shoes and Stockings, &c. His Master, if he has any, is desired to come in four Weeks from the Date hereof, pay Charges, and take him away, otherwise he will be sold for the same, by
ALEXANDER HARVEY, Goaler.

94. February 7, 1763

RUN away, the 6th instant from Stephen Carpenter, in the Northern Liberties, a lusty Negroe Woman, about 45 Years of Age, and looks very gray: Had on when she went away, a black, red and white striped

Linsey-woolsey short Gown, and Petticoat, a light coloured Cloth short Cloak, with a small Leghorn Hat, and Check Apron. It is supposed she is in Town, as she has a Husband, a Baker by Trade. Whoever takes up and secures said Negroe Woman in the Workhouse, so as her Master may have her again, shall have Twenty Shillings Reward, and reasonable Charges, paid by STEPHEN CARPENTER, in the Northern Liberties aforesaid.

95. June 23, 1763

RUN away from Benjamin Jackson and Company, at the Globe Mill, in the Northern Liberties of this City, a Negroe Man, named Friday, about 22 Years of Age, 5 Feet 6 or 7 Inches high, has a Scar on his Cheek, near his Mouth, and some large ones on 'his Arms: Had on when he went away, an Ozenbrigs Shirt, snuff coloured Thickset Coat, Fustian Breeches, old blue Jacket, old Hat, white Yarn Stockings, and good Shoes, and took with him an old Cloth Coat, and Linen Breeches. Whoever takes up and secures said Negroe Man, shall have Twenty Shillings Reward; and whoever is known to harbour him, shall be prosecuted according to the utmost Rigour of the Law.

   N.B. 'Tis supposed he is harboured by some base White Woman, as he has contracted intimacies with severil of that Sort lately.

96. June 23, 1763

FIVE POUNDS Reward.
Philadelphia, June 13, 1763.

RUN away Yesterday Morning from on board the brig Catherine, John Waterman Commander, a Negroe Man, named Joe, about 28 Years of Age, Virginia born, about 5 Feet 10 Inches high, branded on the Right Breast I, and on the Left F: Had on when he went away, a Frock and Trowsers; speaks good English, and will attempt to pass for a free Man. Whoever takes up and secures said Negroe, so that his Master may have him again, shall have Five Pounds Reward, and reasonable Charges, paid by

JOHN WATERMAN,
or
WILLING and
MORRIS

97. August 25, 1763

RUN away from Col. John Read, of Fairfield, in Connecticut, Two Mulatto Fellows; one named Titus, aged 22, of a middle Stature, longish and pale visaged, his Hair cut off, plays well on a Fiddle, and had one with him: Had on, A blue Flannel Coat, with flat Pewter Buttons. The other named Daniel, aged 16, large of his Age, broad Face, high Cheek Bones, long black Hair, cut off on the Top of his Head: Had on, A brown Camblet Coat, red Lining, a white Linen and a mixed coloured Flannel Vest; both had blue Great Coats, with yellow Metal buttons, and Leather Breeches. Any Person that will take and return them to their said Master, or secure them so that he may have them, shall have Five Pounds, New York Money, Reward, and Fifty Shillings for either of them singly, and all needful Charges paid—They had a Gun with them, and a forged Pass; were seen to cross Hudson's River, and travel Westward; whoever takes them, are desired to secure them well, or they will get away, and search well and secure said Pass, for which Two Dollars shall be added to the above Reward.

Any Person that hath a Mind to purchase them, that can take and secure them, and send me Word, shall have them at a reasonable Price. They are healthy able bodied, and understand Husbandry Business well.—All Masters of Vessels are forbid to carry them off.

JOHN READ.

98. September 1, 1763

Marcus-Hook, Chester County, August 23, 1763.

RUN-away from the Subscriber, the First of this instant, A Negroe Wench, named Phebe, about 30 Years of Age, of a small Stature, has three or four large Negroe Scars up and down her Forehead, but is apt to wear a Handkerchief round her Head to hide them: Had on, and took with her, Three fine Shifts, and one coarse Ditto, a Calicoe Gown and Bed-gown, a striped Linsey Bedgown and three Petticoats. She sometimes calls herself Sarah, and pretends to be free. Whoever takes up and secures said Wench in any Goal, so that the Subscriber may have her again, shall have Thirty Shillings Reward, and reasonable Charges, paid by   THOMAS BARNARD.

N.B. It is supposed that she is harboured by some of the free Negroes in or near Philadelphia or Germantown.

99. *September 29, 1763*

FIVE POUNDS Reward.

RUN away the 12th of July last, from Abraham Hewlings, in Evesham, West-New-Jersey, A Negroe Man, named Moses, about 18 Years of Age, about 5 Feet 3 or 4 Inches high, and has a Scar on the upper Side of one of his Feet: Had on when he went away, An Ozenbrigs Shirt and Trowsers, a lightish coloured Cloth Jacket, with a Piece set in the Forebody, an old Felt Hat, and a Pair of strong Shoes. He took with him a Sickle. Whoever takes up and secures said Servant, so as his Master may have him again, shall have the above Reward, and reasonable Charges, paid by   ABRAHAM HEWLINGS.

N.B. He formerly belonged to George Keen, and it is supposed is harboured by some ordinary People; for, while he belonged to said Keen, he was concealed by a Dutchman near Germantown.

100. *September 29, 1763*

RUN away from Samuel Read, living near the new Forge, the 9th instant September, A likely Negroe Man, named Peter, about 5 Feet 8 Inches high: Had on when he went away, A grey Jacket, also a red Stuff ditto, old coarse Trowsers, soaked with Apple-juice, and old Shoes. He is much given to laughing, and has some Marks on his Back and Belly with the Horse-whip. Whoever takes up and secures said Negroe, so that his Master may have him again at the new Forge, shall receive Forty Shillings Reward, and reasonable Charges, paid by me

SAMUEL READ.

101. *October 13, 1763*

Easton Goal, in Northampton County, October 6, 1763.

WHEREAS a certain Negroe Man, who calls himself Spencer Lake, and says he belongs to Colonel Palmer, of Virginia, and was by him hired to John Pennel, of Maryland, from whom he ran away, was committed to this Goal upwards of a Year ago, and advertised in the Pennsylvania Gazette, and particular Notice of his being here given to said Pennel: Now this is to give public Notice to the Master or Owner of said Negroe, that unless they send or come and pay the Charges, and take him away, before the first Day of November next, he will on that Day be sold out, for Payment thereof.   JACOB BAUCHMAN, Goaler.

102. *October 13, 1763*

RUN away from the Subscriber, living in Carlisle, about the 7th of September last. A Negroe Man, of middle Size, and middle Age, a Smith by Trade, named Abel, walks lame in his right Foot: Had on when he went away, an Elkskin Jacket, Buckskin Breeches, pieced on the Knees, Shoes and Stockings. Whoever takes up said Negroe, so that his Owner may have him again, shall have Forty Shillings Reward, and reasonable Charges, paid by THOMAS BUTLER.

103. *October 20, 1763*

RUN away from the Head of Chester River, in Kent County, Maryland, on the 10th of this instant October, a Mulattoe Man, named James, about 19 Years of Age, 5 Feet 9 Inches high, or thereabouts, slim, thin Visage, short curied Hair, a Scar on his Head, talks good English, a saucy Look, he has worked some Time in a Mill, in a Tan-yard, and on a Plantation: Had on, when he went away, a mixt grey Cloth Coat, with Horn Buttons, a Snuff coloured Thickset Vest, Check Shirt, with Sleeves of different Sorts, a halfworn Felt Hat, striped Trowsers, a white Cravat. It is supposed he rode away a black Horse, 14 and a Half Hands high, 5 Years old past, a Star on his Forehead, one grey fore Foot, paces, trots and gallops, and is sprightly. Whoever secures the said Fellow in any Goal, so that his Master may have him again, shall have Five Pounds Reward, and if in Virginia, the Province of Pennsylvania, the Jerseys, or on the Western Shore of Maryland Bay, Ten Pounds Reward, and reasonable Charges, paid by GEORGE GILPIN, living at the Head of Chester River, or THOMAS GILPIN, in Philadelphia.

104. *October 27, 1763*

RUN away, on the 23d of September last, from the Subscriber, living in New Providence Township, Philadelphia County, a lusty Negroe Man, of a very black Colour, speaks very little English: Had on, when he went away, a brownish coloured Cloth coat, with a Patch of Linsey in one of the Corner Skirts before, a lightish coloured Cloth Jacket, Tow Trowsers, old Shoes, and an old Felt Hat. Whoever takes up said Negroe, and secures him, so as his Master may have him again, shall have Thirty Shillings Reward, and reasonable Charges, paid by
JOHN HAMER.

N.B. The said Negroe is named Jupiter, though it is likely he may call himself by his Negroe Name, which is Mueyon, or Omtee.

105. *October 27, 1763*

RUN away from the Subscriber, living in Manatawny, in Berks County, 3 Miles from Thomas Potts's Old Furnace, on the 8th of July last, a Negroe Man, named Henry, about 24 Years of Age, middle sized, and well set, has on each Side a Hole through his Nose, and one through each Ear; speaks neither English nor Dutch. He went away from the Brick kiln, and had on a green Jacket and a Pair of Tow Trowsurs, leaving his Hat and Shoes behind him. Whoever takes up and secures the said Negroe, so that his Master may have him again, shall have Thirty Shillings Reward, and reasonable Charges, paid by
GEORGE ADAM WEIDNER.
N.B. All Masters of Vessels are forewarned to carry him off, at their Peril; and whoever in Town or Country harbours him, shall be dealt with according to Law.

106. *November 3, 1763*
FOUR PISTOLES Reward.

RUN away, on the 17th of October last, from Charming Forge, in Tulpehocken Township, Berks County, a Mulattoe Slave, named Joe, thick set, about five Feet six Inches high, has long black Hair, can speak but little English, and no Dutch: Had on when he went away, an old Castor Hat, Bearskin Jacket, and a striped Linsey one under it, Check Shirt, Cotton Stockings, and new Shoes, and has both Breeches and Trowsers with him, as also a Gun, Tomahawk, and a Pair of Boots. It is supposed he is gone to join the Indians beyond the Mountain. Whoever takes up and secures said Mulattoe in any Goal, and gives Notice thereof to Mr. Steigel, at Elizabeth Furnace, or to Charming Forge, shall have the above Reward, and reasonable Charges, paid by H. W. STEIGEL, or JOHN H. SMITH.

107. November 10, 1763

Dorchester County, Maryland, October 20, 1763.

FIVE POUNDS Reward.

RUN AWAY from the Subscriber, on the 6th Instant, his Mulattoe Waiting-man, named Jem (commonly called James Dyson) about 28 or 30 Years of Age, about 5 Feet 6 Inches high, a likely well-set Fellow, wears his own black Hair, which is commonly tied in a Cue behind, or plaited, and curls on each Side of his Face: Had on when he went away, a Cotton Jacket, brown Roll Trowsers, and old Shoes, but it is supposed he will change both his Name and Dress, as he has been seen with his Hair combed out straight, and an Indian Matchcoat on. I am informed he intends to make for the Jerseys in that Disguise, pass for an Indian, and profess himself a Shoemaker; he took with him some Lasts, and Shoemakers Tools. He is well acquainted both in Maryland and Pennsylvania, and is a very handy, sly, complaisant, smooth-tongued Fellow, can shave and dress a Wig as well as most Barbers, and will (as he is a light Mulattoe) probably pass for a free Man, and profess himself of that Trade. Whoever takes up the said Slave, and brings him to his Master, shall receive Forty Shillings Reward, if taken in the County, or Five Pounds if taken out of it, or secured in any Goal, so that he may be had again, paid by   ROBERT DARNALL.

108. January 26, 1764

ABSENTED from the Subscriber, living near New-port, New-Castle County, a likely Negroe Man, about 23 Years of Age, about 6 Feet high: Had on, when he went away, a blue Coat, and a new red Jacket, old Leather Breeches, old Shoes and Stockings, with a Felt Hat; his Name is Sam, well known in Philadelphia, formerly belonging to Rudeman Robinson. Whoever secures said Negroe, so that his Master may have him again, shall have Twenty Shillings Reward, if taken in, or near Philadelphia, but if 40 Miles Distance, Forty Shillings Reward, and reasonable Charges, paid by   DAVID REYNOLDS.

N.B. He had Liberty of his Master to go and see his Friends at Philadelphia, to return in two or three Days, but has now been about 16 Days.

109. *March 8, 1764*

THREE POUNDS Reward.

RUN away from the Subscriber, living in Hanover Township, Lancaster County, and Province of Pennsylvania, on the 16th of last Month, A Negroe Man, about 28 or 30 Years of Age, a little pitted with the Smallpox, named Abraham, a well-set Fellow, about 5 Feet 7 or 8 Inches high: Had on when he went away, an old Beaver Hat, Flannel Cap, light coloured strait Coat, with red Scrgc laid on the Cape, and bound round the Cuffs with red Serge, white Flannel Jacket, Leather Breeches, blue Yarn Stockings, and had in one Shoe a Brass Buckle, and in the other a carved Pewter Ditto. He is this Country born, and talks good English; it is supposed he will make towards Philadelphia, or the Forks of Delaware, as he was bred near Bethlehem. Whoever takes up and secures said Fellow in any Goal of this or the neighbouring Provinces, and gives Information thereof, so as his Master may have him again, or sends him to his Master, shall receive the above Reward, from

BENJAMIN WALLACE.

110. *May 31, 1764*

RUN away from the Subscriber, living in Upper Freehold, Monmouth County, West New-Jersey, on the 21st of this instant May, two Negroe Men, one named Toby, a well set Fellow, about 21 or 22 Years of Age, 5 Feet 5 or 6 Inches high, of a pleasant Countenance for a Negroe, shews his Teeth frequently, which are very white, is square built, with bow Legs, all the Toes on one Foot are short, as they have been froze, the Toe next to his great Toe on the other Foot lies over his great Toe, his Coat is a redish brown, of bought Cloth, with a green Thickset Lining, a new Ozenbrigs Shirt, a pretty good Felt Hat; had on Leather Breeches, much worn, which he may change; he can play upon the Violin, but not extraordinary well. The other is named Abraham, belonged once to Mr. Emlen, in Philadelphia, to Joseph Steniard, and to John Cox, of Upper Freehold aforesaid; he can write and read, understand Plantation Business; he is older than the other, and about 5 Feet 9 or 10 Inches high, well built; it is likely he will forge a Pass, and pretend to want a new Master for himself and the other. Whoever secures said Negroes in any Goal, or either of them, so as their Masters may have them again, or brings them home, shall have Twenty Shillings Reward for each, with reasonable Charges, paid by JOSEPH GROVER, and JOSEPH COWARD.

111. *June 14, 1764*

WHEREAS Joseph Grover, and Joseph Coward, of Upper Freehold, Monmouth County, West New-Jersey, did advertise, in the public Papers of the 31st of May last, two Runaway Negroes; these are to inform the said Persons, that the Negroes are now in Reading Goal, in Pennsylvania, and they are hereby desired to come and pay Costs, and take them away.   ISAAC WICKERSHAM, Goaler.

112. *August 9, 1764*

RUN away from Dr. Bern Budd, of Hanover, in Morris County, East New-Jersey, a likely well set Negroe Man, about 5 Feet 9 or 10 Inches high, of a yellow Complexion: Had on, when he went away, a blue Broadcloth Coat, with Tortoise-shell Buttons, a double breasted Broadcloth Jacket, with Mohair Buttons, and Leather Breeches. He took with him 3 white Shirts, a Check Ditto, a Snuff coloured Manchester Velvet Jacket, one striped Jacket, and a Pair of wide Trowsers. He speaks good English, understands all Sorts of Farmer's Work, and something of the Sea, and no Doubt will endeavour to pass for a free Negroe, as he can write any Pass he thinks necessary. Whoever takes up the said Negroe, and confines him in any of his Majesty's Goals, and sends his said Master Notice, so that he may have him again, or brings him to his said Master, shall receive TEN DOLLARS Reward, and all reasonable Charges, paid by   BERN BUDD.

N.B. All Masters of Vessels, and others, are forbid, on their Peril, to carry him off, or harbour him.

113. *September 13, 1764*

Carnarven, Berks County, May 18, 1764.

RUN away from the Subscriber hereof, a Mulattoe Servant Man, who passes for a Portugee, named James Johnson, about 35 Years of Age, of short Stature; had on and took with him, a Snuff coloured Coat, red Jacket, Leather Breeches, Beaver Hat, and some other Cloathing, which are all old; he can play on the Violin. Whoever takes up the said Servant, and secures him in any of His Majesty's Goals, so that his Master may have him again, shall have Forty Shillings Reward, paid by
GEORGE HAYS.

N.B. There is a white Woman that keeps with the said Servant, and passes for his Wife, of the Name of Catherine, about 40 Years of Age.

114. September 20, 1764

RUN away on the Ninth of this instant September, from the Subscriber, A Negroe Man, named Frank, alias Francisco, about 5 Feet 7 or 8 Inches high, well set, about 25 Years of Age, walks remarkably upright, can talk but little English, having lived among the Spaniards, and talks in that Dialect. He carried off with him sundry Cloaths, viz. one Cloth Jacket of an Olive Colour, lined with Linsey-woolsey, one red Ditto without Sleeves, with Brass Buttons, one Pair of Leather Breeches, one Knit Ditto, one Pair of Trowsers, three Ozenbrigs Shirts, two Pair Thread Stockings, one Pair new Shoes, one Ditto old: He commonly wears a large Pair of Pewter Buckles. It is supposed he is gone off in Company with a Negroe Fellow that has been lurking about this City some Time (supposed to be a Runaway) as he was seen in Company with the said Negroe the Night before he went off. Whoever takes up the said Negroe, and secures him in the Work-house of this City, shall receive, if taken in, or near the City, Thirty Shillings Reward, if out of the Province, Five Pounds, and all reasonable Charges, paid by

THOMAS PRYOR.

N.B. He commonly wears a white Handkerchief round his Head.

115. September 20, 1764

RUN away, on the 8th instant September, from the Subscriber, living at the Cross Roads, in New-London Township, Chester County, a Mulattoe Servant Man, named Malege Thompson, 5 Feet 3 Inches high, 30 Years of Age, a well set, brisk, mannerly talking Fellow; is bandy legged, and has been in the Army; had on and took with him, a new white coloured Cloth Coat, with blue Cloth Lining and Metal Buttons, a brown Camblet Jacket, with gilt Buttons, Buckskin Breeches, brown Yarn Stockings, one Pair of good Shoes, with large square Brass Buckles, and a Pair of Pumps, lately soaled, two Pair of coarse Trowsers, two coarse Shirts, and one fine one—He took an old roan Mare with him, and has a Certificate from Joseph M'Cullough that he came honestly by said Mare, and it is supposed he will endeavour to pass for a free Man, having his Indenture with him. Whoever takes up and secures said

Runaway, in any Goal, so that his Master may have him again, shall have Three Pounds Reward, and reasonable Charges, paid by

MICHAEL MONTGOMERY.

N.B. All Masters of Vessels and others are desired not to harbour or carry him off, at their Peril.

116. October 4, 1764

RUN away from the Subscribers, living in Amwell, in the County of Hunterdon, West Jersey, five Negroes, two of them are Men, about 30 Years of Age, well set, supposed to have taken a Gun with them; the other three are Women, about 25 Years of Age, one of them has a Child, about four Months old. The above Negroes have been in the Country about two Years, speak bad English, and went all off in Company together.—Whoever takes up and secures said Servants, in any of His Majesty's Goals, so that their Masters may have them again, shall receive Twenty-four Dollars Reward, and so in Proportion, for either of them taken separate, with all reasonable Charges, paid by WILLIAM NORCROSS, GERSHAM LEE, DANIEL READING, THOMAS READING, ISAAC FITZRANDOLPH.

117. October 11, 1764

FIVE POUNDS Reward.

RUN away from the Subscriber, living in Carlisle, in Cumberland County, on the 24th of September last, a Negroe Lad, named Abraham, about 19 Years of Age, 5 Feet high, this Country born, can do a little in Silver Work, is active in any Kind of Farming Business, cut in both Ears; had on an Iron Collar, Blanket Coat, Buckskin Breeches, Stockings, and Shoes with Whitemetal Buckles. Supposed to have gone with a Deserter, as the same night the Shop of John M'Ker, Taylor, was broken, and the following Goods taken, viz. a blue Coat, with white Lining, much worn, a Soldier's light-coloured Coat, with Horn Buttons, a scarlet Jacket newly turned, two Pair of Breeches, one black Cloth, the other Nankeen, supposed by a Deserter, as next Day an old Soldier's Coat, with some other Goods taken out of said Shop, were found in the Woods. Whoever takes up said Negroe and Thief, and secures them in any County Goal, so as his Master may have the Negroe, and the Thief brought to Justice, shall have Five Pounds, or for either of them Fifty Shillings, paid by JOHN GEMMIL.

118. October 18, 1764

York Goal, Oct. 6, 1764.

WAS committed to the Goal of this County the two following Persons, viz. John Stevens, a Frenchman, about 29 Years of Age, about 5 Feet 4 Inches high; has on a coarse Tow Shirt, light coloured Jacket, Ozenbrigs Trowsers, but no Shoes nor Stockings. Moses Grimes (a Negroe) this Country born, about 5 Feet 6 Inches high; has on a green Thickset Coat and Jacket, blue Breeches, with white Metal Buttons, and had with him a bay Horse, and says he is free. Their Masters, if any they have, are desired to come and pay Charges, and take them away, otherwise they will be sold for the same, in 30 Days from the Date hereof, by

JACOB GRAYBILL, Goaler.

119. October 25, 1764

RUN away about two Weeks ago, from the Subscriber, living in Concord, Chester County, a Mulatto Servant Man, named Jacob Jones, by Trade a Mason, about 5 Feet 8 Inches high, a well limbed, well set lissom Fellow, about 22 Years of Age, very active at most Sorts of Exercise, Jumping, Wrestling, &c. he hath a short Nose, and short black Hair, large Feet and Legs, his Shins bending forwards, he is very talkative, apt to laugh, and shew his Teeth, which are very white, had on a good green double breasted Coat, with a small Cape, and yellow Metal Buttons, a good black Hair Plush Jacket without Sleeves; he hath been about three Years ago in the Army, and had two Passes, one from Major Rogers, and about two Years ago worked at Winchester, in Virginia, and perhaps has made that Way. Whoever takes up and secures said Servant, so that his Master may have him again, shall have Three Pounds Reward, and reasonable Charges, paid by   JOHN PEIRCE.

120. November 22, 1764

FIVE POUNDS Reward.

RUN away from the Subscriber on Saturday, the 30th of June last, a young Mulattoe Fellow, about 20 years of Age, named Frank, about five Feet five Inches high, well set, full faced, short black curled Hair, very apt to swear when angry; had on and with him, when he went away, a coarse home made Tow Shirt and Trowsers, a Woollen Jacket, home-made, old Hat and Stockings; it is supposed he has changed his Clothes, and perhaps his Name by this Time; it also is supposed he is some where in the Cedar Swamps in the Jerseys, down Delaware River, as his Mother, and others of his Acquaintance, live near Cohansey, where the Fellow I believe was bred. Whoever secures said Mulattoe in any Goal, or brings him to his said Master, shall have the above Reward, besides reasonable Charges, paid by   THOMAS WITHERSPOON.

121. November 29, 1764

RUN away from the Subscriber, in King and Queen, Virginia, two white indented Servants, a Man and his Wife. The Man is English, about 5 Feet 5 Inches high, of a red Complexion, wears his Hair, is much Sun-burnt, steps short and quick in his Walk, is a Brickmaker by Trade, and has a sett of Shoemaker's Tools; had a short red Coat, red Breeches with Metal Buttons, an old green lappelled Jacket, a Flannel Jacket with red Stripes, new Osenbrigs Trowsers, with other Clothes, as he stole Part of mine; his Name is James Marrington. His Wife is about 30 Years of Age, about 5 Feet high, very thick, looks well, and has got good Clothes; she is an Irish Woman, and her Name is Mary Marrington.

Run away likewise 4 Negroes, viz. Jack, a black thick Fellow, about 30 Years old, about 5 Feet 6 Inches high, speaks broken English; has been used to go by Water, but of late to Plantation Business; had on a blue Cotton Jacket and Breeches, Petticoat Trowsers, Stockings, Shoes with Buckles, and has a Whitemetal Button in his Hat. Dick, a dark Mulattoe, very lusty, about 25 Years old, about 5 Feet 8 Inches high, a Carpenter and Painter by Trade; had on Cotton Clothes, with Petticoat Trowsers, and he has got a red Jacket and Breeches, a good Felt Hat, and Buckles in his Shoes. Daniel, a well set black Fellow, about 5 Feet 10 Inches high, has been used to Plantation Business, and had on Cotton Clothes. Dorcas, a small Wench, about 5 Feet high, has been used to House Business, has got a new brown Linen Jacket and Petticoat, and sundry other Things that she stole. They have all large Bundles, as they stole several Sheets and Blankets, with other Things. They were supposed to be seen crossing from Point Comfort to Little River, in a small Boat, with a Blanket Sail, last Saturday Morning, and I imagine will make for North-Carolina. Whoever apprehends the above Servants and Slaves, and delivers them to me, shall have Ten Pounds Reward, if taken in Virginia, if out thereof Twenty Pounds.   EDWARD VOSS.

If the above Runaways are taken in Pennsylvania, and conveyed in Philadelphia, the above Reward will be paid by RITCHIE and CLYMER.

122. *January 17, 1765*

NOW in Possession of the Subscriber, living in Philadelphia, a Negroe Man, about 5 Feet 6 Inches high, pretty well set, and straight limbed, is a deep black, hath been in and about Philadelphia since September last, is about 26 Years of Age.

Likewise a Negroe Wench, about 5 Feet high, and about 18 Years old, is a little on the yellow; she say she was born in the Jerseys; they both speak good English.   NATHANIEL DONNELL.

123. *March 14, 1765*

TEN PISTOLES Reward.

RUN away from the Subscriber, living near the Great Falls of Potowmack, in Frederick County, Maryland, a Mulattoe Man Slave; he has been gone upwards of two Years, and last January was twelvemonth he was seen near Reading Town, and have since heard he was at Hacket's Iron-works, in West-Jersey; he is about five Feet eight or ten Inches high, he resembles an Indian, as his Father was one, walks very upright, something bow-legged, had very black Hair, which he takes great Care of, and curls, has little or no Beard, broad across his Eyes, a Scar on one Side of his Nose, and several on his Head, one very large; went by the Name of Daniel, but may have changed his Name, very apt to get drunk, and then is bold and saucy; he understands Farming Business, about Forty-three Years of Age. Any Person that will secure him in any Goal, and gives Notice to the Subscriber, shall have the above Reward, paid by
THOMAS DAVIS, Tavern-keeper.

124. *March 21, 1765*

RUN away from the subscriber, living near Prince Frederick Town, Calvert County, Maryland, on the 1st day of October last, a Negroe man, named London, about 35 years of age, and about 5 feet 7 inches high, of a yellow complexion, stammers in his speech, if examined strictly, bow legged, and when he talks, one corner of his mouth stands awry. He may change his name, is very artful, and at no loss for a plausible story, is a cooper and carpenter by trade. Whoever takes up the said negroe, if in the county aforesaid, and brings him to the subscriber, shall receive Forty Shillings reward; if taken 30 miles from home, Five Pounds; if out of this province Seven Pounds, and reasonable charges. As I have some reason to apprehend the above mentioned negroe has been carried off by some ill-disposed person, I hereby promise a reward of Twenty Pistoles to any person who will discover the thief, so as he can be convicted. ROBERT FREELAND.

125. May 16, 1765

RUN away from the Subscriber, living in Upper Freehold Township, Monmouth County, in New-Jersey, a Negroe Man, named Pomp, about 36 Years of Age, about 5 Feet 10 Inches high, he has lost one of his upper Teeth, and has a bald Spot on the Crown of his Head; had on, when he went away, an old light coloured Coat, an old Pair of Leather Breeches, old Ozenbrigs Shirt, a Pair of white Yarn Stockings, a Pair of new Pumps, an old Felt Hat, and he took with him, a small sized Gun. Whoever takes up and secures said Fellow, so that his Master may have again, shall have Thirty Shillings Reward, and reasonable Charges, paid by EBENEZER APPLEGATE.

126. May 16, 1765

NOW in Newtown Goal, Bucks County, a certain Negroe Fellow, who calls himself Pompey, and says he belongs to Ebenezer Applegate, near Allen Town, in East New-Jersey. His Master is desired to fetch him away in two Weeks from the Date hereof, or he will be sold for his Charges. ANTHONY SIDDON, Goaler.
May 14, 1765.

127. May 30, 1765

RUN away from the Subscriber, of Northumberland County, Virginia, on the first of May, three Convict Servant Men, who carried with them a Negroe Man Slave, viz. Matthew Leonard, an Irishman, about six Feet high, well proportioned, his Hair very red and long, which he used to tye behind; but as he carried away several Wigs, it is possible they may all cut their Hair, and wear Wigs; his Face and Hands are very much freckled, and says he has been a Serjeant in the Army; he stole a drab coloured Cloth Frock, with yellow Buttons, several of the Tops off, an old Crimson Cloth Waistcoat, with plain double gilt Buttons, and a Pair of Whitney Breeches, which it is supposed he will wear. Also Samuel Holmes, an Englishman, a Taylor by Trade, about 5 Feet 6 Inches high, has a remarkable yellow Spot on one of his Knees, and on the Instep of the other Leg has been a very great Sore, which is now dried up, and has left a large Scar; he stoops a little, rocks very much in his Walk, is bow-legged, and stammers in his Speech; as he carried off a great many Clothes out of his Shop, belonging to different People, it is impossible to describe any of their Dresses exactly. Dennis M'Cartey, an Irishman, he professes the Trades of a Blacksmith, Coppersmith, Brazier and Tinker, and has worked at each since he came into the Country, about 5 Feet 5 Inches high, has a very crooked Nose, a well made little Fellow, and pretends to play the Slight of Hand. Sam, a Negroe, of a yellowish Complexion, about 5 Feet 6 Inches high, about 28 Years of Age, very wide between the Knees, and had on a red Pea Jacket. They carried away with them two Guns, a large Pack-sheet, made for cleaning Grain on, and several Carpenter's Tools. Whoever apprehends them, or any of them, and secures them, so as I get them again, shall receive Three Pounds Reward for each, from   WILLIAM TAITE.

N.B. It is suspected they have a forged Pass.

128. June 13, 1765

Philadelphia, June 5, 1765.

RUN away, last Night, from Captain Hugh Wright's Ship, a Mulattoe Fellow, named Dick, about 5 Feet 6 Inches high, well set, very crafty, talks much, and is remarkable for a Cast in his Right Eye; he wears a red Jacket, white Breeches, Check Shirt, new Shoes and Stockings, and an old Beaver Hat. It is supposed he is gone to Dover, as he has a Wife there. Whoever secures said Fellow in any Goal, or brings him to JAMES HARDING, in Philadelphia, shall have Forty Shillings Reward, besides Charges.

N.B. Masters of Vessels are cautioned against taking him away.

129. June 27, 1765

Chester Goal, Pennsylvania, May 20, 1765.

IN Custody of the Subscriber, the three following Persons, viz. Matthew Leonard, an Irishman, 6 Feet high, Samuel Holmes, an Englishman, 5 Feet 6 or 7 Inches high; by Sundries found in his Bueget, a Taylor by Trade, stammers in his Speech; Negroe Sam, nearly the same Height of the latter, very wide between the Knees, and bow legged; committed as Runaways, and say they came from Virginia. Their Masters, if any, are desired to come, pay Cost, and take them away.

SAMUEL RAINE, Goaler.

N.B. The Property of William Taite, Esq; Virginia.

130. July 4, 1765

New-Castle, June 19, 1765.

IN Custody of the Subscriber, a Mulattoe Fellow, named Dick, advertised by Mr. James Harding, in Philadelphia. His Master is desired to send for him, by   ALEXANDER HARVEY, Goaler.

131. July 4, 1765

RUN away from the Subscribers, on Sunday, the 9th of last Month, two likely Negroe Fellows, the one named Begill, about 5 Feet 10 Inches high, slim built, has been in the Country near 4 Years, speaks tolerable English for the Time, aged about 35 or 40 Years; had on, when he went away, a Linsey Coat, of black and blue Colours mixed, with Brass Buttons, a Felt Hat, white Shirt, Sheepskin Breeches, Stockings of mixed Colours, and double soaled Shoes. The other named Jerry, aged about 25 Years, near the Height and Size of the former, has been in the Country about 3 Years, speaks very broken English; had on, when he went away, a striped Linsey Waistcoat, white Shirt, and narrow short Trowsers, old Shoes, no Stockings, an old Felt Hat, with a red String or Garter round the Crown. Whoever takes up the said Negroes, and brings them to the Subscribers, in Reading, in Hunterdon County, New-Jersey, or secures them in any Goal, giving Notice to the said Owners, so that they may have them again, shall have Six Dollars Reward, and reasonable Charges, or Three Dollars for each, paid by SAMUEL HERRIOT, or LAWRENCE POOL.

132. July 11, 1765

RUN away from the Subscriber, living in Amwell Township, Hunterdon County, West-Jersey, on the 20th of May last, a Negroe Man, named Sambo, about 30 Years of Age, near 6 Feet high, slim built, a single Mark on his Right Cheek; he is a new Negroe, and can speak but little English; he is very apt to speak the Words that are spoke to him again. It is supposed that he is either stolen or decoyed away. Whoever takes up said Negroe, so that his Master may have him again, shall have Three Pounds Reward; and if stolen, Ten Pounds, provided the Thief be brought to Justice, with reasonable Charges, paid by
ISAIAH QUINBY.

133. August 1, 1765

Lancaster, July 23, 1765.

WAS committed to my Custody, on the 22d Day of this instant July, the following Negroes, viz. a Negroe Man, named Jack, alias Tobias, and a Negroe Woman, Named Jane, Wife to the said Jack, alias Tobias, and her two Children, a Boy, five Years old, or thereabouts, and a Girl about four Years old. The Man is about Thirty four Years of Age, and the Woman about Thirty; they have sundry good Clothes with them; they say they belong to James Campbell, in Conegocheague, near Fort Loudoun. The said Campbell is hereby desired to come and pay the Charges, and take them away, or they will be sold for the same, in four Weeks from this Day, by me   MATTHIAS BUCH, Goaler.

134. September 26, 1765

FIVE POUNDS Reward.

RUN away from the Subscriber, living in Baltimore County, Maryland, on the 24th Day of June last, a Country born Negroe Man, named Shadwell, about 45 Years of Age, but looks older, bald on the Head, and has lost his upper fore Teeth: Had on when he went away an Iron Collar, and a Pair of Iron Fetters doubled rivetted, but 'tis likely he has got them off. His Cloathing is very uncertain, as he will change it if he can, as also his Name, and wants to pass for a Freeman. He can give a pretty good Account of Annapolis, as he was born near that Place; also of Baltimore County, Part of Frederick County in Maryland, Marsh-creek Settlement, and Part of Connawaga, as he did Harvest there two Years together when he was run away; he likewise has been at Anteaton, and many Miles beyond it, and was in Carlisle Goal. He seemed inclined to go among the French or Indians in the Time of War, but was prevented; and as I am informed he was seen near the South Mountain, it is probable he will make for Pittsburgh, or the back Inhabitants. Whoever apprehends said Negroe, and secures him in any Goal, if out of the Province, shall have Forty Shillings Reward, or Five Pounds Pennsylvania Currency, if brought Home, paid by   THOMAS COCKEY.

N.B. He can walk upon his Hands, with his Feet upwards, but perhaps may not do it now, being formerly taken up by it.

135. October 24, 1765

RUN away from Charles Town, Cecil County, Maryland, on Friday, the 11th of this instant October, two Negroe Fellows; one named Cuff, about 5 Feet 3 Inches high, a thick, well set Lad, about 17 Years of Age, very thick Lips; had on, when he went away, a blue Cloth Jacket, without Sleeves, Ozenbrigs Shirt and Trowsers, and about 4 Weeks ago was brought home (after running away) from Philadelphia Work-house, where he was taken up and confined, and formerly belonged to Mr. Charles Moore, Hatter there. The other a well set, down-looking Fellow, about 5 Feet 9 Inches high, 22 Years of Age, and Country born; had on, when he went away, a new blue Sailor's long Pea Jacket, and new Linen Shirt and Trowsers; he has a large fresh Wound on his Left-hand. Whoever takes up and secures said Negroes, or either of them, so as the Subscribers, may have them again, shall receive Twenty Shillings Reward, and reasonable Charges, for each, paid by ABRAHAM VAN-BEEBER, or THOMAS BRUCE.

136. December 12, 1765

FOUR DOLLARS Reward.

RUN away from the Subscriber, living at the Sign of the Buck, In Worcester Township, Philadelphia County, on the 28th of November, a lusty likely Negroe Wench, named Hannah, 18 Years of Age, bred in Michael Hulings's Family, in Philadelphia, and bought of him last October: Had on, and took with her, a striped Camblettee Gown, a brown Linsey Petticoat, an Ozenbrigs Shift, green Yarn Stockings, several Caps and Handkerchiefs, and a Straw Hat; can tell a plausible

Story, and is well acquainted in Philadelphia, Jerseys, and Wilmington; it is supposed, if not secreted by Negroes in Philadelphia, she is gone to Wilmington, she having a Brother and Sister living with Mr. Hulings, on the Plantation of William Empson, deceased. Whoever secures said Wench in any Goal or Workhouse, so as she may be had again, shall have the above Reward, and reasonable Charges, paid by PHILIP FITZ-SIMMONS.

137. December 19, 1765

WENT away from Joseph Sharp, of Salem County, West Jersey, the 10th Day of November last, a Negroe Man, named Sambo, under Pretence to get a Master; he is a thick short Fellow, limps with his Right Knee, and one of his Buttocks bigger than the other, about 40 Years of Age, talks much, and cannot count above 15, if you ask him how much 10 and 5 is, he can't tell such Question; he has had many Masters, and lived at Mount-Holly, when the Furnace went with Mr. Bard; it is thought that he will endeavour to get to Philadelphia, or is gone to New-York. Whoever takes up the said Negroe, and secures him in any Goal, so that his Master may have him again, shall have Three Pounds Reward; if taken in this County, or Cumberland, Forty Shillings, paid by   JOSEPH SHARP.

138. January 30, 1766

Lancaster, January 15, 1766.
THREE POUNDS Reward.

RUN away, last Night, from the Subscriber, a Servant Girl, named Ann Broughton, aged about 20 Years, 5 Feet 4 or 5 Inches high, is tolerable likely, her Hair is light brown, and curls much, has taken with her different Kinds of womens Apparel, served her Time in Salem, in New Jersey. Also a Negroe Man, named Bob, very well made, about 5 Feet 6 Inches high, aged about 30, but looks older, he is a Skinner by Trade; had on, when he went away, a redish brown Country Cloth Coat, with yellow carved Buttons, red Jacket, and Buckskin Breeches, took with him other Breeches and Trowsers, Yarn Stockings, new Shoes, and yellow coloured Buckles; he appears a civil good natured Fellow; they will probably pass for Man and Wife. Whoever brings them home, or secures them in any Goal, so that their Master may have them again, shall receive Thirty Shillings Reward for each, from   GEORGE ROSS.
   N.B. They are both this Country born.

139. February 6, 1766
FIVE PISTOLES Reward.

RUN away from the Subscribers, living at the Nanticoke Iron-works, in Worcester County, Maryland, about the 9th of September last, a Negroe Man, named Abraham, and often calls himself Abraham Dobson, about five Feet six Inches high, about 24 Years of Age, of a yellowish Complexion, well set, and talks good English: Had on when he went away, a Leather Cap, or Felt Hat, Cloth Jacket, Country made Linen Shirt and Trowsers; also took with him a Pair of Leather Breeches. He is supposed to be taken away by a certain John Mears, about 23 Years of Age, about five Feet eight or nine Inches high, down Look, appears to be a sober orderly Person, not very talkative, and was sometime ago advertised for some Misdemeanors done in Virginia. Whoever takes up said Negroe, and secures him in any Goal in this Government, or in Pennsylvania, so that the Subscribers may have him again, shall have the above Reward, and reasonable Charges, and if out of the said Governments, the Five Pistoles abovementioned, paid by WILLIAM DOUGLASS, or JONATHAN VAUGHAN.

140. February 6, 1766
TEN POUNDS Reward.

BROKE Goal, at Dover, in Kent County, on Delaware, on the 28th of this Instant, two Irishmen named William M'Laughlin, and Patrick Gillaspy; the said William is a lusty Man, but looks very poorly, having been in Goal some Time; had on, when he went away, a Saggathy Coat and Breeches, very much worn, and took with him a Pair of blue Breeches, and old Shoes and Stockings; wears his Hair, which is black, bushy or curled, and is very much Pock-marked. Patrick is a stout well set Fellow, born in Dublin, said to be a Servant, and very impertinent; both of said Men are very much given to Drink, and have stole, or took out of Goal, two New Negroes, which they will sell, if they meet with an Opportunity, likewise a Gun, and sundry other Things, to the Amount of Four or Five Pounds: Said Patrick had on, when he went away, a blue Coat and Breeches, a large Racoon Hat, a cut Wig, new Shoes and Thread Stockings, which he stole. By his Looks he may be supposed to be a Robber or Highwayman. Whoever takes up the said Irishmen and Negroes, and secures them so as the Goaler may have them again, shall have the above Reward, paid by   JOHN WINTERTON.

141. *May 1, 1766*

RUN away from the Subscriber, the 15th Day of April last, a Negroe Man, named Beaver or Bevis, about 5 Feet 10 or 11 Inches high, between 30 and 40 Years of Age, a smart lively Fellow, and is a midling Scholar, talks very good English and Dutch; had on and took away with him, a Blanket Coat, old Beaver Hat, Buckskin Breeches, and grey Yarn Stockings, half worn Shoes, and Buckles; likewise a bay Horse, Saddle and Bridle, from his said Master. Whoever takes up said Servant, and secures him in any Goal, so that his Master may have him again, shall have Forty Shillings Reward, or Twenty Shillings for the Horse, paid by
NATHANIEL RING.

142. *June 19, 1766*

FIVE POUNDS Reward.

RUN away from the Subscriber, living in the City of Burlington, a Mulattoe Servant Man, named Lewis, about 5 Feet 10 Inches high, stoops in his Walk, round Shins, the Calves of his Legs very high up to his Hams, long Visaged, grey Eyes, very much freckled: Had on when he went away, a Homespun Cloth Coat, of a redish brown Colour, black Jacket and Breeches, new Pumps with large Silver Buckles in them; it is supposed he went off with one John Sidenham, lately enlisted in one of the Royal American Battalions. Whoever takes up said Servant, and secures him in any of his Majesty's Goals, so that his Master may have him again, shall receive the above Reward, and reasonable Charges, paid by me, SAMUEL HOW.

N.B. The above Servant is so white, that he hardly would be taken for a Mulattoe, only by his Hair.

143. *June 26, 1766*

Reading, June 24, 1766.

RUN away from Berkshire Furnace, in Berks County, about the last of May, a Negroe Man, named Dublin, aged 24 Years, 5 Feet 6 Inches high, well set; had on, when he went away, an Ozenbrigs Shirt and Trowsers, green Jacket, a half worn Felt Hat, and new Shoes, with Brass Buckles. Whoever takes up and secures the said Negroe, so that his Master may have him again, shall receive Forty Shillings Reward, and reasonable Charges, paid by JOHN PATTON.

144. July 3, 1766

RUN away from the subscriber, in Paxton Township, Lancaster County, on Monday, the 19th of May last, a certain Negroe man, named Dick, about 5 feet 6 inches high, a slim built black fellow, about 23 or 24 years old, speaks good English, some Low Dutch, and some French; had on, when he went away, an old hat, blanket coat, good leather breeches, old stockings, good shoes, but a good deal too large for him, tied with strings. As he formerly lived with one Mr. Hunt, in the Jerseys, it is thought he will make that way, or towards Philadelphia. Whoever takes up said Negroe, and secures him, so as his master may have him again, shall receive Six Dollars Reward, and reasonable charges, paid by
JOHN POSTLETHWAIT.

145. July 3, 1766

RUN away from the subscriber, living on Bohemia manor, Cecil county, Maryland, a Mulattoe man, named Joe, about 25 years of age, 5 feet 10 inches high, loves strong liquor; had on, and took with him, an old felt hat, a white linen cap, or a wig, old whitish home-made cloth coat, some mohair buttons on it, coarse tow shirt and trowsers, white yarn stockings, new shoes, and carved buckles. It is supposed he has a pass. Whoever takes up said fellow, and puts him in any goal, or brings him to his master, shall have Three Pounds reward, paid by
EPHRAIM LOGUE.
   N.B. All masters of vessels are forewarned not to carry him off at their peril.

146. July 17, 1766

Chester County July 12, 1766.

WAS committed to the Goal of this County, a Mulattoe Man, who says he belongs to Mr. Ephraim Logue, living on Bohemia Manor, Caecil County, Maryland. His Master is desired to come and pay Charges, and take him away.   JOSEPH THOMAS, Goaler.

147. September 11, 1766

TEN DOLLARS Reward.

RUN away from the Subscribers, living in Nottingham Township, Burlington County, West New-Jersey, on the 26th Day of April last, a Mulattoe Servant Man, named John Johnston; he is about 5 Feet 8 or 10

Inches high, has a remarkable Lump on his under Lip, and a Scar on one of his Hands, he is given to Drink, and when in Liquor is very talkative; he ran away from the Subscribers last December, and was taken up, and put into Easton Goal, but broke Goal, and went to Reading, in the Jerseys, when he was taken up, and put into Easton Goal again, from whence his Masters got him; he stole and took with him, a blue Surtout Coat, with Hair Buttons, and Velvet Cape, about half-worn, also a red Flannel Waistcoat, two new Ozenbrigs Shirts and Trowsers, a half-worn Castor Hat, Yarn Stockings, a Pair of dark ribbed Worsted Ditto, and several other Things. He was advertised in the Pennsylvania Gazette last December, and continued for three Months. Whoever takes up said Servant Man, and secures him in any of his Majesty's Goals, so as his Masters may have him again, shall receive the above Reward, and all reasonble Charges, paid by

ABIA BROWN, and JOSEPH CLAYTON.

N.B. All Masters of Vessels are forbid to carry him off at their Peril.

148. November 6, 1766

RUN away, on the 7th of September, from the Subscriber, living in Baltimore Town, a Negroe Girl, named Hagar, about 14 Years of Age, of a brownish Complexion, has remarkable long Fingers and Toes, and a Scar under one of her Breasts, supposed to be got by Whipping: Had on, when she went away, an Ozenbrigs Shift and Petticoat, very much patched, and may now be very ragged, an Iron Collar about her Neck, which it is probable she may have got off, as it was very poorly rivetted; she is supposed to be harboured in some Negroe Quarter, as her Father and Mother encourage her in these Elopements, under a Pretence that she is ill used at home. Whoever takes up said Girl, and brings her to me, shall have, if taken ten Miles from home, Twenty Shillings Reward, if 20 Miles Forty Shillings, if further Three Pounds, and if out of the Province Five Pounds, paid by   WILLIAM PAYNE.

N.B. All Persons are forbid to harbour the said Girl, as they shall answer the contrary at their Peril.

149. November 6, 1766

FORTY SHILLINGS Reward.

RUN away from the Subscriber, living in Worcester township, Philadelphia county, on Thursday, the 16th of October last, a Negroe man, named Jack, about 26 years old, about 5 feet 4 or 5 inches high, a thick set fellow; had on, when he went away, a light coloured lincey jacket, a striped lincey under jacket, without sleeves, tow trowsers, good shoes and stockings, a good felt hat, wears it cocked; one of his legs is thicker than the other from the ancle to the knee. Whoever takes up the said Negroe, and secures him in any goal, or brings him to the Subscriber, shall have the above Reward, besides Charges, from   PETER WENTZ.

150. November 13, 1766

Burlington, Nov. 10, 1766.

NOW in the custody of the subscriber, a certain Negroe man, who is advertised in last week's papers by the name of Jack, and says he belongs to Peter Wentz, of Worcester Township, and county of Philadelphia; this is to give notice, that except his master comes and pays the charges, and takes him away, he will be sold out for the same, by

EPHRAIM PHILLIPS, goaler.

151. November 13, 1766

Somerset County, Maryland, October 19, 1766.

RUN away, about the 16th of June last, from the Subscriber, living at Princess Ann Town, in Somerset County, Maryland, a Mulattoe Wench, named Ibbe, about 19 Years of Age, very fat and clumsy, with large Cheeks, short Nose, and Holes in her Ears; her Dress uncertain, as she had several Changes with her. She has been seen at Indian River with a free Negroe, pretended to be his Wife, and called herself Sabrah Johnson. Whoever takes up said Mulattoe, and secures her, so as her Master may have her again, shall have Five Pounds Reward, and reasonable Charges, paid by Captain George Noarth, in Philadelphia, or the Subscriber.   ARNOLD ELZEY.

152. December 4, 1766

RUN away from the Subscriber, living at Grubb's Forge, in Lancaster County, about the 7th of October last, a young Negroe Man, named Cato, about 18 Years of Age, about five Feet six Inches high, well set, three remarkable Sc[ar]es on each Cheek; had on, when he went away, a new Felt Hat, new Ozenbrigs Shirt, old Trowsers, new Shoes, a Jacket of Bird eyed Stuff, without Sleeves. Whoever takes up said Negroe, and secures him in any Goal, so that his Master may have him again, shall receive Three Pounds Reward, and reasonable Charges, paid by

SAMUEL JONES.

153. December 11, 1766

New Castle County, Dec. 5, 1766.

NOW in the custody of the subscriber, the three following persons, viz. Samuel Galloway, about 35 years of age, about 5 feet 9 inches high, wears a cap, a blue cloth coat, with white metal buttons, thickset waistcoat, and light coloured cloth breeches, was committed the 10th of July last as a vagrant, and on suspicion of horse stealing, and it is suspected that he has escaped from some goal.

Also a certain William Muheaw, about 20 years of age, about 5 feet 4 inches high, light brown hair, by trade a tinker; had on, when committed, a brown broadcloth coat and waistcoat, with mohair buttons, striped Holland trowsers, white worsted stockings, and half boots, committed 21st of October last as a runaway; says his master's name is Thomas Beech, and lives in Arundel County, in the province of Maryland.

Also a negroe lad, about 19 years of age; about 5 feet 6 inches high, slender made, speaks bad English, pretends to be foolish, to obtain his freedom, calls himself Cato, and says he belongs to Samuel Jones, at Grubb's Iron Works, in Lancaster County; had on, when committed, an Indian blanket coat, ragged tow trowsers, and old shoes, with strings. Their masters (if any they have) are desired to come, pay charges, and take them away in six weeks, or they will be sold out for the same by

THOMAS PUSEY, Goaler.

154. December 18, 1766

Maryland, November 29, 1766.

RUN away from the Subscriber (in Dorchester County, Ennalls's Ferry) a Negroe Man, named Charles, about 6 Feet high, between 40 and 50 Years of Age; had on a black Broadcloth Coat, but it is supposed he will change his Clothes; he can read, write, and cast Accounts, has a small Notion of Surveying and Music, and took with him a Flute; he is very talkative, vastly affable, and very fond of letting those he talks with know what he understands; he has a remarkable Scar on one of his Feet, occasioned by the Cut of an Axe, and it is likely he may have a Pass. Whoever secures the said Negroe in any Goal, so as his Master may have him again, shall have Forty Shillings Reward, and if brought home, the above Reward, and reasonable Charges, paid by

RICHARD KEENE.

N.B. It is likely he may attempt to get on board some Vessel, therefore all Masters of Vessels are forewarned not [to] take him off, at their Peril.

155. January 8, 1767

Burlington, January 2, 1767.

NOW in the Goal of the City and County of Burlington, a certain Negroe Man, who calls himself Charles Cornish, and can read and write; had on, when committed, a black Broadcloth Coat, and says he belongs to Richard Keene, at Ennalls's Ferry, in Dorchester County, Maryland. He was advertised in this Paper the 29th of November last. His Master, if any he has, is desired immediately to come and pay Charges, and take him away, otherwise he will be sold out for the same, by me

EPHRAIM PHILLIPS, Goaler.

156. January 29, 1767

Easton, January 19, 1767.

ON the 4th of November last was committed to the goal of this county, a negroe man, who calls himself John Lyndsay, about 26 years of age, and about 5 feet 7 inches high; he is said to belong to one John Postlewait. The owner is desired to take him away, otherwise he will be sold for his charges, by the 17th of March next.   JACOB BACHMAN, Goaler.

157. June 25, 1767

FIVE POUNDS Reward.

RUN away from the Subscriber, the 13th instant June, a Negroe Man, named Richard or Dick, aged about 25 Years, about 5 Feet 9 Inches high, of a yellowish Complexion, and grave Countenance, very stout and well set, walks a little stooping, and is a good Farmer; had on, when he went away, a good Nap Coat, dark coloured, with Mohair Buttons, Ozenbrigs Shirt and Trowsers, a Pair of new Shoes, and a good Felt Hat. Whoever takes up said Fellow, and secures him in any Goal on the

Continent, so that he may be had again, or brings him to his Master at Whitehill, Burlington County, West-Jersey, shall have the above Reward, and reasonable Charges, paid by   ROBERT FIELD.

N.B. It is probable he will get in Company with my Indian Slave Jack, advertised runaway the 18th Instant, Three Pounds Reward for taking him up. All Masters of Vessels, and others, are forewarned not to employ or secret them at their Peril.

158. October 1, 1767

Sussex county, on Delaware, Three Run Mills, Sept. 22, 1767.
TEN POUNDS Reward.

RUN away, from the subscriber, on the 13th instant, a mulattoe slave, named HARRY, about 40 years of age, 5 feet 6 Inches high, and well set. Had on, when he went away, a brown cloth coat, white linen jacket, and brown breeches; he was bred a miller, and understands very well how to manufacture flour, and can invoice the same; is much given to strong drink, and playing on the violin; understands the carpenter's and millwright's business middling well; was removed from East New-Jersey in the year 1762, by one Nicholas Veight, who lived at Rockey-Hill, and kept a mill. The said fellow has a free mulattoe wife, named Peg, and two children, and I expect they will endeavour to get together (though they did not run away at one time) it is expected they will endeavour to get to the province of East New-Jersey; it is imagined said mulattoe has a pass. Any person or persons that takes up and secures the said mulattoe, and delivers him to CHARLES WHARTON, merchant, in Philadelphia, or to the subscriber, shall have the above reward of Ten Pounds, if taken in the province of New-Jersey, and Six Pounds if in the province of Pennsylvania, paid by   LEVIN CRAPPER.

N.B. The said mulattoe woman, named Peg, has run away from her bail, at Lewis Court, in Sussex county.

159. May 26, 1768

THREE POUNDS Reward.

RUN away, the 3d of May ultimo from the Subscribers, in Cumberland County, West New-Jersey, two Negroe Men, one about 5 Feet 10 or 11 Inches high, named PETER; had with him two Felt Hats, 1 fine Shirt, 1 Woolen, and 2 coarse Ditto, a Thickset Coat, with a Cape, a black Cut-Velvet Jacket, blue Plush Breeches, a Pair of Leather Ditto, 2 Pair

of Woollen ribbed Stockings, 1 Pair of Thread Ditto, 2 Pair of Shoes, Brass Buckles, and 5 or 6 Caps. The other named WILL, is a stout well set Fellow, not quite so tall as Peter; had with him, when he went away, one brown Jacket, 1 old Ditto, without Sleeves, blue Breeches, no Hat. As they are artful Fellows, it is not unlikely they may change their Cloaths and Names, the latter came from Carolina, and it is likely they may try to get there again; and as he can write, and they have taken Pen and Ink with them, it is not unlikely they will produce a Pass. Whoever secures said Negroes, so as their Masters may have them again, shall have the above Reward, or Thirty Shillings for either of them, paid by
EPHRAIM SEELY, ISAAC ANTRIM.

160. December 15, 1768
TWENTY POUNDS Reward.

RAN away from the Neabsco Iron-Works, in Virginia, on, or about the 10th of October last, a country born Negroe man slave, named BILLIE, the property of the Hon. John Tayloe, Esq; he is about 30 years of age, very black, well made, 5 feet 8 inches high, puts on a sour look when taxed with any thing amiss; he had on and took with him, when he went away, a blue broad cloth coat, black cotton velvet jacket, and sundry other sorts of cloths, besides shoes and stockings of various kinds: He is by trade a Shipcarpenter, and is such a proficient in that business, as not only to repair, but to build all sorts of small craft. The day that he went off, he was accompanied by a dark Mulatto fellow, named Scipio, the property of Mr. John M'Millian, of Prince William county, in Virginia, of much the same age and size as himself. They crossed Potowmack-River together, in a schooner's boat, to the Maryland shore, where they left her, and have, from that time, kept themselves undiscovered. As BILLIE was some time last summer brought from Carolina (to which place, under the sanction of a forged pass, he had travelled as a freeman) it is more than probable that if he is not now engaged by some shipbuilders to the northward, that he will endeavour to get on board of some craft, bound for Charles-Town, or to some place in Carolina, where he expects to be free.

Whoever takes up the said Negroe, or Mulatto, and brings one, or both to the subscriber, or to Mr. John Calvert, manager of Col. Tayloe's mine-bank, in Baltimore county, or will secure them, so as they may be had again, shall receive, for each, a reward of Five Pounds, if taken 40 miles from home, or the above reward, if taken at a greater distance, from the said Mr. John Calvert, or from   THOMAS LAWSON.

161. March 30, 1769

RUN away last night from the subscriber, living in York Town, a Negroe MAN, who calls himself MOSES GRIMES, about 5 feet 4 or 5 inches high, about 29 years of age; had on and took with him, a white coloured broadcloth coat, a green ditto, much torn, a flowered silk jacket, a half silk red striped ditto, a brown broadcloth ditto, a nap ditto, one pair of broadcloth blue breeches, a pair of cotton stockings, and a pair of ash coloured ditto, two pair of shoes, with a pair of brass buckles, and a pair of boots, two linen shirts, an old hat, with a hole in the crown. Whoever takes up said Negroe, and secures him in any of his Majesty's goals, so that his master may have him again, shall receive FORTY SHILLINGS reward, and reasonable charges, paid by me

PHILIP GRAYBILL.

March 20, 1769.

162. April 13, 1769

RUN away from Berkshire Furnace, in Berks county, on the 27th of March last, a Negroe man, named Dublin, 26 years of age, 5 feet 6 inches high, is a remarkable strong chunky fellow, speaks but indifferent English; had on, and took with him, a leather cap, felt hat, ozenbrigs and check shirts, spotted under jacket, a blue coarse ditto, blanket coat, two pair of Germantown made stockings, and old shoes. Whoever takes up said Negroe, and brings him to the works aforesaid, shall have FORTY SHILLINGS reward, and reasonable expences, or if secured in any goal, so that he may be had again, shall have THIRTY SHILLINGS, paid by   JOHN PATTON.

N.B. All masters of vessels, and others, are forbid to carry him off, or harbour him.

163. May 4, 1769

Chester Goal, April 29, 1769.

NOW in Custody of the Subscriber, a NEGROE Man, named Dublin, who says he belongs to Mr. John Patton, at Berkshire Furnace, in Berks County. His Master is desired to come, pay Charges, and take him away.

JOSEPH THOMAS, Goaler.

164. June 1, 1769

Hobb's Hole, Virginia, May 20, 1769.

RUN away from the Subscriber, the 2d instant, a Negroe boy, named Billy, about 15 years old, he is a likely, stout, well made lad, and not very black; had on, when he went away, a brown cloth coat, with red sleeves and collar, and green plains waistcoat and breeches. He was seen in Richmond county, going upwards, with David Randolph, a cooper by trade, who run away from this town the 5th instant; he is a stout made fellow; had on, a blue serge coat, lappelled, with yellow buttons, a white waistcoat, striped with blue (which appeared to be country made) and leather breeches; he had other clothes with him, and some cooper's tools. He worked last at Mr. James Hunter's, but am told served his time in Philadelphia, and I apprehend will carry the boy to Maryland or Pennsylvania, to sell him. Whoever takes up the said boy, and secures him, so that I may get him again, shall receive Five Pounds, if taken in the colony, if out of the colony TEN POUNDS, from

JOHN BROCKENBROUGH.

165. June 1, 1769

RUN away from the Subscriber, living near the head of Chester river, Queen-Anne's county, Maryland, in the night of the 14th instant, a convict servant man, named William Prees, about 50 years of age, 5 feet 6 or 7 inches high, is broad set, his hair almost white, the top of his head bald, and has a particular wink, or leer, with his eyes, when talking. Also a Negroe fellow, named Ben, between 30 and 40 years of age, about 5 feet 8 inches high, and very black. They took with them 4 pair of old leather breeches, a new white shirt, the linen about 3s. per yard, 2 white, and 2 brown shirts, much worn, 2 white country kersey jackets, not milled, a dark coloured fearnought jacket, a white Welsh cotton ditto, a claret coloured and brown ditto, both cloth, a brown camblet coat, 3 felt hats, and 4 pair of shoes. Whoever takes up and secures the said convict and Negroe, or either of them, so that the Subscriber may have them again, shall receive Twenty Shillings each, if taken in the province, or Forty Shillings each, if taken out of the province, and reasonable charges.   JOHN SEALE.

May 22, 1769.

166. *June 22, 1769*

Sussex County, on Delaware.

ON the sixth day of June instant, was taken up a Negroe BOY, by John Wood, of Lewis Town, on suspicion of being a runaway, and committed to the goal of the county aforesaid; and upon examination, he is found to answer every description (except his cloathing, which he says is changed) of a boy advertised in the Pennsylvania Gazette, No. 2110, by John Brockenbrough, of Hobb's-Hole, in Virginia. His master may have him again, by applying to   BOAZ MANLOVE, Sheriff.

167. *June 22, 1769*

New-Castle, June 16, 1769.

RUN away on the 6th instant, at night, from Joseph Enos, a Negroe man, named Congamochu, alias Squingal, about 25 years of age, 5 feet 10 inches high, straight and slim, large white teeth, he has many large scars on his belly and arms, in his country fashion, talks very bad English, has a hole through one of his ears, and thought to be the right one, he has been inoculated for the small-pox in the left arm, but took no infection; had on, when he went away, an old cloth vest, without buttons, and a good pair of cloth breeches, open at the knees, both of a light colour, and a tow shirt; he was seen at the river shore, near New-Castle, the day after he went off; as he talked much of his wives, and country, it is thought he will endeavour to get off by water; this is to desire all masters of vessels, and others, not to carry off, nor harbour the said Negroe. Whoever takes up the said Negroe, and secures him in any of his Majesty's goals, so that he may be had again, shall have Twenty Shillings reward, and reasonable charges, paid by JOSEPH ENOS.

168. *June 29, 1769*

Somerset County, New-Jersey, June 19, 1769.

RUN away, on Saturday, the 10th day of this instant, from the Sub-scribers, two Negroe men, one named Ben, of a yellow complexion, flat faced, bushy hair, about 5 feet 2 inches high, aged about 19 years; had on, when he went away, a brown homespun coat, lined with striped homespun, with metal buttons, black flowered everlasting jacket, a pair of linen breeches, or trowsers, a felt hat, and some other clothes; speaks good English and Dutch. The other named Jack, also of a yellowish complexion, aged about 21 years, about 5 feet 9 inches high; had on, when he went away, a blue coat, with white metal buttons, buckskin breeches, and several other cloathing, so it is likely he may change his dress; took with him a fiddle, and speaks good English and Dutch. They have both obtained a false pass, by which they pass for free mulattoes. Whoever apprehends the said Negroes, and secures them, so as their masters may have them again, and gives notice by a letter, by the post, to the Subscribers, near New-Brunswick, shall have Ten Dollars reward for both, or Five for either of them, and all reasonable charges, paid by LEFFERT WALDRON, ERNESTUS VAN HARLINGEN.

N.B. Their pass is signed with the name of Lefferty, a justice of the peace in the county of Somerset. They came over the Ferry at Bordentown, on Tuesday, the 13th instant, and went the post road to Philadelphia, and it is supposed they will try to push to sea. All masters of vessels are forbid to carry them off at their peril.

169. *July 13, 1769*

RUN away, on the 12th of June last, from the subscriber, living near Wright's Ferry, in York county, a Negroe man, that calls himself Moses Grimes, country born, is about 28 years of age, 5 feet 6 or 7 inches high, is very talkative, and given to lying, has been used to be an hostler, and to wait in a tavern; had on, and took with him, an old felt hat, without lining, two white diaper caps, a new hemp shirt, an old flax ditto, two pair of tow linen trowsers, a pair of old leather breeches, a pair of white cotton stockings, a pair of blue ribbed ditto, a pair of boots, a pair of channel pumps, a light coloured cloth coat, a short green cloth ditto, a brown broadcloth jacket, one ditto flowered silk, one striped cotton and silk ditto, a grey cloth double breasted ditto; it is likely that he will pass for a free man, and get sombody to forge a pass for him. Whoever apprehends said Negroe, and secures him in any goal, so that his master may have him again, shall receive Thirty Shillings reward, and reasonable charges, paid by   THOMAS MINSHALL.

N.B. He is very yellow, and has passed for a Mulattoe.

170. *July 27, 1769*

TAKEN up, on Saturday, the 15th Instant, at the Blazing Star, and now is in Perth-Amboy Goal, a Negroe Man, that nearly answers the Description of one advertised in this Gazette, by Thomas Minshall, living near Wright's Ferry, in York County; he will not tell his Name, nor own he has a Master, but passes as a Freeman. His Master may hear further, by applying to JOHN KINSEY, in Woodbridge.

171. August 17, 1769

August 4, 1769.

RUN away from the Subscriber, living in Donegall, Lancaster county, an Irish servant man, named JOHN ROBESON, about 22 years of age, about 5 feet 6 inches high, of a fresh complexion, red hair, and commonly wears it tied behind, and cued; had on, when he went away, a shirt and trowsers, a linen jacket, with 4 rows of buttons on the breast, and a pair of old shoes; he is a good scholar, and perhaps may pass for a Doctor. There went off with him, a Negroe man, named NED, well set, and strong, but not very tall, aged about 28 years, born in the Jerseys, speaks very good English, and can read and write, of a down look, and thick lips; had on, when he went away, a coarse shirt and trowsers, a hat, bound round the edge, and a hood worked in it; he may be taken for a Mulattoe, by his colour, and probably both may have provided other clothes. Likewise ran away in company with them, a Negroe man, belonging to Joseph Chambers in York town, named JAMES JONES, about 28 years of age, about 5 feet 11 inches high, slim made, born in this country, and has a good countenance; he took with him a blue broadcloth coat, black velvet jacket and breeches, a pair of leather ditto, two fine shirts, one of them ruffled, 2 coarse ditto, two pair of coarse trowsers, a pair of pumps, with silver shoe-buckles, a pair of strong shoes, a blanket, and a gun, with a split in the stock, near the butt. It is likely they may have forged passes, as the white man writes a good hand. Whoever takes up and secures the said servants, so that their masters may have them again, shall have SIX POUNDS reward for the three, or Forty Shillings for either, if taken separate, and reasonable charges, paid by us, ALEXANDER LOWREY, JOSEPH CHAMBERS.

172. September 14, 1769

Bohemia, September 1, 1769.
THREE POUNDS Reward.

RUN away from the Subscriber, living on the Bohemia Manor, in Cecil county, Maryland, a Mulattoe SLAVE, named JOE, about 30 years of age, 5 feet 10 inches high, a slim straight built fellow, has several bumps or knots on his chin and throat, readily to be seen when new shaved, somewhat pitted with the small pox, has several scars of the whip on his back, likes strong drink, can read print, and is a forward talkative fellow; had on, and took with him, when he went away, an old felt hat, a white fine shirt, and coarse tow ditto, and wide trowsers, a new silk handkerchief, a light coloured over jacket, the collar lined with blue velvet, metal buttons, a red under vest, without sleeves, white metal buttons, blue fine yarn stockings, half worn, with some darns in them, and half worn shoes, without heels. He has been used to the water, and it is supposed has with him, or will endeavour to procure, a pretended pass, and get on board some vessel; all masters of vessels are forbid to carry him off at their peril. Whoever takes up said fellow, and secures him in any goal, or brings him to his said master, shall have the above reward, and reasonable charges, paid by   EPHRAIM LOGUE.

173. October 19, 1769

Baltimore Town, September 19, 1769.
FORTY POUNDS Reward.

BROKE goal last night, about eleven o'clock, the following prisoners, viz. JOHN NAILING, a tall thin faced square set young fellow, about 20 years of age, born in Ireland, and imported from Dublin, speaks much on the brogue, is remarkably talkative, addicted to drinking and swearing, brags much of his manhood, and is a great bruiser; this was the fourth time of his being committed to goal in one year that he has been in the country. WILLIAM STALING, a well set man, about 5 feet 8 inches high, by trade a Leather-breeches maker, born in Ireland, and about 30 years of age, both his eyes have lately been bruised in fighting, and one of them very blood shotten, he has a very ill look, and at present appears very sickly. JOHN STINSON, who says he was born in Pennsylvania, near Schuylkill, about 5 feet 10 inches high, a portly well set man, wears his own black hair, tied behind, has a down look, goggle eyes, thick lips, and a mole on one cheek; he has a wound on the back of his left hand, by which he has lost the use of one finger; he is a notorious horse-thief and house-breaker, has twice been tried for his life in Virginia, under the name of SHEPHERD, but constantly broke goal; he has with him, a light coloured Wilton coat, without lining, also a green saggathy coat, and leather breeches. JOHN DOUGLAS, born in Ireland, about 6 feet high, stoops much in his shoulders, has sore eyes, he was detected in carrying servants from this town to Virginia, he speaks a little on the brogue, and is very drunken and talkative, he chiefly goes by water, and says he lived in Norfolk. ROBERT COALE, a Negroe, who pretends to be a freeman, but is the property of David Chevis, of Caroline county, Virginia, whose house and property he destroyed by fire, in April, 1767, for which he was sentenced to die. He broke goal, and was afterwards confined in Port Tobacco goal, from whence he also escaped, and came to Baltimore, where he continued near two years working as a labourer to Masons, before he was committed to this goal, he has a certificate of his freedom, signed by a certain Tomkins, who broke goal with him, in Charles county; he is about 26 years of age, of a good countenance, is a very civil handy fellow, can wait at table, and plays the fiddle with his left hand, has a remarkable large foot, he has been sometime in irons, and may still carry the marks of them, he has several suits of cloaths, particularly a brown broadcloth suit, a black ditto, with sundry fine white linen shirts, &c. RICHARD WHEELER, was born in this county, about 25 years of age, a tall thin young man, he has a very down cast look, and has been in goal near 14 months, much pitted with the small pox, which he has had not long since. THOMAS ELTON, a servant of Mr. Rutland's, near Annapolis, a short square set man, he is a very sober orderly fellow, had on a blue ragged coat, old shirt, and leather breeches, which are very old, and too short for him, without shoes or stockings, one of his eyes appears much bruised by fighting, by trade a Farmer, and has a very pale countenance, thick faced. As many of them have been long confined, they appear pale, and their shins tender, tho' they are tolerable well in Flesh, their cloathing is uncertain, as many of them had scarce any, and most of them barefooted. Whoever secures and brings back said prisoners, shall have Forty Pounds reward for the whole, or Five Pounds for each, paid by

DANIEL CHAMIER, Sheriff of Baltimore County.

174. December 7, 1769

FIVE DOLLARS Reward.

RUN away from the subscriber, living at Upper Freehold, in Monmouth county, East Jersey, the 20th of November last, a Negroe man, named SYRON, middle aged, about 5 feet 10 inches high, a stout, well set bold-looking fellow, very talkative, smooth face, and remarkable large feet; had on, when he went away, a light cloth coloured coat, wore out at the elbows, a spotted swanskin jacket, and brown cloth coloured breeches, wool hat. He had a pass, without a limited time, to look for a master. Whoever takes up and secures the said Negroe man, so that his master may have him again, shall receive the above reward, and all reasonable charges, paid by   RICHARD BRITTAIN.

175. *January 11, 1770*

FOUR DOLLARS Reward.

RUN away, on Christmas day last, from the subscriber, living in Worcester township, Philadelphia county, a Negroe man, named JACK, about 34 or 35 years of age, about 5 feet 5 or 6 inches high, and his left leg much thicker than the right; had on, a new white linsey jacket, an under ditto, without sleeves, buckskin breeches, light blue yarn stockings, new shoes, with large brass buckles, and a good wool hat. He says he has liberty from me to look for another master. Whoever takes up said Negroe, and brings him to me, or secures him in any of his Majesty's goals, so that I may get him again, shall have the above reward, and reasonable charges, paid by   PETER WENTZ.

N.B. All Masters of Vessels are forbid to carry him off, at their peril.

176. *January 18, 1770*

MADE his escape from the subscriber, living in Caecil county, in the province of Maryland, at Bristol, in Bucks county, in the province of Pennsylvania, on the 24th of October last, as he was bringing him home, from Somerset county goal, in East New Jersey, a Negroe man, named Pen, but had changed his name, by a forged pass, and called his name James Pemberton, it is likely he may pass by the same name; he is about 25 years old, a chunky and well set black fellow, very talkative, and pretends to be very religious; he had on, when he made his escape, a brown jacket, with a blue cape, blue cloth trowsers, white yarn stockings, old shoes and buckles, and an old beaver hat, cocked on two sides.

Likewise run away, from the subscriber, on the 27th of December last, a Negroe lad, aged about 20 years, his name Cuff, he is a small thick lipped fellow, branded on one of his cheeks something like PR; had on, when he went away, an old great coat, a blue jacket, an old spotted jacket, three pair of trowsers, blue, white and check, a grey cloth cap, nits and lice yarn stockings, good shoes, and tolerable buckles; has had a scalded head, which has occasioned the wool on the top of his head to be white. He has run away several times, and has each time endeavoured to ship himself on board vessels in Philadelphia harbour.

Whoever takes up Pen, and secures him in any goal, or brings him home, shall have Fifty Shillings; and for Cuff, Forty Shillings, and reasonable charges, paid by me   THOMAS SAVIN.

N.B. All masters of vessels are hereby forbid to harbour or take them on board, at their peril.

177. April 12, 1770
SIXTEEN DOLLARS Reward.

RUN away, on the 5th of April last, from the subscriber, living in East Whiteland, Chester county, a Negroe man, named PEDRO, about 27 years of age, about 5 feet 10 inches high, a well set, stout, active, lively fellow, very mannerly when abroad, talks poor English, being brought up among the Spaniards: Had on, when he went away, a blue nap cloth coat, with yellow metal buttons, and red lining, a calicoe jacket, a fine castor hat, half worn, a fine white shirt, one homespun ditto, a pair of trowsers, with a pair of good buckskin breeches under them, brown yarn stockings, a pair of ribbed ditto, one pair of shoes, half soaled, a pair of plated buckles, one silk cap, one linen ditto, ruffled, &c. But as he is a crafty, subtle fellow, it is likely he will change his cloaths in many respects, if not his name. Whoever takes up and secures the above Negroe, in any of his Majesty's goals, so that his master may have him again, shall have the above reward, and reasonable charges, paid by
                              ROBERT POWELL.

N.B. All masters of vessels, and others, are forbid against harbouring or carrying off said Negroe, at their peril.

178. May 10, 1770

RUN away on the 19th day of March last, from the Subscriber, living in Cumru township, Berks county, within 5 miles of Reading town, a NEGROE man, about 28 years of age, and about 5 feet 9 inches high, has lost several of his fore teeth, and his right foot is frost-bitten; had on, when he went away, a blanket coat, whitish cloth jacket and breeches, homespun shirt, and is named Dick, alias John Linch; had a collar round his neck, and a chain to his leg; he pretends to be free, and is very much given to lying. Whoever takes up and secures said Negroe, so that his master may have him again, shall have Three Dollars reward, and reasonable charges, paid by me   DAVID EVANS.

N.B. Said Negroe took with him a hammer and chisel.

179. May 17, 1770

THREE POUNDS Reward.

RUN away from the subscribers, living in York county, near Wright's Ferry, a Negroe man, called Moses Grimes, about 30 years of age, about 5 feet 5 inches high, his head is a little bald, very talkative, a great liar, this country born, and will pass for a free Negroe; had on a felt hat, a blanket coat, broken about the arm and shoulder, old tow linen shirt, a pair of tow trowsers, and old shoes. Likewise went off in company with the above Negroe, Jacob Davis, who is an apprentice to Henry Davis, is a mason by trade, about 5 feet 6 or 7 inches high, well set, black hair, and full faced; had on, when he went away, an old felt hat, old blue coat, much broken about the sleeves, a blue jacket, the back parts much lighter coloured than the fore parts, a new sheepskin apron, a pair of new striped trowsers, new shoes, pieced on one of the toes, a pair of half worn ash-coloured lincey breeches; he took with him a mason's hammer and trowel. Whoever apprehends the above runaways, and secures them, so that their masters may have them again, shall receive Three Pounds reward for both, or Thirty Shillings for each, with reasonable charges. THOMAS MINSHALL, and HENRY DAVIS.

May 8, 1770.

180. June 28, 1770

TWENTY SHILLINGS Reward.

RUN away from the subscriber, a Negroe man, named Sharper, a short, thick, well-set fellow, his clothes uncertain; he formerly belonged to Robert M'Lonan, in New-Castle; he has got a piece of writing drawn, setting forth, that I sold him to Samuel Shoemaker, Esq; Mayor of Philadelphia; by which Means he has imposed on several that knew him to be my Property. Any person lodging said Negroe in any of his Majesty's goals, or otherwise secures him, so that I may get him, shall have the above reward. Likewise run away from the subscriber, an old Negroe man, named Philip. Whoever secures said fellow, shall be handsomely rewarded, by   THOMAS LENNON.

N.B. As I live a small distance from town, by applying to Mr. TIMOTHY CARROLL, Merchant, at the corner of Chestnut-street, in Water-street, Philadelphia, will be properly directed.

181. August 2, 1770

RUN away, about 5 weeks ago, from the subscriber in Front-street, Society-hill, a Negroe man, named TOM, a likely fellow, about 5 feet 8 inches high, by trade a bisket baker; had on, and took with him, a blue cloth jacket, one of the shirts pieced, 2 ozenbrigs shirts, and a pair of trowsers, buckskin breeches, thread stockings, and new shoes; his hands a little crooked, speaks good English, was formerly the property of Mark Cook, biscuit baker, of Parson Sturgeon, and John Elton, carpenter; he was accustomed to elope, when he followed whitewashing; it is believed he is lurking about this city, all persons are forbid to employ or entertain him. Whoever brings said Negroe to his mistress, shall have Fifteen Shillings reward, from ANN REARDON.

To be LETT, by said Ann Reardon, a new bake-house with two new ovens, and all utensils necessary for the business.

July 16, 1770.

182. August 30, 1770

West-Pennsborough township, Cumberland county, August 22, 1770.

RUN away from the subscriber, about the 26th of July last, a Negroe man, named ABEL, of middle age and size, a smith by trade, has a little halt as he walks, and turns out his toes, had, sometime ago, a large wart under his waistband, and I think a bit hath been taken out of his ear. Whoever secures said Negroe in any goal, so that the owner may get him again, shall have FOUR DOLLARS reward, and reasonable charges, paid by me THOMAS BUTLER.

183. September 13, 1770

Chester, September 5, 1770.

THIS day was committed to my custody as a runaway, a Negroe man, named Abel, who says he is a slave to Thomas Butler, in Cumberland county, who lives within about 10 miles of Carlisle; his master is desired to come and pay charges, and take him away, by

JOSEPH THOMAS, Goaler.

Also was committed to my custody on the 22d day of August last, a Woman, who calls herself Mary Sanderson, alias Heyney, for stealing clothes from sundry persons, which have been owned; and as there are many clothes still in my custody, supposed to be stolen, viz. 3 good shifts, of about 900 linen, 2 linen handkerchiefs, one lawn, 2 muslin, and 1 cambrick ditto, 2 holland aprons, 1 long lawn, 2 home made linen ditto, and 1 linen petticoat, 2 pair of India calicoe pockets, 2 white linen short gowns, a pink coloured calimancoe quilt, a lincey jacket and petticoat, with two sorts of stripes in the petticoat, and several pair of linen and yarn stockings; whoever has lost the said clothes, proving their property, may have them again, by applying in six weeks from the date hereof, or they will be disposed of according to law, by

JOSEPH THOMAS, Goaler.

184. September 27, 1770
FIVE POUNDS Reward.

RUN away the 13th of this instant September, from the subscribers, living in Leacock township, Lancaster county, a Negroe man and woman; the man is about 30 years old, 5 feet 4 inches high, speaks good English, has long hair; had on an old hat, his other clothes uncertain;— the woman who went with him, has with her a young female child, about 8 months old (a good mark to know them by) she is about 23 years old, middling size, has good clothes, two long gowns, one striped cotton, the other calicoe, two short gowns, and new low heeled shoes. Also a white servant man, named Adam Jacobs, who run away the 13th of June, is about 18 years of age, 5 feet 4 inches high, is somewhat marked with the small-pox; had on, a white wool hat, a light coloured cloth jacket, with cuffs on the sleeves, old buckskin breeches; had also a pair of coarse linen trowsers, but what is most distinguishing, he has a large scar on his left leg, it having been run over by a waggon, also that knee is much larger than the other. Whoever secures them, so that their owners may get them again, shall receive the above reward, or Forty Shillings for the white man, Thirty for the Negroe man, and the same for the woman and child, paid by SAMUEL LEFEVER, or DAVID WATSON.

185. October 11, 1770
FORTY SHILLINGS Reward.

RUN away from the subscriber, living at Pine Forge, in Berks county, Pennsylvania, on Monday, the 1st of this instant October, a Negroe man, called Wetheridge, but generally calls himself Jacob, about 5 feet 7 or 8 inches high, middling slender, very black, and much marked with the small-pox, about 23 or 24 years of age, walks remarkable straight and quick, and speaks good English, has been brought up to cooking and waiting in a gentleman's family, which business he understands very well, as a gentleman in Philadelphia, from whom he was lately bought, brought him up to that business only; had on, and took with him, 1 fine white shirt, 2 ozenbrigs ditto, an old pair of ozenbrigs trowsers, old leather breeches, one red and white striped linen jacket, one white linen ditto, with sleeves, 2 brown cloth ditto, without sleeves, lined with shaloon, a snuff-coloured broadcloth coat, almost new, with yellow metal buttons, a coarse brown great coat, with white metal buttons, good strong shoes, with brass buckles, a half-worn beaver hat, which he generally wears cocked; he likewise took with him, a very old silver watch, without a chrystal, silver faced, the hour and minute hands both brass, the maker's name Moore, London, number forgot, and on the outside of the inner case is badly engraved I I, and some figures. Whoever takes up said Negroe, and secures him in any goal, and gives notice thereof to the subscriber, shall have the above reward, paid by

THOMAS MAY.

186. November 1, 1770

RUN away on the 25th day of August last, from the subscriber, living in East Nantmell township, Chester county, a Mulattoe man, named Thomas Bucher, aged 35 years, about 5 feet 10 or 11 inches high, hath short black curled hair, very large feet, his legs not equal, the one considerably thicker than the other, is pretty much marked with the small-pox; had on, and took with him, when he went away, a whitish coloured thick cloth coat, with mohair buttons, one under jacket, without sleeves, one fine linen shirt, one tow ditto, one pair of tow trowsers, one pair of coarse leather shoes, with brass buckles, one new castor hat, and one half worn ditto. Said Mulattoe took with him a white woman, which he says is his wife, she is very remarkable, as all the fingers are cut off her right hand, and is a thick-set, chunky, impudent looking, red haired hussey, pretty much given to strong drink. Whoever takes up said Mulattoe man, and secures him in any of his Majesty's goals, shall have Eight Dollars reward, and reasonable charges, paid by

JOHN STARRETT.

N.B. It may be supposed some evil designing person hath drawn him a pass.

187. November 22, 1770
FORTY SHILLINGS Reward.

RUN away from the subscriber, in East Nottingham, Chester county, on the 18th of this instant November, a Negroe man, known by the name of Jack, or John Richison, about 5 feet 7 inches high, a well set fellow, about 30 years of age, and speaks good English; he is supposed to have on a short brown coat, and buckskin breeches, or black stocking pattern breeches; he is marked on the forehead, and one of his feet frost-bitten, and has a lump on one of his wrists; he is a smart active fellow, and will endeavour to pass for a free man, and has a letter for that purpose, which he reports he got from Ireland, and probably a forged pass, supposed to be given him by some of my honest neighbours, and will pretend he is going to Philadelphia for justice, as some of his confederates persuaded him the letter will set him free. Whoever secures the said Negroe in any goal or work-house, so as his master may have him again, shall have the above reward, and reasonable charges, paid by
WILLIAM BEAN.

N.B. It is supposed he may endeavour to get to sea, all masters of vessels are forbid to carry him off at their peril.

188. January 10, 1771
TEN DOLLARS Reward.
(Purchased by Doctor Bouchell, as he runs)

A PALE Mulattoe man (a slave for life) named JOE, but now passes by the name of PRINCE ORANGE, and often changes his name; was seen in April last, at Blackford Town, and worked near that place for some weeks; was born at Cambridge, in Dorchester county, and sold in Kent, on Delaware; he is a tall, slender, boney fellow, about 30 years old, very talkative when in drink, can read a little, and pretends to be a seaman, has a small stoop in his shoulders, thin face, high nose, a little pitted with the small-pox, is a drunkard, swearer, and liar; had on a whitish brown country cloth jacket, and a red under jacket. Whoever delivers the said fellow at Mr. WITHERSPOON'S, in New-Castle county, shall receive the above reward, and reasonable charges, paid by
SLUYTER BOUCHELL.

January 1, 1771.

189. March 7, 1771

TWENTY DOLLARS Reward.

RUN away from the sloop Tryall, in Rappahannock river, Virginia, on the 2d day of December last, a bright Mulattoe man slave, named SAM, about 25 years of age, 6 feet 2 inches high, strong, and well made, has a small scar on his forehead, over one of his eyes, I think it is the left, and a large quantity of long wool on his head, which he sometimes shears about the crown; his cloathing is such as is worn by seamen, and were imported from England ready made, the under jacket of spotted swanskin, the sleeves of which are much too short for his long arms; he had also with him, a new spotted rug, and some mixed coloured broadcloth, which he had stolen, and I believe was the cause of his flight, and may probably induce him to go a great distance, to avoid punishment; he was bred to plantation and farming business, and sometimes employed as an axe man and sawyer in ship-building, has only been about six months by water, so that he cannot be supposed a compleat sailor. Whoever apprehends and secures him in goal, or otherwise, and gives notice thereof, to Mr. Charles Yates, of Fredericksburg, so that he may be delivered safe to him, or his order, shall be paid the above reward of Twenty Dollars.   STAFFORD LIGHTBURN, junior.

190. June 6, 1771

SIXTEEN DOLLARS Reward.

RUN away, from the subscriber, living in Lancaster, on the 21st of May last, an indented Negroe man, named *Anthony Sernetor*, about 28 years of age, 5 feet 7 inches high, well shaped, but pretty slim, is very talkative, speaks good English, and also reads and writes it; he is a tanner by trade; had on, when he went away, a felt hat, a brown linsey coat, with pockets in the folds, brown cloth jacket, blue and white striped trowsers, good shoes, with buckles. It is supposed he is gone to Philadelphia, as it has been observed that he has a pass about him, in order to go on board some vessel, having formerly been in the sea service for some time. Whoever takes up the said Negroe, and secures him in any goal, so that his master may have him again, shall have the above reward, paid by   CASPER SINGER.

N.B. All masters of vessels are forbid to carry him off at their peril.

191. *July 4, 1771*

Perth-Amboy, July 1, 1771.
FIFTEEN POUNDS REWARD.

RUN away from the subscriber, in the month of October, 1762, a Mulattoe Woman SLAVE, named VIOLET, about 35 years of age; she is very active, and rather tall. Some time afterwards she was seen in company with one James Lock somewhere on the Sasquehanna, and by information was apprehended and committed to goal, in the year 1764, in Frederick-Town, in Maryland, on suspicion of having run away. From that goal she was reported to have made an escape, and about two months ago was discovered about 15 miles from Ball-Fryer's ferry, in Frederick county, in Maryland aforesaid, where she had three children. Edward Bonnel, of Monmouth county, in the province of New-Jersey, was formerly her owner, and after his decease, she was sold by his executors to the subscriber. Any person who may take her up must secure her strictly, or she will certainly escape again, being remarkably artful. Whoever delivers her, and her children, to the subscriber, or to THOMAS M'KEAN, Esq; in New-Castle, on Delaware, shall receive the above reward, or TEN POUNDS for the wench only, and reasonable charges, from   PHILIP KEARNEY.

192. *August 1, 1771*

July 26, 1771.

RAN away from the Subscriber, living in the Fork of Gunpowder, Baltimore County, a Negroe Man, named Jem, born in Maryland, about 5 feet 8 inches high, and 25 years of age; had on, when he went away, a white broadcloth coat, brown waistcoat, ozenbrigs trowsers, and old shoes, but it is probable will change his dress, as he was (since he ran away) concerned with several other Negroes in breaking open a store in Joppa, from which they have taken money and goods, to the amount of Forty Pounds. Whoever will apprehend the said Negroe, and have him secured in any goal, shall have a Reward of Three Pounds, and if brought home, Five Pounds, and reasonable charges, paid by SAMUEL YOUNG.

193. September 5, 1771

Chester county, August 21, 1771.

RUN away last night, from the subscriber, living in East-Nottingham township, a Negroe man, known by the name of JACK or JOHN RICHARDSON, he is a smart likely fellow, about 5 feet 6 inches high, and about 30 years of age; had on, when he went away, a dark coloured cloth jacket or coat, a white linen shirt, ozenbrigs trowsers, grey yarn stockings, good shoes, and an old hat; he has a lump on the under part of one of his wrists, and wants the first joint of one of his great toes; he is well known about Chester, by a trial he had for his freedom, but being disappointed of his expectations, he was sent home, and continued till about the 18th of November last, when he absconded from his master, and was put in the public gazettes; but a few days before they came from the press, he was met by a certain public friend, known by the named of James Rigbee, who took him into Maryland, and kept him in his employ for near 9 months, but finding he could no longer keep him, without being put to trouble, or his ungenerous actions appearing more in the public, he delivered him up to his master, on the 17th of this instant— Whoever takes up said Negroe, and secures him, so as his master may have him again, shall have SIX DOLLARS reward, and reasonable charges, paid by me   WILLIAM BEAN.

N.B. It is possible the Negroe may endeavour to pass for a freeman, by some writings he may have for that purpose, therefore, all masters of vessels are forbid to carry him off, at their peril.

194. December 26, 1771

RAN away, on the morning of the 14th of December instant, from the subscriber, an English servant boy, named *James Winterbottom,* by trade a chimney sweeper: Had on, and took with him, when he went away, a chimney frock and trowsers, blanket, brush and scraper. He is about 17 years of age, 4 feet 7 inches high, wears his own hair, of a brown colour, is weak and hollow-eyed, waddles in his walk, and stammers much when talking, and has a down speaking look. Also ran away, and went with him, a Negroe boy slave, named *Prime* or *Primus,* aged a[bout] 16 years, 5 feet 3 inches high, by trade a chimney sweeper: Had on, and took with him, a chimney frock and trowsers, blanket, brush and scraper. He is straight limbed, cushion kneed, and speaks broken English. Whoever takes up the said servants, and will bring them to the subscriber, living

near the corner of Race and Fourth-streets, Philadelphia, shall receive
Five Pounds for both, or Fifty Shillings for either of them, and reasonable charges, paid by   GEORGE BEATHO.

195. February 20, 1772

Pottsgrove, February 15, 1772.

WHEREAS the subscriber did, on or about the 2d of November last,
give his Mulattoe wench Hagar Jones, a pass for 8 days, in order to visit a
child of her's in the city of Philadelphia, but never returned; he, about 4
weeks ago, had her taken up and sent to the work-house, but neglecting
to get a commitment from the Mayor, was discharged; she is a very lusty
Indian looking hussy, remarkable fond of spirituous liquor, very turbu-
lent in her temper, drunk or sober, is supposed to have gone to New-
Jersey or New-York, and being an artful jade, may probably obtain a
pass under pretence of being a free woman; she has a large scar on her
forehead, is about 34 years of age. Whoever secures her in any of his
Majesty's goals, so that her master may get her again, shall have Twenty
Shillings reward, and reasonable charges, paid by
                                          THOMAS CULLEN.
   N.B. The said Cullen has to dispose of 150 acres of land, very good in
quality, situate in York county, about 12 miles from York-Town, in
Warrington township, joining lands of Thomas Edmonson, Joshua
Brown, Thomas Brunton, and Edmund Philips, on which is erected a
good log house, 21 feet square, 7 acres cleared, and the whole well
watered and timbered. For terms, apply to Thomas Doyle, in Lancaster, or to Robert Stephenson, Tavernkeeper, near the premises.

196. July 2, 1772

RUN away on the 23d of June, 1772, from on board the sloop William,
in Baltimore harbour, a NEGROE MAN SLAVE, named DICK, near 6
feet high, with an uncommon *large head* and *feet*, many *scars* on his face
and body; is a very lusty fellow, of a yellowish complexion; had on a *red
jacket, frock, trowsers,* and half worn *castor hat.* He was seen taking the
road to Philadelphia, intending it is thought to get into some vessel, as he
followed the sea. Whoever shall apprehend the said Negroe in the
province of Maryland, and deliver him to Mr. John Smith, of Baltimore-
town, merchant, shall receive *Three Pounds* as a reward; or if taken in or

near Philadelphia, and delivered to Captain William Allison, the same reward, and reasonable charges, from either of the above Gentlemen, or
WILLIAM DUNSCOMB.

N.B. He may change his dress, as he had a blue coat, a blanket, check shirt, &c.

197. July 2, 1772

June 13, 1772.
TWENTY DOLLARS Reward.

RUN away from Occoquan Furnace, in Virginia, a Negroe fellow, belonging to the estate of Presly Thornton, Esq; named LEAMAN (or CLEM) a short well made fellow, yellow complexion, about 30 years of age, can turn his hand to many sorts of trades, and particularly that of a Carpenter; had on, when he went away, a blue fearnought jacket, a hat with a white metal button to it, the rest of his dress as is common for Negroes; he will probably pass for a freeman, is now under the predicament of an outlaw, for not returning to service. Whoever takes up and secures said Negroe, so that I get him again, shall receive the above reward, and reasonable charges, if taken out of the colony.
THOMAS LAWSON.

198. August 5, 1772

FIVE POUNDS REWARD.

RUN away the 15th of July, at night, from Elk Forge, in Caecil county, Maryland, a Mulattoe SLAVE, named JEM, about 28 years of age, and about 6 feet 2 inches high, and well proportioned to his height, can read pretty well, and talk Dutch, was born in Kent county, Maryland, is a cunning ingenious fellow, and probably will endeavour to pass for a freeman, is a good workman in a forge, either in finery or chafery, can do any kind of smith's or carpenter's work, necessary about a forge, can also do any kind of farming business; had on, and took with him, a felt hat, of the best kind, Philadelphia make, a black broadcloth coat, blue and white striped linen vest, fine white shirt, new buckskin breeches, thread hose, good pumps, and narrow trimmed plain silver buckles; he also took with him, one tow shirt, one pair of tow trowsers, and a coarse brown cloth jacket. Whoever takes up said Slave, and secures him in any goal, and gives notice thereof to the subscriber, at said forge, shall have the above reward; and if secured in Philadelphia goal, or brought home, reasonable charges besides, paid by ISAAC ATTMORE, in Philadelphia, or   THOMAS MAY.

199. *August 12, 1772*

RUN away from the subscriber, living in Hanover township, Lancaster county, near Jones's-town, a NEGROE man, named TONY (but sometimes calls himself Anthony) he is about 5 feet 5 inches high, 40 years old, has a scar across his throat, lost some of his teeth, is a butcher by trade; had on and took with him, when he went away, a lightish blue broadcloth coat, a striped jacket, two pair of striped trowsers, one pair of tow ditto, a half-worn beaver hat, a leather cap, and a hunting shirt, also one old velvet jacket, a lincey ditto, a new linen shirt, and an old shirt, a butcher's steel, a hone, two pair of buckles, and a pair of shoes; he talks good English and Dutch, and is this country born. Whoever takes up said Negroe, and secures him, so that his master may have him again, shall have FORTY SHILLINGS reward, and reasonable charges, paid by   BENJAMIN CLERK.
    July 27, 1772.

200. *September 9, 1772*

Gloucester, New-Jersey, September 1, 1772.

WERE committed to my custody two men, one on suspicion of being a runaway servant, and calls himself JOHN HANDLIN, about 30 years of age, a short well set fellow, of a dark complexion, and black curled hair; had on, when committed, a pair of new shoes, coarse shirt and trowsers, striped jacket, without sleeves, and old felt hat, and says he was born in Ireland. Likewise a Negroe man, says he belongs to BENJAMIN CLARKE, in Hanover township, Lancaster county, calls himself ANTHONY WELSH, and says he was born in Burlington, in the Jerseys. This is therefore to desire their masters or mistresses, if any they have, to come within three weeks from this date, pay charges, and take them away, or they will be sold out for the same, by me
RICHARD JOHNSON, Goaler.

201. *October 14, 1772*

RUN AWAY from the subscriber, the 20th day of August last, a NEGROE slave, called CATO, middle sized, bowlegged, and speaks good English. The said Negroe was formerly in the possession of — Brisbane, of Chester county, and afterwards of Hieronimus Echman, of Lancaster county, and is a great rogue, having committed several daring burg-

laries. He is supposed to have broke into the shop of the subscriber since he absconded, and to have stolen from thence 3 Half Johannes's, and other money, a silver watch seal, and several paste or stone buttons, set in silver. Whoever apprehends the said Negroe, and delivers him to the Goaler of York county, shall receive FOUR POUNDS reward, and reasonable charges, and One Third the value of the money or things stolen, as they shall secure for the owner.   DAVID JAMESON.
York-Town, Sept. 30, 1772.

The said Negroe broke into a house in York-Town, and stole from thence upwards of Ninety Pounds, belonging to Nicholas Shaffer, who has offered a very considerable reward for apprehending him.

202. October 21, 1772

RUN away from the subscriber, on the 18th of October, a Negroe man, named JACK, about 22 years of age, 5 feet 9 or 10 inches high, has a scar under one of his eyes, is a strong well built fellow, talks very good English; took with him, when he went away, a blue cloth coat, cotton velvet jacket of the flowered kind, two pair of breeches, the one white plush, the other ticken, two check shirts, a pair of blue yarn stockings, one pair of new shoes, with silver plated shoe and knee buckles, a half worn beaver hat, with a black silk band and silver buckle. Whoever takes up the said Negroe, and brings him to me, shall have Three Pounds reward, if taken up out of Philadelphia county, and reasonable charges, paid by   JOHN ZELLER, distiller.

N.B. As the said Negroe was born in Maryland, and purchased here from Zephaniah Bond, living in Maryland, it is supposed he is on his way to his old master, to see his father and mother.

203. November 25, 1772

THREE POUNDS Reward.

RUN away on the 10th of August last, from the subscriber, living in Lombard-street, Philadelphia, a Negroe man, named *MOSES GRIMES*, about 32 years of age, about 5 feet 6 inches high, of a yellowish complexion, the fore part of his head shaved, and is rather bald, he sometimes wears a wig, is very religious, preaches to his colour, walks before burials, and marries; he is very artful, pretends to be free, and will no doubt get a forged pass; he is very fond of liquor, and if spoke familiarly to pretends to simplicity and laughs; he had on, when he went away, an ozenbrigs shirt, and jacket, with sleeves, bound with green binding. Whoever apprehends the said Negroe, and confines him in any of his Majesty's goals, so as his master may have him again, zshall receive the above reward, and reasonable charges, paid by JOHN HALES.

N.B. It is supposed he is gone to Carolina, or Carlisle in this province.

204. December 30, 1772

Fredericksberg, in Virginia, December 23, 1772.
TWENTY DOLLARS Reward.

RUN away the 3d instant, from the subscriber, living in Spotsylvania county, Virginia, a NEGROE fellow, named BOB, of a yellow complexion, about 22 years of age, and 6 feet 2 inches high; had on, when he went away, a white Bath coating coat, a snuff-coloured cloth jacket, and black stocking breeches; he carried with him some striped jackets, and sundry fine shirts and stocks, marked W. H. I am informed he has a general pass, signed William Smith, and goes for a freeman, under the name of Robert Alexander; he likewise pretends to have a discharge, and says he served his time in Augusta county; but, I do hereby certify, he is a slave for life; I am informed he has been seen travelling towards Philadelphia. Whoever takes him up, and secures him in any goal, and gives me notice thereof, shall have the above reward, paid by
WILLIAM HESLOP.

N.B. All masters of vessels are hereby forwarned from taking him on board.

205. January 20, 1773

Christiana Ferry, New-Castle County, January 8, 1773.

RUN AWAY, last night, from the subscriber, a lusty yellow fellow, part Indian and part Negroe, about 5 feet 11 inches high, calls himself JERRY CLARK, is a thick strong made fellow, a great liar, fond of strong liquor, and boasts much of his having been at sea; had on a pair of trowsers and a jacket, both made of blue duffil, tow shirt, coarse white yarn stockings, good shoes, old hat; has a cut on one side of his head, which is sore at this time, and has several scars, one in particular on his left hand. Whoever apprehends said fellow, and secures him in any of his

Majesty's goals, so that his master may get him again, shall be entitled to a reward of Four Dollars, paid by   MORTON MORTON.

206. *February 24, 1773*

THREE POUNDS Reward.

RUN away from the subscriber, living near Canawingo Creek, Little-Britain Township, Lancaster County, on Friday, the 15th of January, a Mulattoe woman, about 18 or 19 years of age, she calls herself HANNAH CAMBEL, is a bold well tongued hussy, of a whitish cast, very much freckled in the face, has a brown spot on one of her little fingers, and commonly wears her hair tied; had on, when she went away, a light coloured lincey jacket and petticoat, and it is supposed she had other clothes, she wore white stockings, with blue clocks, high heeled shoes, and it is thought she will dress herself in mens clothes. Whoever takes up said wench, and brings her home to her master, or secures her in any of his Majesty's goals, so as he may get her again, shall have the above reward, and reasonable charges, paid by   MOSES DAVISON.

207. *March 3, 1773*

Lancaster Goal, February 11, 1773.

THIS day was committed to my custody, a certain JERRY CLARK, a Negroe MAN, who is advertised in the Pennsylvania Gazette, by Morton Morton, living at Christiana Ferry, New-Castle County, with a reward of Four Dollars for taking up the said Negroe.

Also was committed to my custody, on the 8th day of September, 1772, a certain JAMES HENDERSON, as he called himself but now confesses that his name is JAMES SHEHEE, and that he is a servant to David Morgan, Esq; near Mr. Jones's tavern, on the Horseshoe road, in Lancaster County. The masters of the said Negroe man, and the other servant, are desired to come, pay their fees, and take them away, or they will be discharged, on paying their own fees, in four weeks from this date, by   GEORGE EBERLY, Goaler.

208. *March 31, 1773*

RUN AWAY from the subscriber, living in Southwark, on the 19th day of February last, a Negroe man, named Quaco, but calls himself William

Murrey, a yellow fellow, 5 feet 5 or 6 inches high, knock kneed; went off with a new snuff coloured coat, with small cuffs, with a short blue coat, several jackets, breeches, check and white linen shirts, new shoes, and several pair of stockings; he has a certificate of his being baptized, which he shews as a pass, and says he is a free man; and, as he is a sly arch fellow, may have a forged pass from me of his freedom; he has been seen in several parts of the town, and on Friday last he was seen at the barracks. Whoever takes up said Negroe, and secures him, so that his master may get him again, shall have THIRTY SHILLINGS reward, and reasonable charges, paid by   JOSEPH JOHNSON.

N.B. Whoever harbours or conceals said Negroe, may depend on being prosecuted to the utmost rigour of the law; and all captains of vessels are forbid to carry him off at their peril.

209. April 7, 1773

THIRTY DOLLARS Reward.

RUN away from the subscriber, the 15th of March last, a Negroe man slave, named Brit, is the same fellow that the Salmons has had at Wyoming for 3 years, he is a very stout well made fellow, near 6 feet high, about 33 years of age; had on, when he went away, a red great coat, half worn, a blue coat, and a blue kersey jacket, with flat white metal buttons, buckskin breeches, black and white stockings; he can read and write, and it is supposed he will forge a pass. Whoever will secure him in Philadelphia or Easton goals, so that his master may get him again, shall have the above reward, and all reasonable charges for bringing him to the subscriber, near Elizabeth-Town, in New-Jersey. Whoever takes him up are desired to be very careful in pinioning him, as he will undoubtedly make his escape if he can. All persons are forbid harbouring or entertaining said slave, as they will do it at their peril; he is supposed to be gone in the back parts of Pennsylvania, to Shamokin or Wyoming, where he is well known; he was seen to cross Delaware the Monday after he run away.   JACAMIAH SMITH.

210. April 28, 1773

FORTY SHILLINGS REWARD.

RUN away from the subscriber, on Saturday, the 24th instant, a negroe, named JACK, between 21 and 22 years of age, about 5 feet 10 inches high, a well set likely fellow, he has a scar under one of his eyes; had on when he went away, a dark brown jacket, with small metal buttons, tow linen trowsers, and old beaver hat; he likewise took with him about £16 in money, and may probably change his dress. Whoever takes up the said negroe, and secures him, so that his master may get him again, shall have the above reward, and reasonable charges, if brought home, paid by   JOHN ZELLER, Distiller.

211. April 28, 1773

THREE DOLLARS Reward.

RUN away from the subscriber, in Londonderry township, Lancaster county, a Negroe Man, called PERO, about 23 years old, the insides of both his wrists are remarkably white, though one is whiter than the other; one knee is bent in towards the other, is a great talker and liar; had on a good lappelled jacket, and half-worn breeches, both of a light colour, the button holes wrought with red, two shirts, one fine, the other coarse, half-worn stockings, and bad shoes; he had an iron collar about his neck, but it is supposed the collar is taken off by some ill-disposed neighbour. Whoever takes up said Negroe, and secures him in any goal, so that his master may have him again, shall have the above reward, paid by   JOHN ROAN.

N.B. All masters of vessels are forbid to harbour or carry him off at their peril.

212. May 26, 1773

RUN away last night from the subscriber, living in York county, near Peach-Bottom Ferry, a MULATTOE slave, named JACK, about 22 years of age, well set, about 5 feet 5 inches high, and very white of the sort; had on, when he went away, an old home made cloth-coloured coat, tow shirt and trowsers, an old hat, no shoes that I know of; but it is expected that he will break houses and change his apparel, he being a very great rogue, and intends to steal a currying knife, and pass for a currier. Whoever takes up said slave, and secures him in any goal, so as his master may get him again, shall have *Three Pounds Ten Shillings* reward, and if brought home *Five Pounds,* paid by
                                          HUGH WHITEFORD.

May 1, 1773.

213. June 23, 1773

WE do hereby certify, that a certain Negroe man, named BOB, formerly the property of M[a]chimines Porter, of the county of Somerset and province of Maryland, but now the property of Miller and Heslop, of the county of Spotsylvania, and colony of Virginia, Merchants, is a SLAVE; that he was born such, that his mother and all her children are such, and that any thing to the contrary of their being any thing else than actual slaves, during their natural lives, they know not. Given under our hands, this 14th day of October, 1772.

William Vennables, William Horsey, John Mitchell, Caleb Balding, Zach. Maddux, Peter Cullaway, William Figgs, John Hamilton, William Vaughan. (Copy) .

RUN away, early last December, from Mount-Pleasant, Spotsylvania county, Virginia, the abovementioned NEGROE. I will give *Ten Pounds* reward, Virginia currency, to have him secured in any goal on this continent, on notice given in this GAZETTE; *Twenty Pounds*, if brought to Fredericksburg. When he went off he produced a forged pass, signed with the name of William Smith, Gentleman, one of his Majesty's justices of the peace for the county of Spotsylvania, called himself and passed as a free man, by the name of ROBERT ALEXANDER; but the above certificate will show him to be a slave, as it is signed by several people who were formerly his owners. The dress he went off in was a drab Bath coat, a brown broadcloth waistcoat, buck breeches, yarn stockings, shoes and brass buckles; but as he is a cunning artful villain, he may have changed his dress: He stole sundry fine linen shirts, the property of Mr. William Heslop, marked W. H. He is above six feet high, slim made, a very likely fellow, and is handy at all sorts of plantation work, is by trade a sawyer, having been bred to it from his infancy, and attended several saw-mills on the Eastern-shore (of which place he is a native) he likewise understands the house-carpenter's business. I expect he has pushed to the northward, indeed he was followed as far as Annapolis, from whence I imagined he crossed the Bay; if taken up in Maryland or Pennsylvania, and delivered to Mr. DAVID KERR, near Annapolis, Mr. JAMES JAFFRAY, in Baltimore, or Mr. WILLIAM TURNBULL, Merchant, Philadelphia, the above reward will be paid.   JOHN MILLER.

Virginia, May 25, 1773.

All masters of vessels are forewarned not to carry him off at their peril.

214. June 30, 1773
FORTY SHILLINGS REWARD.

RUN AWAY, on Saturday, the 26th instant, a Negroe man, named PETER, about 20 years of age, about 5 feet high, a clumsey looking fellow, stoops a little in his walk; had on, and took with him, a light coloured Wilton coatee, a red nap ditto, a clouded knit waistcoat, light coloured jean breeches, with silk garters, black plush ditto, almost new shoes, clouded stockings, check shirt, plated buckles, old beaver hat, and other articles; as he is a cunning artful fellow, will endeavour to pass for a free man; he has a mother living in Trenton, a free woman, named Violet, it is likely he is gone that way. Whoever apprehends the said Negroe, and secures him in any of his Majesty's goals, so that his master may have him again, shall have the above reward, and reasonable charges, if brought home, paid by   JOHN M'CALLA.
    Philad. June 29, 1773.
    N.B. All masters of vessels, and others, are forbid to harbour or carry off the said Negroe, at their peril.

215. September 1, 1773

RUN AWAY from the subscriber, in the lower end of Buckingham county, Virginia, between 4 and 5 years ago, a young NEGROE fellow, named ESSEX; he is a middle sized fellow, very straight, has large eyes, and had many places broke out and cured under his jaws; I have never heard of him till lately, and that was by a gentleman's servant, who was at Philadelphia, and saw the said runaway in that city, about twelve months ago, who knew him perfectly well, and says he went by the name of JOE SCOTT, was a sailor in Captain Atcheson's vessel, or ship, and passed for a freeman; I always imagined he was gone to some of the distant colonies, or the West-India Islands; I will give a reward of FIFTY POUNDS, to any person that will prove the Captain of a ship or vessel that carried him out of Virginia, so that he is legally convicted of the same, and can be brought to condign punishment; I will give a reward of TWENTY POUNDS, to any person that will deliver the said slave to me; and I do forewarn all persons from employing the said slave, or in any wise harbouring of him; in case no person will deliver him to me, I will thankfully pay any Captain of a vessel, that will put the said runaway in irons, and deliver him to Col. WILLIAM WAGER, at Hampton; to Mr. GEORGE DONALD, at Richmond town; Mr.

JOHN JOHNSON, at Hanover town, or Col. GEORGE TAYLOR, at Conway's warehouse, on Rappahannock river. I request the favour of the gentleman to whom he is delivered, to pay the charge, and hire some safe hand to deliver him to me, or to put him in goal and advertise him.

ANTHONY WINSTON.

July 3, 1773.

216. September 1, 1773

Queen-Anne's County, near Queen's-Town, Maryland, August 21.
THREE POUNDS Reward.

RUN away, on the 21st of July, 1773, a salt water Negroe man, about 5 feet 3 or 4 inches high; and 25 years of age; he has been in the country six years, and talks not quite plain; his name is JOE, though he has passed by the name of DICK in some parts of this county, as a freeman; he is black and smooth faced, spare, active, clean limbed, and runs fast; his fore teeth long and turning outwards, he has lost two of his under teeth before, chews tobacco much; the crown of his head shaved, with a ridge of wool left all round, and a foretop, which he turns back; a brass or iron ring in his left ear; a scar near his right eye, and another on his breast; he has lost an old fearnaught jacket and wears two shirts, brown roll petticoat trowsers, and a half-worn felt hat, cocked two ways; he has been taken up once on Kent-Island, and got away; it is said he was seen near Tuckahoe Bridge, in this county, lately, and may be lurking there, and the adjacent parts of Talbot and Dorset counties, for some time. Whoever takes up and secures the said runaway, so that I may get him again, shall have Four Dollars; if brought home, Three Pounds, and reasonable expences paid, if 20 miles from home.

ROBERT SAUNDERS.

N.B. He may get into Worcester or Sussex counties, in the other province.

217. March 9, 1774

Roxbury, Morris County, East New-Jersey, Jan. 25, 1774.
SIX DOLLARS Reward.

RUN away from the Subscriber, the 19th instant, a Negroe man, named JOE, about 25 years old, 5 feet 9 or 10 inches high, a stout strong fellow, of a yellowish black: Had on, when he went away, a new flannel shirt, old leather breeches, a light coloured over waistcoat, lined with flannel,

an under ditto black, all of homespun, grey stockings, new shoes, with a pair of campaign soals; he is an arch fellow, this country born, and has a scar in his forehead, near his eyebrow; about 7 years ago he ran away, and got to New-York, where he continued two years, and went by the name of Levi; as he is known in New-York, perhaps he may go to Pennsylvania. Whoever secures the said Negroe, so that he may be had again, shall receive the above reward, and all reasonable charges, paid by
AUGUSTINE REID.

218. April 27, 1774

Neabsco Furnace, Virginia, April 15, 1774.

RUN away from the Neabsco Furnace, on the 16th March last, a light coloured Mulattoe man, named BILLEY, the property of the honourable JOHN TAYLOR, Esq; when I tell the public he is the same boy who for many years waited on me in my travels through this and the neighbouring provinces (and by his pertness, or rather impudence, was well known to almost all my acquaintances) there is the less occasion for a particular description of him; however, as he is now grown to the size of a man, and has not attended me for some years past, I think it not amiss to say he is a very likely young fellow, about 20 years old, about 5 feet 9 inches high, stout and strong made, has a remarkable swing in his walk, but is much more so by a knack he has of gaining the good graces of almost every body, who will listen to his bewitching and deceitful tongue, which seldom or ever speaks the truth; he has a small scar on the right side of his forehead, and the little finger on his right hand quite straight, by a hurt he got when a child; had on, when he went away, a blue fearnaught and an under jacket of green baize, light coloured cloth breeches, with silver basket buttons, a pair of cotton ditto, ozenbrigs shirts, a mixed blue pair of yarn hose, country made shoes, and yellow buckles.—From his ingenuity he is capable of doing almost any kind of business, and for some years past has been chiefly employed as a founder, stone mason and miller, as occasion required; one of which trades, in the character of a freeman, I imagine he will profess. Whoever apprehends the said fellow, and delivers him to me, or his master at Mount-airy, or secures him so as to be had again, shall have double the reward allowed by law, and all reasonable charges, if brought home.
THOMAS LAWSON.

219. July 20, 1774
FIVE POUNDS Reward.

RUN away from the subscriber, living in Kent county, in the province of Maryland, about the middle of May, in the year 1773, a Mulattoe Slave, named BEN, about 32 years of age, of a thin visage, hollow eyed, with a black beard, and black curled hair, has lost one of his fore teeth, about 5 feet 8 or 9 inches high, much addicted to strong liquor, and has been much whipped on his back; he understands most parts of the farming business, has been much used to minding horses and waiting in houses; he is likewise a good sailor, especially in small vessels. I am apprehensive that he is in or about Philadelphia, as he was seen there about five weeks past, at which time he had on a blue coat, and a striped waistcoat. Whoever apprehends and secures the said slave, so that the subscriber gets him again, shall receive the above reward, besides all reasonable charges.   ROBERT READ.
   July 9, 1774.

220. August 17, 1774
SIXTEEN DOLLARS Reward.

RUN away from the subscriber, living in Baltimore county, Maryland, about 12 miles from Baltimore-town, about the 7th of June, 1773. A salt water NEGROE man, named SOLOMON, aged about 22 years, he has been in the country about three years, and talks pretty good English for the time, is of a middle size, a little upon the yellowish cast; it is needless to say any thing about his clothes, as he has been gone so long. He was, in July last, in New-Castle, supposed to be in the possession of Robert Bail, and had changed his name to *George*. Whoever apprehends the said Negroe man, and secures him in any goal, so that his master may get him again, shall receive the above reward, paid by THOMAS COCKEY.
   August 10, 1774.

221. August 31, 1774
Caecil County, Maryland, August 24, 1774.
EIGHT DOLLARS Reward.

RUN away from the subscriber, living at Elk Ferry, in the county aforesaid, a Negroe man, named Penn, about 5 feet 6 or 7 inches high, he is country born, well set, very talkative, and may probably make a great show of religion; he is a very black small eyed fellow; had on, when he went away, a snuff coloured jacket, without sleeves, an ozenbrigs shirt, and tarry canvas trowsers; and for some years past has rowed in the Ferry-boat at Elk Ferry.

Said Negroe ran away some years ago, and passed himself for a freeman, by the name of James Pemberton, and got a forged pass, signed Thomas Franklin, of Baltimore, on account of which he was employed by one Merchant, a Tanner, near Correyllis Ferry, and afterwards indented himself to another Meredith, a Currier, in Philadelphia, and as he has been in New-York with said Meredith, he may now probably be making that way.

Whoever takes up said Negroe, and secures him in any of his Majesty's goals, so that his master may have him again, shall have the above reward, and reasonable charges, paid by   THOMAS SAVIN.

All masters of vessels are forbid to carry him off.

222. September 28, 1774

FIVE POUNDS Reward.

ON Sunday, the 18th of September, absconded from his service, at Franklin Park, near Bulington, a NEGROE slave, the property of the subscriber, by name Frank, was purchased of a certain John Davan, Haccansack township, Bergen county, New-Jersey. Whoever secures the said Negroe in any of his Majesty's goals in America, shall be entitled to the above reward. He is a likely fellow, about 5 feet 10 inches high, bushy hair, and of the Indian cast; has had several masters, and never staid long in one place, when abroad imposes himself on the public for a free man. At the time of his elopement he stole a horse from out of the pasture, turned him adrift near Bordentown, which is since come home, and is supposed to have stolen another near the place where he turned mine off, the property of one Mr. Quicksey, near Bordentown, an iron grey mare, about 14 hands high, natural pacer, a star in her forehead, neither brand or ear-mark, quite sound, one of her hoofs a little twisted.—It is not known what he went off in, but took a bundle with him, which is supposed to contain the following articles, viz. 3 or 4 shirts, 3 or 4 pair of linen trowsers, a pair of red ditto, a brown cloth jacket, a striped lince ditto, 2 or 3 pair of worsted stockings, a pair of good shoes, and a good hat.   BALDWIN WAKE.

223. *November 2, 1774*

FIVE POUNDS for the Negroe, with reasonable charges, on
delivering him at Philadelphia, and
TEN POUNDS for the Person who took him away, if convicted of
the crime.

RAN away, about the 24th of June, 1774, from the subscriber, living in
Philadelphia, a Negroe man, named CAESAR, of a middling black
colour, about 22 years of age, 5 feet 3 or 4 inches high, well made, with a
long neck and falling shoulders, walks very upright, has bandy well
made legs, with thick muscular calves, a large mouth and lips, is much
inclined to laugh, and when he laughs shews much of his gums and
teeth, is talkative and impertinent, with often an elevated voice, where
he dares to make free, is insolent, and ready to box amongst his compan-
ions, and is fond of playing scraps of tunes on the fife. He having taken a
Bristol pipe box, about two feet and an half long, with sundry clothes,
may change his dress, but may have on either a mended cloth colour, or
an old dark blue superfine cloth coat, a blue nap round about or sea
jacket, lined with white flannel, and a red and white narrow striped
ditto, green plush or black stocking breeches, remarkably narrow
striped Irish ticken breeches and trowsers, thread stockings, &c. The
above reward of £5, and charges, on delivering the Negroe at Philadelphia, and also the £10, on proving and prosecuting to conviction the
person, who aided, assisted, or carried him off, will be punctually paid
by   PHILIP WILSON.
    N.B. He is supposed to be gone to the West-Indies. He was born in
Jamaica, lived at the Grenades with Thomas and James Lucas, who sold
him to Captain Godfrey M'Donnell about the year 1766.

224. *April 12, 1775*

Baltimore County, Patapsco-Neck, April 3, 1775.
TWENTY DOLLARS Reward.
For apprehending a RUNAWAY.

JAMES, a Mulattoe Slave, sometimes known by the name of VULCAN,
but commonly answers to the name of BUCK, took an abrupt leave of
his overseer last Wednesday, and has not yet returned; he is a dark
mulattoe, about 5 feet 9 inches high, strong made, sensible, artful, and
deceptive in conversation, firm and daring in his efforts to perpetrate
villainy, though of mild temper, and plausible in speech. He has fre-

quently travelled through this and some part of the Province of Pennsylvania; is well known, it is supposed, in the borough and county of Lancaster, and is acquainted with Philadelphia; may probably therefore re-visit those places. His working cloaths were a home manufactured long cloth waistcoat with sleeves, and breeches, yarn stockings, ozenbrigs shirt and good shoes, nailed with hobs; he is possessed of and has taken with him, a blue German serge coat, a green broadcloth vest, two pair of cotton and one pair of thread stockings, two white shirts ruffled at the breast, a good castor hat with band and buckle, a pair of good pumps, with a pair of double rimmed silver buckles. He has a mark of distinction, which from modesty, or some other motive, he is careful to conceal; one of his ears (but which is forgot) is remarkably less than the other. The above reward will be paid if he should be taken up out of the province, or 60 miles from Baltimore Town in the province and brought home; Five Pounds if at the distance of 40 miles; Three Pounds if 30, and Forty Shillings if 20 miles, with reasonable travelling expenses, including the legal charge under the Act of Assembly, by

THOMAS JONES.

225. April 26, 1775

FORTY SHILLINGS Reward.

RUN away, on the first day of this instant April, from the subscriber, living near Bethlehem, Northampton county, a Negroe man, named George Lux, but commonly known by the name of Chubb or Chubby, about 40 years of age, 5 feet 8 inches high, stout, active and well made, can shave and bleed well; took with him a case of spring lancets, he was seen in several parts of New Jeresy, had a forged pass, said he was free, and was going to New-York, from thence to London; had on, when he went away, a blue cloth upper, and a spotted swanskin double breasted under jacket, without sleeves, a white linen shirt, leather breeches, white yarn stockings, good shoes, with silver buckles in them, and a half-worn castor hat. Whoever takes up the said slave, and secures him in any of his Majesty's goals in America, or in the work-house in Philadelphia, shall have the above reward, paid by

JAMES CRUIKSHANK.

226. May 17, 1775

New-Castle, April 29, 1775.
FIFTEEN DOLLARS Reward

FOR apprehending a runaway JOE, a likely young Negroe SLAVE, this country born, had leave in writing to go [to] Mr. Andrew Yeatman's, in the upper part of Christiana Hundred (with whom the said JOE has lived for a number of years last past) on Saturday last, and was to return the Monday following, but has not yet come back to New-Castle; he is a light pale or yellow Negroe, about 5 feet 8 inches high, well proportioned and genteely made, has regular features and a good countenance; he is about 20 years of age; had on, or took with him from Yeatman's his late master, a brown drugget coat, with hair buttons, lined with a country coloured stuff, made of worsted and linen, the coat appears short for him, as he has grown since it was made, a brown lincey jacket, buckskin breeches, tied at the knees with strings, and cut without seams between the thighs, two flaxen shirts, a red and white linen handkerchief, an old felt hat, a pair of brown yarn stockings, two pair of white thread ditto, one plain the other ribbed, one pair footed with brown thread, a pair of coarse shoes, with hob nails, and a pair of half-worn pumps, with white metal buckles. He is unacquainted with the country, except in some parts of New-Castle and Chester counties; he was seen on the King's road between Wilmington and Chester, on Sunday, the 23d instant, being the day after he went from New-Castle; as he is very artful, it is supposed he will endeavour to go to Philadelphia, New-York or Boston, and will probably change his apparel, and endeavour to pass for a freeman. The above reward will be paid, if he should be taken 60 miles from the town of New-Castle, and brought home; *Four Pounds*, if at the distance of 40 miles; *Three Pounds*, if 30 miles; and *Two Pounds*, if 20 miles, and reasonable charges (including the legal charge under the act of assembly) by

JOHN THOMPSON.

227. May 24, 1775

RUN away the 8th of May, 1775, from Birdsborough Forge, a Negroe man, named *Cuff Dix*, a smart well set fellow, about 5 feet 5 inches high, speaks good English, has a little stopage in his speech; had on, and took with him, an old felt hat, iron collar round his neck, it is likely he will soon get that off, a cinnamon coloured jacket, ozenbrigs shirt and trowsers, leather breeches, good shoes; is a Hammerman by trade, he always changes his name, and denies his master. Any person that takes him up must be careful in examining of him. Whoever takes up said Negroe, and brings him home, or secures him in any goal, so that his master may have him again, shall have *Forty Shillings* reward for taking him, and if brought home *Six pence* per mile for travelling charges and expences, paid by   MARK BIRD.

228. *July 5, 1775*

Burlington, June 24, 1775.

WAS committed to the goal of the county of Burlington, on suspicion of being a runaway, the 21st day of this instant, a certain Negroe man, he says his name is *Willis Brown,* and has lived some years in Princess-Ann's county, Virginia, but been from there some time; has been a preacher, as he says, among the Indians, and is about 30 years of age, about 5 feet 5 inches high, speaks good English, but has a stopage in his speech, he brought with him 3 yards of red and white striped linen, which he says he bought at Wood's-town, Salem county; had on, when committed, an old felt hat, old double-breasted swanskin jacket, one pair of old woollen trowsers, one pair of broad striped ticken ditto, one Russia sheeting shirt, one check ditto, old shoes, with brass buckles in them. His master (if any he has) is desired to come in 3 weeks from the date hereof, pay charges, and take him away, otherwise he will be sold out for the same.   EPHRAIM PHILLIPS, Sheriff.

229. *August 16, 1775*

FORTY SHILLINGS REWARD.

RUN away from the subscriber, living in Reedy-Island, Neck, New-Castle county, on the 28th of July last, a NEGROE man, named *Jacob Purkins,* about 26 years of age, 5 feet 9 inches high, of a yellowish colour, he chews tobacco and is very apt to ask any person he sees use it for a chew; he had an iron collar about his neck, when he went away, a pair of old striped holland trowsers, an old felt hat, and an old blue coat. Whoever secures the said Negroe, so as his master may have him again, shall be paid the above reward, and reasonable charges, by

WILLIAM M'KEAN.

230. August 30, 1775
SIXTEEN DOLLARS Reward.

RUN away from the subscriber, living at Elk-Ferry, in Caecil county, Maryland, two NEGROE MEN, who both rowed in the Ferry boat at said Ferry; one named CUFF, the 8th of May last; he is about 5 feet 3 or 4 inches high, a straight well set fellow, with thick lips and the letter R marked on one of his cheeks, he has had a scald head, which he commonly keeps covered, is artful and talks a little in the Negroe dialect; had on, when he went away, a lead coloured jacket and breeches, ozenbrigs shirt, old stockings, but no shoes. The other named PENN, the 19th of August, he is about 5 feet 6 or 7 inches high, country born, well set, very talkative, and may probably make a great shew of religion; he is a black small-eyed fellow; had on, and took with him, a country cloth light coloured upper jacket, a dark flowered flannel under ditto, a patched check shirt, an ozenbrigs ditto, one pair of tarry canvas trowsers, one pair ozenbrigs ditto, an old small brimmed tarry hat, old shoes, and carved brass buckles. Said Negroe ran away some years ago, and passed himself for a freeman, by the name of James Pemberton, and got a forged pass, signed Thomas Franklin, on account of which he was employed by one Meredith, a Tanner near Corryel's Ferry, and afterwards indented himself to another Meredith, a Currier, in Philadelphia, and as he has been at New-York with said Meredith, he may now be making that way. Both or either of them, as they have many acquaintences, may probably get forged passes. Whoever takes up and secures said Negroes, so that their master may get them again, shall have the above reward, or Eight Dollars for either of them, and reasonable charges, paid by   THOMAS SAVIN.
    August 20, 1775.

231. September 6, 1775
Queen-Anne's County, Maryland, August 21, 1775.

THERE is a Mulattoe Man in Queen's-Town Goal; he is about 5 Feet 10 Inches high, and says he belongs to William M'Keene, on Reedy-Island; he has an ozenbrigs shirt and trowsers. The owner is desired to come and take him away, and pay Charges.   JOHN BUTLER, Goaler.

232. October 11, 1775

TEN POUNDS Reward.

RUN away on the 17th of September last, a salt water Negroe man, named JOE, slave to the subscriber, about 5 feet high, spare and active, a black Negroe; he has long teeth before, and has lost two or three of his under fore teeth, thin visage, a scar on one of his temples like a burn, the crown of his head commonly shaved, having a foretop, and ridge of wool round his head, chews tobacco much; holes in his ears for rings; he is artful and cunning, talks not quite plain, and changed his name to DICK, when he ran in the year 1773, and endeavoured to pass for a freeman; he had on a new shirt of good crocus, and an old pair of black breeches, which were all his cloathing. Whoever takes up the said fellow, and secures him in any goal, so that I may get him again, shall receive FIVE POUNDS; if brought home safe, and delivered to me, the above reward of TEN POUNDS, paid by ROBERT SAUNDERS, living in Middle-River-Neck, in Baltimore County, on Gunpowder-River, Maryland.

233. October 11, 1775

SIXTEEN DOLLARS Reward.

RUN away, the 8th of May, 1775, from Birdsborough Forge, a Negroe man, named *Cuff*, goes by the name of *Cuff Dix*, a smart well set fellow, about 5 feet 4 or 5 inches high, speaks good English, but has a little stoppage in his speech; had on, and took with him, an old felt hat, an iron collar round his neck, it is likely he soon got that off, a brown jacket, ozenbrigs shirt and trowsers, leather breeches, and good shoes; is a hammerman by trade. Also a Negroe man, named *Chester*, on Saturday night, September 9, 1775, a stout fellow, about 5 feet 8 inches high, speaks good English, is pock-marked, and flat footed; had on, when he went away, a good beaver hat, a light coloured Wilton coatee, ozenbrigs shirt and trowsers, and good shoes. *Chester* formerly belonged to one Keys, in the Jerseys, and was seen on the road to Philadelphia. Whoever takes up said Negroes, and brings them home, or secures them, or either of them, in any goal, so that their master may have them again, shall have THREE POUNDS reward for each, and reasonable charges, paid by   MARK BIRD.

234. November 15, 1775

Chester, November 7, 1775.

WAS committed to my custody, on the 23d day of October last, a certain *Frances Lyons,* on suspicion of being a runaway servant, she is of a darkish complexion, and middle size. Likewise a Negroe man, on the 29th, who calls himself *Cuff Dicks,* and says he belongs to Mark Bird, Esq., in Berks county. Their masters (if any they have) are desired to come, pay the charges, in three weeks from this date, otherwise they will be discharged, on paying their fees, by   JOEL WILLIS, Goaler.

235. November 15, 1775

Lancaster, November 7, 1775.
SIX DOLLARS REWARD.

RUN away on the 5th instant from the subscriber, in the borough of Lancaster, a Negroe man named BOB, about 5 feet 8 inches high, 26 or 27 years of age, a well made stout fellow, this country born. Had on when he went away, a drab coloured coatee, elk-skin breeches, Germantown stockings, and good shoes. Whoever secures said Negroe in any goal out of this county, so that his master may have him again, shall have the above reward and reasonable charges, paid by
GEORGE MOORE, Tavern-keeper.

It is supposed he is gone towards Fort-Pitt, as his former master Daniel Elliot followed the Indian trade, with whom he hath been frequently there. He served some time with John Miller, near Carlisle.

236. January 10, 1776

Reading Goal, January 1, 1776.

WAS committed to my custody, a certain Negroe Man, who calls himself WILL, and says he belongs to JOHN HUSBAND, in South-Carolina; he is supposed to be about 25 or 30 years of age; he says he run from his master in December 1774. His master, if he has any, is desired to come, within two months from the date of advertising, pay charges, and take him away, or else he will be sold for the same, by
PAUL KERBER, Goaler.

237. *February 21, 1776*

Philadelphia, February 20th, 1776.
FORTY SHILLINGS REWARD.

RUN AWAY, last Thursday evening, from the subscriber, living in Second-street, near Market-street, a NEGROE woman, named Hannah, about 22 years old, a stout made, hearty girl, full faced, but rather down countenance, scars on her cheeks (the marks of her tribe in Guinea) had only her work clothes on, being a green baize short gown, striped lincey petticoat, an old pair of men's shoes, and stockings, a plain linen cap. Whoever will bring said Negroe woman to her master, shall have the above reward and reasonable charges.

ROBERT [COSPAR].

It is supposed that she is lurking in town, as she has been seen since she went off.

238. *April 17, 1776*

RUN away on the 6th of April, 1776, from the subscriber, living in Salem county, a Negroe man, named Toney, about 40 years of age, and about 6 feet high; had on when he went away, a light coloured waistcoat, and a striped under ditto. He was born in Gloucester county, and brought up in James Hinchman's family; he was seen at James Talman's, on Oldman's-creek, in Gloucester county, on the 8th instant, and told said Talman he would get on board a man of war if he could. Whoever takes up and secures said Negroe, in Gloucester or Salem goals, so that his master may get him again, shall have Forty Shillings reward, or Three Pounds, if taken in any other county in the province, and secured in goal there, paid by   JOSEPH SHARP.

N.B. All persons are forewarned taking him by water out of the province.

239. *May 1, 1776*

RUN away from the subscriber, living in Philadelphia, a Mulattoe man, named *Ned*, but calls himself *Ned Levy*, about 21 years of age, 5 feet 6 inches high, he squints much, or rather has a cast in his eyes, bow legged, with a scar on the leftside of his nose, and is very apt to shut his left eye; had on, when he went away, a superfine blossom coloured broadcloth coat and breeches, black cotton-velvet jacket, holland shirt, white thread stockings, and took with him two white dowlas shirts, a pair of new buckskin breeches, with some other clothes; he can beat on the drum, and is very fond of that exercise; he has been harboured in the Northern Liberties and Passyunk for 3 months, but has left that some time. Whoever takes up the above runaway, and brings him to the subscriber, shall have *Three Pounds* reward, paid by

BLATHWAITE JONES.

All persons are forbid to harbour or conceal the said Mulattoe, as they will be prosecuted with the severity of the law.

240. *May 15, 1776*

Philadelphia, April 20, 1776.

ON the 29th of January last was committed to my custody, a certain Negroe Man by the name of JOHN BROWN, who says he ran away from Joseph Milburin, in St. Mary's county, Maryland, about ten years ago: And as I have sent several letters to acquaint his master thereof, I now publicly advertise and give notice to his master, that unless he comes, pays charges and takes him away, he will be sold for the same in one month from this date. THOMAS DEWEES, Goaler.

241. *July 17, 1776*

THREE POUNDS Reward.

RUN away from Birdsborough Forge, in Berks county, Pennsylvania on the 16th of June, 1776, a Negroe Man, commonly called CUFF DIX; he is an active well made fellow, and most excellent hammerman; he is about 5 feet 5 or 6 inches high, fond of liquor, understands English well, though he stammers in his speech; there is an iron ring in one of his ears, which if he can take out, a hole will remain [in] it, large enough to receive the small end of a pipe stem, in which case he will very probably endeavour to conceal the hole by filling it up; he wore, when he went away, a small old hat, light coloured homespun jacket, tow shirt and trowsers. He has often run away, changed his name, denied that the subscriber was his master, and been confined in several goals in this province; he was employed the greatest part of last summer by a person near Dilworth's town, in Chester county. Any person who shall harbour said Negroe shall be dealt with as the Law directs, and his name not omitted in a future advertisement. As Negroes in general think that Lord Dunmore is contending for their liberty, it is not improbable that

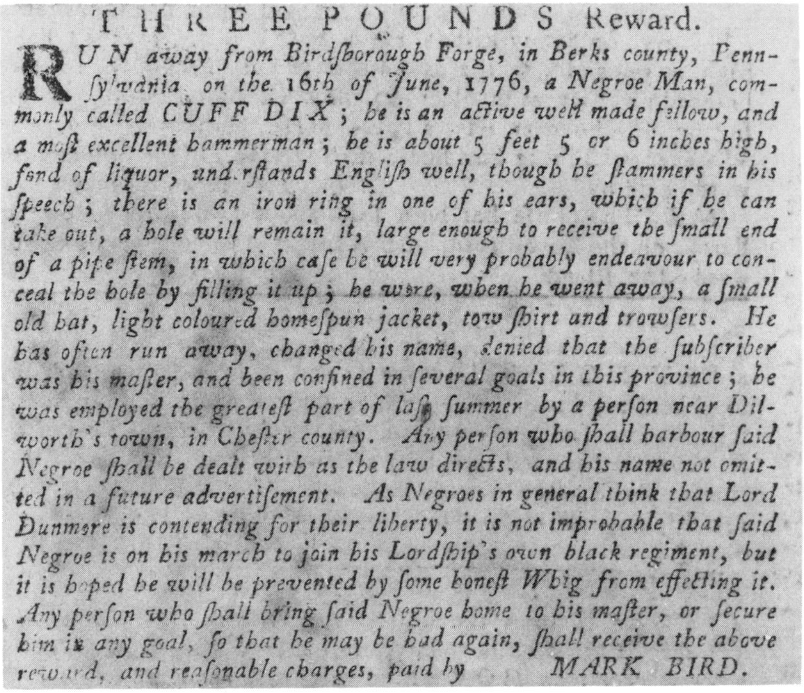

FIGURE 5: Advertisement from the *Pennsylvania Gazette*, July 17, 1776. *Courtesy of The Historical Society of Pennsylvania.* (See case 241.)

said Negroe is on his march to join his Lordship's own black regiment, but it is hoped he will be prevented by some honest Whig from effecting it. Any person who shall bring said Negroe home to his master, or secure him in any goal, so that he may be had again, shall receive the above reward and reasonable charges, paid by   MARK BIRD.

242. July 24, 1776

May 1, 1776.
SIX DOLLARS Reward.

RUN away from the subscriber, living in Harford county, Maryland, a Mulattoe Slave, named *JACK*, well set, is about 5 feet 6 inches high, very white for one of his kind, speaks good English; is a very great rogue. The said Slave was taken up and put in Lancaster goal on the first of July 1775, and made his escape from William Whiteford coming home.—

The said fellow said he had been in New-York goal as a runaway, but, by reason of my advertisement not going there, was let out; and says he has been on board the king's ships of war, and that he was at the West-Indies; it is thought he will endeavour to get to the ministerial army; he has changed his name to *Jacob Kelly*. Any person who takes up said Slave is requested to deal severely with him, and if he is taken up by this advertisement, is desired to put him in Dunlap's paper. Whoever takes up said Slave shall have the above reward, paid by

HUGH WHITEFORD.

N.B. The subscriber requests this advertisement may be carefully kept and taken notice of for several years.

243. *August 7, 1776*
IN MENS CLOTHES.

RUN away the 30th of July last, from the Jerseys to Philadelphia or New-York, a MULATTOE Woman Slave, named *Maria;* had on a white or red and white jacket, white oken breeches, white stockings, old mens shoes, and an old beaver hat; she is hardly discernable from a white woman, is rather thinish visage middle size, thick legs, long black hair, and about 35 years old; she hath left behind her three young children, a good master and mistress, and is going towards New-York after a married white man, who is a soldier in the Continental service there. Whoever secures the said Mulattoe in goal, and will immediately advertise the same in this paper, shall have FOUR DOLLARS reward.

244. *September 25, 1776*
TEN DOLLARS Reward.

RUN away from the subscriber, living in Evesham, in the county of Burlington, on Monday, the 9th of September instant, a Negroe man, named Moses, about 4 feet 4 inches high, a thick set fellow; had on, when he went away, a short light coloured coat, with binding of the same colour, a pair of strong new shoes, with large plated buckles, homespun linen trowsers, a black stock with steel buckle. He also stole, and took with him, a blue great coat, with white metal buttons; the other part of his clothes not known. As he has been endeavouring to prevail upon the Negroes in this neighbourhood to go with him and join the ministerial army, it is hoped every lover of his country will endeavour to apprehend so daring a villain. Whoever will secure him in any goal in this State, shall be entitled to the above reward, with reasonable charges if brought home, paid by   CHARLES READ.

245. *October 30, 1776*

CAME to the house of the subscriber, in Springfield township, Bucks county, Pennsylvania, some time in September last, a NEGROE LAD, who says his name was JAMES, and that he ran away from his master in Virginia, to Dunmore, and that his master's name is Samuel Morgan.— His master is desired to come, prove his property, pay charges and take him away.   WILLIAM BRYAN.

246. *February 5, 1777*

Chester, November 23, 1776.
FIVE POUNDS Reward.

RUN away from the subscriber, living in the Borough of Chester, in the beginning of August last, a Mulattoe man, named *Jack Jones,* upwards of 24 years of age, a Cooper by trade, about 5 feet 7 inches high, wears his hair tied in a cue behind, has a hobbling gait when he walks, occasioned by the rheumatism formerly in his hips, this country born, speaks good English, can read, and write a tolerable hand, and can play pretty well on a fife, is a sly, smooth tongued fellow, and may probably forge a pass, and pretend to be a freeman; he went on board the Providence privateer, commanded by Captain Jones, when she lay opposite to Chester, outward bound on her cruize, and am since informed by one of the hands, that he escaped from on board the first prize taken by the privateer, when she was retaken by the English, and came ashore at or near Egg-harbour, in Jersey, so that it is supposed he is lurking somewhere in Jersey, or perhaps may have come to Philadelphia in expectation of getting his prize money. Whoever takes up said fellow and brings him home, or secures him in any goal in this province, so that his master may have him again, shall receive the above reward, and reasonable charges, paid by   ELISHA PRICE.

N.B. His clothes cannot be well described, as he left the most of his old clothes at home, and is supposed to have got new.

247. July 30, 1777
TEN DOLLARS REWARD.

RUN away, July 22, from the subscriber, living in Byberry township, Philadelphia county, a Negroe Boy, named JESS, about ten years of age; had on a white linen upper waistcoat, a grey worsted under ditto, and black breeches; he took a very precipitate resolution to decamp, insomuch that he did not stay to put on his hat or shoes; he has a very modest pleasant countenance, is a trim active cunning lad, and remarkably handsome for one of his colour; he is subtle enough to give a good account of himself, can furnish a very indifferent story, with an excellent complexion, and answer intricate questions without hesitation. Whoever takes up and secures said Boy, so that his master may get him again, shall have the above reward, and reasonable charges.

ENOCH EDWARDS.

248. August 13, 1777
THIRTY DOLLARS Reward.

RUN away from the subscribers, living in Springfield township, Chester county, Pennsylvania, on the night of the 4th instant, two Mulattoe young men, one named Caesar, about 18 years of age, 5 feet 7 inches high, a well set, good looking active fellow; had on, and took with him, two tow shirts, two pair of tow trowsers, a white hunting shirt of the same, two jackets, without sleeves, of thick cloth, one grey and the other a reddish colour, a new wool hat, cocked, a red and yellow handkerchief, and good shoes. The other named Anthony Welsh, but is commonly called Tone, about 18 years of age, 5 feet 9 inches high, a likely fellow, two fingers on his right hand very crooked; had on, when he went away, a new wool hat, cocked, tow shirt and two pair of trowsers, one striped lincey jacket, without sleeves, good shoes, and a silk handkerchief. It is probable they will change their names. They are both very careful in combing their wool; the latter keeps his mostly tied. It is thought they are gone towards the camp with a design to enlist, but it is hoped they will not meet with a Dunmore there. Whoever secures said Mulattoes, so that their masters may have them again, shall have the above reward for both, or Fifteen Dollars for either of them, and reasonable charges, from

JAMES CROZER,
JAMES ANDERSON.

August 6, 1777.

249. May 30, 1778

RUN away from the subscriber, living in Carlisle, on the 18th of May, a Negroe man, named Nat, about 30 years of age, of a slim make, much addicted to strong drink; is an artful fellow, speaks very good English, rather of a tawney than proper black colour, and about 5 feet 6 or 7 inches high: Had on and took with him, an old light coloured coat, a shirt of seven hundred linen, a pair of tow trowsers, a pair of shoes and an old felt hat.—Likewise a green sagathy coat and breeches, the coat very good, but the breeches much worn. Whoever takes up and secures said negroe, that his master may get him again, shall have *THIRTY DOLLARS* reward, paid by   WILLIAM LYON.

250. February 24, 1779
SIXTY DOLLARS REWARD.

RUN away from the subscriber, living in *Kent* county, in the State of *Maryland*, a Mulattoe man, named *JAMES*, about 22 years old, country born, about 5 feet 5 inches high, full faced, by trade a tanner; it is supposed he went on board the *English* shipping when in *Chesapeake Bay* in *August* 1777. I have been informed he has since left the army, and lurks about *Philadelphia*. Any person securing the said Mulattoe, or bringing him to his master, shall have the above reward, and reasonable charges, paid by   DAVID CRANE.
    December 7, 1778.

251. June 2, 1779
SIXTY DOLLARS Reward.

RUN away from John M'Calla, senior, the day before the British army came into this city, a Negroe man, named Peter, about 24 years of age, five feet four or five inches high, a stout looking fellow, and has remarkably large feet; he was seen in this city the latter end of last winter, and may yet be lurking about town. Whoever takes up and secures said Negroe in any goal, so as his master gets him again, shall have the above reward, and reasonable charges, paid by   JOHN M'CALLA, junior

252. *June 30, 1779*

Lancaster, June 21, 1779.
FIFTY DOLLARS REWARD.

RUN away from the subscriber last evening the 20th instant, a negro man named DAN, about 24 years of age, 5 feet 4 or 5 inches high, much pitted with the small-pox; his dress when he went off is uncertain, as he took sundry cloaths with him, amongst which are, two coats, a light sagathy and a brown with yellow buttons, two jackets light blue and brown, a pair of new buckskin breeches, several pair of old striped and a pair of tow trowsers, 3 good shirts and a round hat. Said Negro is fond of playing the fiddle, and has a good deal of money with him, which he acquired that way; no doubt he will be particular in changing his dress, and endeavour to pass as a freeman. Whoever takes up and secures said slave in any Goal, so that his master may have him again, shall have the above Reward, and if delivered to me in Lancaster, One Hundred Dollars.   CHRISTIAN WIRTZ.

N.B. A white man is in company with said negro, for which there is a reward offered.

253. *July 7, 1779*

ONE HUNDRED POUNDS REWARD.

RUN away from the subscriber, near the Head of North-East Caecil County, Maryland, a Negroe Man, call TONEY, about 5 feet 10 inches high, slim built, and his wife RACHEL, with a young child, she is about 5 feet 8 inches high, of a tawny complexion, has some of her fore teeth out, has a very sour look and is very bold and saucy; they are both between 30 and 40 years of age; their clothes is uncertain; it is thought they have a pass with them and may change their names and pass for free Negroes. Whoever will give information where they are concealed, or secure them in any gaol on the continent, shall have the above reward, paid by   JOHN HALL.

April 14, 1779.

254. *July 7, 1779*

RUN away about 19 months ago, and went into Philadelphia, whilst the British troops were there, a young Negroe Wench, named PEG, about 20 years old, very lusty of her age, was born in Chester county, there is great reason to believe she is in, or at no great distance from, Philadelphia, possibly in the Jerseys, as she was seen last winter in the market. Whoever takes up and secures said Wench, so that I may have her again, shall have *One Hundred Dollars Reward,* and all reasonable charges paid, on applying to Colonel WILLIAM HENRY, in Philadelphia, or the subscriber, in Thornbury, Chester county. PERSIFOR FRAZER.

Any person who harbours or conceals her may depend upon the severest prosecution.

255. *August 4, 1779*

CAME to the plantation of Robert Jones, near York-Town, in the State of Pennsylvania, a NEGROE man and woman, can speak but very bad English, so as they cannot be well understood, but from what can be gathered from their dialect, it is apprehended they left some part of Maryland or Virginia about the time the enemy made their last excursion into the said States. Whoever owns the said Negroes, by applying to ROBERT JONES aforesaid, on his plantation, proving property, and paying charges, may have them again.

256. *January 19, 1780*

Sunbury, December 19, 1779.

WAS committed to my custody four Negroe men, one named JAMES HAYS, 5 feet 10 inches high, talks good English, and is a sensible mannerly fellow, about 23 years of age; another named RICHARD LINCOLN (formerly advertised by the name of Pierpoint) about 26 years of age, 5 feet 4 inches high, seems to have been bred a barber; it is alledged they belong to one Mr. Dorsey, near to Frederick-Town, in Maryland. They were committed in October, 1778, on suspicion of their designing to go to the enemy, and were advertised in March last in Mr. Dunlap's paper. The other two were committed this day, also upon suspicion of their going to the enemy; one named WILL, 5 feet 8 inches high, stout made, about 28 years of age; the other named BEN, 5 feet 6 inches high, about 35 years of age. They say they belonged to a certain [Nantfield], at or near Baltimore. Their master or masters (if any they have) are desired to come, prove their property, pay the charges, and take them away in six weeks from the date hereof, otherwise they will be sold out as the law directs.   JOHN MORRISON, Goaler.

257. May 24, 1780

Fifteen Hundred Dollars Reward.

RUN away, on the 16th of October last, from the subscriber, living near the Trap in St. Georges Hundred, New-Castle County, a Negroe man, named BILL, about 24 years of age, five feet five or six inches high, strait and well made, a right jet black complexion, and speaks good English. He formerly belonged to the estate of Samuel Vance, deceased. It is thought he has an old pass of his father's, who has travelled over most parts of the continent. Whoever takes up and secures said Negroe, so that he may be had again, shall have the above reward, and reasonable charges if brought home, paid by

ABEL MILES,
or WILLIAM
WORKMAN[N].

258. May 31, 1780

Princeton, May 23, 1780.
Five Hundred Dollars Reward

A MULATTO SLAVE, who it is supposed has been seduced to undertake to carry letters or intelligence into New-York, ran away from the subscriber, and took off with him a dark bay horse, 6 years old, 14 and an half hands high, with two white feet and a blaze, and is a natural trotter. The Slave is near 6 feet high, strong and well made; had on, and took with him, a variety of cloaths, but those he will most probably wear are, a suit of superfine mixt broad cloth, a new red great coat, white stockings, half boots, a black velvet stock and a beaver hat, but little worn. He appears to be 40 odd years of age, speaks good English, reads and writes a tolerable hand, and is a decent and well behaved ingenious fellow, capable of a variety of works. His name is Michael Hoy, but may go by some other, and it is probable he may travel as a servant to a white man who is supposed to have gone off with him; and as such may change his dress. He went off in the night of the 20th instant. *Five Hundred Dollars* will be given, and all charges paid for securing the slave and the horse, or *Two Hundred* and *Fifty Dollars* for either, paid by

GEORGE MORGAN.

P.S. A deep blood bay mare, with a black mane and tail, was stolen the same night the above mentioned slave went off, supposed by him or his accomplice. She has a short dock and a lump, that looks like a wind gall or small wen, on the hindermost part of one of her thighs. She is half-blooded, pretty old, trots, and is with foal. Six Hundred Dollars will be paid by the Rev. Mr. Smith, of this town, to the person who shall return the mare and convict the thief, or Three Hundred Dollars for the mare alone.

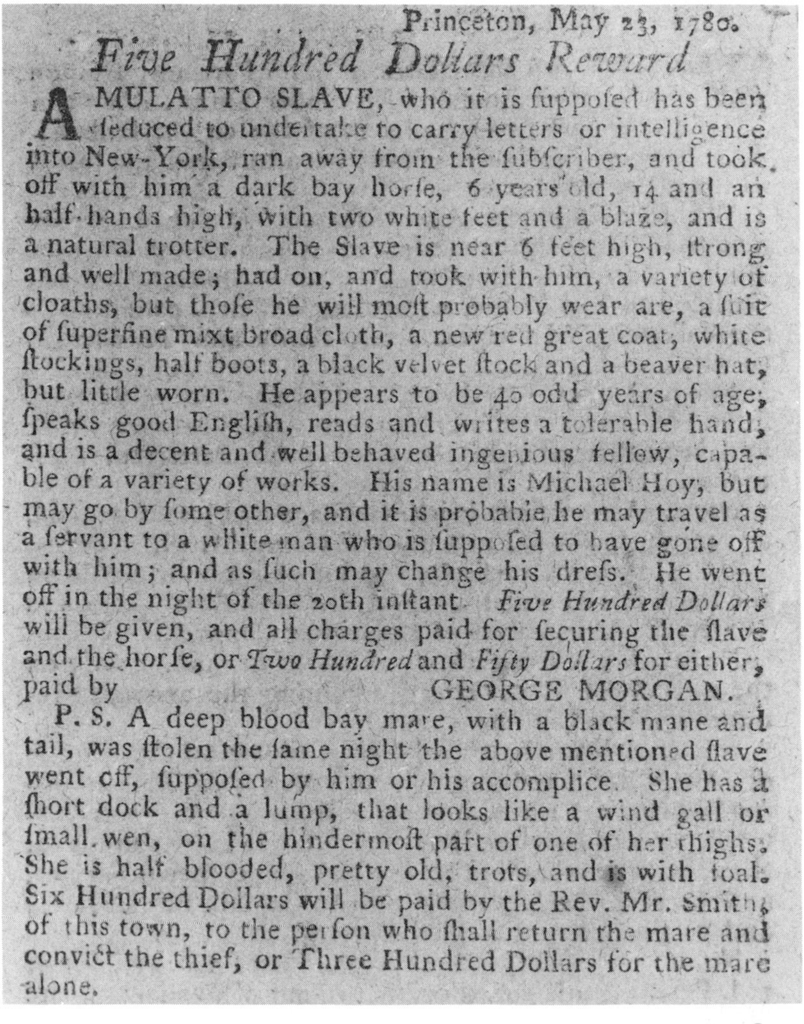

FIGURE 6: Advertisement from the *Pennsylvania Gazette*, May 31, 1780. *Courtesy of The Historical Society of Pennsylvania.* (See case 258.)

259. *May 31, 1780*

Four Hundred Dollars Reward.

RUN away, on Sunday, the 28th instant (May), from the subscriber, in Philadelphia, a Negroe MAN, named Kit (alias Christopher) about 35 years of age, 5 feet 10 inches high, the crown of his head bald, stout built, and somewhat round shouldered, has a down look, is very serious, moves slow and rocks in his walk, talks much of past difficulties, and presumes to say he was once free; he is a Guinea Negroe, but was sometime in New-England, and speaks upon that dialect; had on, and took with him, a blue knap coatee, with basket buttons, a light mixed brown German serge jacket and breeches, with worked basket buttons, a check shirt, and a brown country made linen ditto, the sleeves of which are finer than the body, two pair yarn hose, good shoes, plated shoe buckles, and two round hats, one bound with black velvet; there is great reason to suppose he will try to get to New York; all masters of vessels are charged not to carry him off. Whoever brings home said Negroe, shall receive the above reward, and reasonable charges, paid by

JOHN SHIELDS.

N.B. Strayed away, the 18th instant, a brown and white COW, about 7 years old, has a white belly, and sharp pointed horns. The person that informs where she is will be handsomely rewarded.

260. *June 7, 1780*

Baltimore, May 30, 1780.
FIFTY POUNDS Reward.

RAN away from the subscriber's plantation, about nine miles from this town, a mulatto fellow named JOE. He is very likely and stout made, 25 years old, about 5 feet 10 inches high, has a scar on one of his wrists, and walks very erect.—Had on and took with him, a white cloth surtout coat, an old blue regimental coat, faced with red, and the sleeves, from the elbows, mended with white cloth, white cloth waistcoat, a striped waistcoat, lined with blue linsey woolsey, a pair of linen corded breeches, one pair of linen and one pair of blue worsted overalls, one pair of tow linen trowsers, three shirts, a black stock, a pair of blue ribbed worsted stockings, a new wool hat, with a brass button to it, and a pair of French leather shoes, with brass buckles. He has much the appearance of having been in the army, where he was some time a waggoner. He is very plausible in speech, and will probably attempt to pass as a free man, by the name of JOSEPH HANSON. It is likely he may attempt to pass towards Bush-Town, near where his mother lives.—Whoever takes up the said runaway, and secures or brings him to my plantation, WILLIAM ANDREW, overseer, or to me in this town, shall receive the above reward, and all reasonable charges.   MATTHEW RIDLEY.

261. March 28, 1781

Philadelphia, March 20, 1781.
Five Hard Dollars Reward.

RAN-AWAY, the eleventh instant, from the subscriber, a Negroe Man, named HARRY, of a yellow complexion, about five feet seven inches high, stoops a little, has a large wen on one of his shoulders, and is very talkative when in liquor: Had on when he went away, a brown coatee, two waistcoats, one blue, the other striped lincey, leather breeches, and blue stockings. He has been since seen, and changed his apparel. Had on when seen, a sailor's blue jacket, trowsers and woolen cap.

Whoever brings home said Negroe, shall have the above reward, and Five Hard Dollars more for discovering who hath harboured him.
GEORGE MEADE.

N.B. All masters of vessels and others are requested not to harbour said negroe.

262. April 25, 1781

One Ton of BAR-IRON Reward,
(or the value thereof in currency)

RAN away from James Sharps, in Sadsbury township, Chester county, on the 10th day of April, 1779, a remarkable likely Negroe Man, very black, named ABEL, about 24 or 25 years of age, 5 feet 10 or 11 inches high, with a mole on one of his cheeks, his clothes unknown; it is supposed he harbours between New-Castle and St. George's, or about Apoquinimink, in Delaware State, as he has some friends that are freemen living in a cedarswamp in that neighbourhood. Whoever takes up said Negroe, and secures him in any goal, or brings him to his master, living at Hopewell forge, in Lancaster county, shall have the above reward, paid by   PETER GRUBB.

N.B. It is probable he will pass for a freeman, he having got a pass from a free Negroe, named NAT, and may pass by that name.
March 31, 1781.

263. May 16, 1781

Ten Pounds Specie Reward.

RAN AWAY in July last, a Negroe Woman, named SUE, about 45 years of age; has a down look, remarkable large breasts, and a wen upon the temple; but as she is very artful, she may endeavour to hide it by a long ear'd cap she generally wears; she discovers the loss of some of her teeth when she laughs: She had a variety of clothes, among which are, a tartan, a white linen, and a calico gown, and a striped silk jacket. She passed in Baltimore, where she remained for some time, by the name of Free Poll. She is now about Philadelphia, waiting for the return of her husband, as she calls him; a free Mulattoe, named Mark Stubbs, who sailed from Baltimore in a ship called the Enterprize: He is a short thick talkative fellow, about 50 years of age, and a most notorious villain. She is a good cook, can wash and iron well; he is a butcher, and it is probable they may set up for themselves about the city. Any person who will secure her in any goal in the United States, shall have a Reward of Five Pounds Specie, or if delivered to Mr. James Heron, in Philadelphia, or to the subscriber, at Greenburry's-Point, near Annapolis, Ten Pounds Specie.

DAVID KERR.

Maryland, May 15, 1781.

264. May 23, 1781

Thirty Spanish Milled Dollars Reward.

RUN AWAY from the subscriber, about five weeks ago, A Mulattoe fellow, named JACK, about five feet two or three inches high, fair complexion, black bushy hair. Had on when he went away, a drab coloured cloth coat, leather breeches, a red surtout coat, very large for him; a good tempered fellow when sober, but sulky and quarrelsome in liquor; he is well acquainted with the country, having been two or three times at Boston, and was servant to Doctor Hutchinson when the army were at Valley Forge; he is a good taylor, and probably may be sculking in some part of the country, working at that trade. Whoever takes up said fellow and delivers him to the subscriber, shall receive the above reward. And all persons are forbid harbouring him, as by so doing they will be prosecuted as the law directs.   ANDREW CALDWELL.

N.B. Said fellow would have been advertised before, but he had a trick of absenting himself for two or three weeks at a time and then returning home; it was thought he might do the same now.

Philadelphia, May 13.

265. January 23, 1782

WAS left at the subscriber's house, at the sign of the Battle of Monmouth, in Market-street, Philadelphia, on the 16th of October last, a MULATTOE BOY, by a person who called himself John Park, and offered him for sale; he said he was obliged to go to the southward with some dispatches, and left the boy in my charge, but on his return he was taken up, and is now in Lancaster goal; as soon as the boy heard that Park was confined, he acknowledged that Park had taken him from Mr. Lyons, living near Pe[dee] River, South Carolina, and says his name is John, but Park called him Dick. His master is desired to come, prove his property, pay charges and take him away.   PETER SUMMERS.
    Philad. Jan. 23, 1782.

266. February 6, 1782
One Hundred Dollars, Specie, Reward.

RAN from Elk-Forge, near the Head of Elk, the 23rd of April, 1782, Negroe DICK; about 28 years old, 5 feet 9 or 10 inches high, thin visage, hollow ey'd, straight bodied, speaks pretty quick and a little stammering: Had a variety of good clothes with him, and plenty of money; was bro't up to farming, as a very good ax-man, and handy at most kinds of country work. About 6 years ago was brought from the branches of Nanticoke river, in Sussex county, where he had been brought up, and it is supposed he is now hovering between the bays of Delaware and Chesapeak.
    Also ran from the same place, the beginning of Sept. 1777, and joined the British then at Head of Elk, another Negroe named DICK; near 6 feet high, a straight, well proportioned fellow, not very black, about 30 years old, apt to smile when speaking, was brought up in [Pent]cador Hundred, New Castle county, to farming and driving team, at which he is expert, as well as drinking strong liquor.—'Tis thought he is now hovering about Philadelphia, or in the Jerseys. Any person securing the above described fellows, or either of them, in any goal, and will give notice to the subscriber, at said forge, so that he may recover him or them, shall have FIFTY DOLLARS for each, and if brought home, reasonable charges.   THOMAS MAY.
    N.B. If they return of their own accord, this offence shall be forgiven.
    January 23, 1782.

267. June 5, 1782
FIVE POUNDS Reward.

RUN away from the subscriber, in Amity township, Berks county, and State of Pennsylvania, on the night of the 19th instant, a Negroe MAN, named Caesar, a stout lusty well made Negroe, about 24 years of age, 5 feet 8 or 9 inches high, has lost one of his upper teeth before, and remarkable long hair used to have tied it behind, can talk both Dutch and English; it is supposed he has got a forged pass, and it is thought he has a white woman along with him who passes for his wife; took with him when he went off, a white hunting shirt, a blue under jacket without sleeves, good pair of tow trowsers, new shoes and silver plated buckles, a new felt hat, a hairy jockey cap, &c, and it is thought he will try to get on board some ship; all masters of vessels are forbid to carry him off at their peril. Whoever takes up said Negroe, and secures him in any goal, so that his master may have him again, shall have the above reward, and reasonable charges, paid by   JACOB WEAVER.
  N.B. He is a great fidler.   May 24, 1782.

268. June 5, 1782

RUN AWAY, last night, from the subscribers, in the township of Hopewell, county of Hunterdon, and State of New-Jersey, A Negroe Man, named TOM, about five feet ten inches high, of a yellow complexion: Had on when he went away, a light blue home made broadcloth coat and vest, his other clothes unknown; and at the same time went off, a Negroe Wench, named LIDD, a wife to the above named fellow, likewise of a yellow complexion, something like an Indian: Had on a light chintz gown and a large black bonnet, and took with her a white dimity jacket and petticoat, and other clothes unknown. Whoever takes up and secures the said Negroes, so that their masters get them again, shall have a reward of FOUR HALF JOES, or TWO for either of them, paid by
                    JOHN WELLING,
                    JONATHAN BUNN.
  May 20, 1782.

269. June 5, 1782

CAME to the house of the subscriber, living in East-Nantmill, Chester county, some time in April last, A Negroe Man, called CAESAR, about

22 years of age, five feet six inches high, marked with the small pox, was born in Galena, and speaks very much in that dialect; says he come last from the southern army, and that he is a freeman: Had on, a blue regimental coat, faced with red, black worsted breeches, light coloured jacket, tow cloth shirt, and an old hat; has sundry other clothes, such as, one pair buckskin breeches, one tow cloth hunting shirt, and one scallop'd hat, pretty good; was much indisposed with sickness when he come to my house; is now under a surgeon's hands, and is much recovered; therefore as I doubt the truth of his being free, his master, if any he has, is desired to come, prove property, pay charges and take him away, otherwise he will be sold for the same, in three weeks from the date hereof.

May 22, 1782.   WILLIAM STARRETT.

270. September 18, 1782
EIGHT DOLLARS Reward.

RUN, the 20th of August last, from the subscriber, living near the head of North-east River, in Caecil county, Maryland, a Negroe MAN, named Simon, but may perhaps change his name to Johnson, this country born, is about 27 years of age, nearly 6 feet high, coarse featured, a little pitted with the small-pox; had on, when he went away, a light coloured cloth coat, short made, tow shirt and trowsers, and a cloth cap the same colour of his coat; he was seen at Christiana Bridge in company with some straggling troops belonging to the French army, on his way, as is supposed, to New-York. Whoever takes up and secures said Negroe, so that his master may have him again, shall have the above reward, and reasonable charges, paid by   SAMUEL MAFFITT.

Sept. 10, 1782.

271. January 22, 1783
TWENTY DOLLARS Reward.

RAN AWAY, on Christmas eve, from the subscriber, living in Wilmington, New-Castle county, and Delaware State, A Negroe Man, named CHARLES, formerly LONDON, a spare genteal fellow, about 5 feet 10 or 11 inches high, has a high nose and forehead, very well made, is talkative and bold in appearance, fond of strong liquor, has a small scar over one of his eyes. He had and took with him, two white linen shirts, one ruffled, the other plain, one old tow linen ditto, one pair of old leather breeches, one pair fine white worsted stockings, and one pair dark yarn ditto, a pair of good boots, new shoes, a new fine hat, an old round ditto, a scarlet coat and waistcoat, an old blue cloth great coat with a white velvet cape, an old brown round made jacket with wooden buttons, and lined with tow linen; also a brass barrel'd pistol, has been broke at the butt and mended.

At the same time a Negroe Man, named SAM, belonging to Mr. Ganning Bedford, run off with the above described Negroe, who were both seen in the city of Philadelphia. Sam has since been taken up on board of a brig in the city, and was just going to sea, and it is supposed that Charles will endeavour to make his escape the same way. Sam informed he had obtained a pass from a free Negroe in this town, by the name of Pott, under which pass and name he now passes. All Captains of vessels are forewarned taking the aforesaid Negroe off. Whoever apprehends and secures the above Negroe so that the master may have him again, shall receive the above reward, and all reasonable charges if brought home, paid by the subscriber.

Wilmington, Jan. 7, 1783.   DANIEL I. ADAMS.

272. May 14, 1783

RUN away from the subscriber's plantation, near Chester Town, on Sunday night last, a negroe man named WILL, about 25 years of age, 5 feet 4 or 5 inches high, well set, large white teeth, flat forehead, had on, when he went away, a country kersey jacket and breeches of black and white wool mixed in the [?], the jacket fulled, the breeches not fulled, thick double soaled shoes, tied with leather strings, small hob nails in the soals near the toe, and large ones in the heels, white yarn stockings, round felt hat, bound with black worsted binding, ticklenburg shirt; he did endeavour to get other cloaths before he set off, but cannot tell whether he succeeded, he had an iron collar on but suppose he got it off. Whoever takes up and secures him in any goal, shall receive what the law allows, and if brought home, reasonable charges, paid by

JOHN BOLTON.

N.B. His back is cruelly scarred with severe whipping, for running away before I got him.   April 30, 1783.

273. October 8, 1783

Reading, September 29, 1783.
Committed this day, in the Goal of the county of Berks, The
following Negroe Men, viz.

POMPEY BELL, speaks good English, about 24 years of age, says he lived in Newark with Mr. William Allen, left that place about two years ago, and that he was a freeman, and was persuaded from that place by a certain Allison; the other named PRINCE FREDERICK, says he belong'd to Doctor B[enat] of Newark, and became a freeman, and also taken away by said Allison, who was going to sell him for seven years to Mr. William B[oxon] of Northumberland county; said Negroe Prince Frederick is about 35 years of age, and speaks good English: A Mulattoe Woman, who calls herself BETSY, says she was born in Paxton, Lancaster county, and that she was free; is about 24 years of age, and married to Negroe Prince Frederick. Any person that owns said Negroes and Mulattoe woman, or either of them, as slaves or servants, are desired to reply, prove their property, in four weeks from the date hereof, pay costs, and take them away, otherwise they will be sold to discharge the same, by   PHILIP KREMER, Sheriff.

274. June 2, 1784

THREE POUNDS Reward.

RAN away from the Subscribers living in Wilmington, New-Castle County, on Monday the 19th of March last, from Duck-Creek in said County, where he was sent on Business, and from whence he took a considerable Sum of Money with him the Property of his Master, a Negroe Lad named BEN VALENTINE, bred in Wilmington, about 16 Years of Age, 5 Feet 7 Inches high or thereabout, slim-made, somewhat bow leged, one of his Ancles a little thicker than the other, has an agreeable Countenance, is smart and active, and can read and write tolerably well; having had a big cut off the End of one of the Fingers of his left Hand, a very remarkable Nail has grown thereon: Had on when he left Home, a white Linen Shirt and Stock, with a black or cross-bar'd Silk Handkerchief, a good Londonbrown Forestcloth Coat, with flowered top'd Buttons, a double breasted Jacket, of a redish Colour, with different Metal buttons, Buckskin Breeches, black Wolten Stockings, with white Ones under them, strong Shoes, the Toes capt, large square Blackrim Buckles, a small round Wool Hat, and an old

Surtout Coat, of a Snuff colour. Whoever takes up said Negroe, and secures him in any Goal, so that his Master may get him again, shall have the above Reward, and reasonable Charges (beside Half of the Money found with him) if brought to   JAMES ADAMS.

N.B. As the above described Negroe has been at the Printing Business upwards of a Year it's probable he may offer his Service as a Print-man one Place or other. If he should take a Notion of going to Sea, all Masters of Vessels are forbid to engage him in that Service.

To be LETT, a House in High-street, opposite the upper Market house in the [flourishing] Borough of Wilmington, New-Castle County, well admitted for the mercantile Way; and on Account of its Situation for Business, and a delightful prospect of the river Delaware and Christiana Creek from the Door, is equal to any in the place.—Inquire of the Printers there.

275. July 28, 1784

July 13, 1784.

RUN away last night, from the Administrators to the estate of John Evans, of Uwchland, deceased, a Negroe man, named BOB, about 38 years old, imported from Guinea, and marked in his face, of a middle stature, has learned the tanning business, and is very handy at farming, says that his late master promised he should be set free; had on, when he went away, a tow shirt and trowsers, a new wool hat, and a pair of good shoes with strings. Whoever takes up said Negroe and secures him in any goal, so that the subscribers may him get again, shall have Three Pounds reward, and reasonable charges, if brought to DANIEL EVANS of Uwchland, Chester county, or to EDWARD CARTER of Chester, or JERE[Z]IAN EVANS of East Nantmell, in said county, Administrators.

N.B. It is supposed that there is a Negroe woman with him, as they went both together.

276. August 4, 1784

TWENTY DOLLARS Reward.

RAN away on the second day of May last, from the subscriber, living in the borough of Chester, a Negroe man named PETER, about 27 years of age, 5 feet 6 or 7 inches high, a square well built fellow, a little bow-legged, had on his dirty working cloths, viz. a coarse shirt and trowsers, old hat and jacket, and old shoes with strings, though he possibly may have taken better cloaths with him; he has been used to all kinds of farming work, is a great liar, and boasts much of what he can do. He has been hired with farmers in different parts of Chester county, and lived two years with Mr. Thomas Watson, near Newark, in New-Castle county: He is an artful fellow, can play on the fife, and may probably change his name, and pass for a freeman, as he did once before on a like occasion. Whoever takes up said Negroe and brings him home, or secures him in any goal in this state, so that his master may have him again, shall have the above reward, besides reasonable charges, paid by

ELISHA PRICE.

Chester, July 26, 1784.

N.B. All masters of vessels, and others, are forbid to harbour or carry him off, at their peril.

277. August 18, 1784

Three Hundred DOLLARS Reward.

NEGROE GEORGE ran away from Elk forge near Head of Elk, Cecil county Maryland, on the 2d of August, 1784; is about 40 years of age, 5 feet 7 or 8 inches high, slender bodied thin visage, not very black, plausible and complisant, fond of strong liquor, can speak pretty good English, a little French and a few words of High Dutch; has been in the West-Indies and Canada, also in several of the Northern States, in capacity of waiter; his employ latterly in the kitchen at cooking, at which he is compleat; is also a good barber; has a variety of clothes with him; he will attempt to get off by sea or make to the frontiers.

Negro CATO ran away from the same place the 24th of May, 1783; is a well set fellow, now about 28 years of age, about 5 feet 8 inches high, longish visage, eyes prominent, a blemish in one of them occasioned by a hurt some years ago, heavy eye-brows and down look, perhaps can speak Dutch; he was bred in Albany county, State of New-York, by Mr. Richard Spore, of whom he was brought about the year 1779: he is a compleat farmer and good axman; took none but working clothes with him, but his invention, no doubt, soon furnished others.

Negroe DICK ran away from the same place, the 23d of April, 1781; is now about 31 years of age, 5 feet 9 or 10 inches high, thin visage, hollow eyed, straight bodied, speaks pretty quick and a little stammering; had a variety of good clothes with him and plenty of money, was brought up to farming, is a good axman, and handy at most kinds of country work; was born and brought up about the branches of Nanti-coke river, and supposed may yet be hovering between the bays of Delaware and Chesapeak, or is going by water, probably, in small craft.

All the above Slaves were discovered carrying on illicit traffic with infamous whites in the neighbourhood, and ran off for fear of punishment. There is great reason to believe those vile receivers have furnished them with forged passes, wherewith, they will endeavour to pass for freemen: And whereas it is become too much a practice to employ Negroes without examining or caring whose property they are, all such employers, harbourers or concealers, of the above mentioned Negroes, may be assured they shall be proceeded against with all possible rigour; on the contrary, any person securing in goal, within two years after date, any or either of said Negroes, and giving notice, so that the subscriber may have them again, shall receive One Hundred Dollars for each of them, and if brought home reasonable charges.   THOMAS MAY.

Cecil County, Maryland, August 4, 1784.

278. November 10, 1784
TWENTY DOLLARS Reward.

RAN AWAY from the subscriber, living in Queen Ann's county, Maryland, on Tuesday, the 25th day of October, a well set dark Mulattoe Man, named JEM, but calls himself James Ferguson, and sometimes James Hays, about 5 feet 6 or 7 inches high, 36 years of age, has a large good sett of teeth, and is apt to smile or laugh, with a down look when talking or spoken sharply to; he had several scars cut in his head about the first of September, which time he run away before, and resisted being taken, and one over his left eye, which reaches below the edge of his wool; he understands something of the cooper trade, and it is like will want to get in that employ; he is very fond of strong drink, and very quarrelsome when in liquor. He had on when he went away, an old wool hat, two kersey jackets much worn, two shirts, one of them very narrow at the wristbands, an old pair of trowsers, his other clothes unknown, but it is likely he may change his clothes and name. Whoever takes up the said slave, and secures him in any goal, so that his master may get him again, shall have the above reward, and reasonable charges, paid by
JAMES SETH.

Oct. 29, 1784.
N.B. All masters of vessels are forbid to carry him off.

279. *January 26, 1785*

EIGHT DOLLARS Reward.

RAN AWAY from the subscriber, living in St. George's hundred, New-Castle county, Delaware state, on the 25th ultimo, a Negroe Man, named SIMON, formerly called Dick, 32 years of age, about 5 feet 9 or 10 inches high, he is fat and very strong made, very active and complaisant, apt to tell lies, very fond of telling fortunes, and can alter his voice on each extreme, understands working on a farm, but more especially house and kitchen work, is an excellent cook, can wash, spin, sew, knit, &c. it is probable he may change his clothes and put on womens, in order for better concealment, as he did so once before; he takes a great quantity of snuff, and is subject to fits. Had on when he went away, a large black hat, a fulled linsey short coat, without pocket flaps or cuffs, a calicoe jacket, buckskin breeches, new shoes and stockings, also a check apron. Whoever takes up said fellow, and brings him home, or secures him in any goal, shall receive the above reward, from

WILLIAM MOODY.

January 22, 1785.

280. *May 25, 1785*

TEN POUNDS Reward.

RUN away, on the 22d of April, from Dubartes Shepherd, living near James's river, in Botetourt county, Virginia, a Negroe man, named CHARLES, but supposed to have changed his name. He is about 30 years of age, 5 feet 9 or 10 inches high, strong made, with large hands and very large feet, and when he laughs or smiles his eyes appear very small; he is not so black as some Negroes. It is thought he will pretend to have been set free by the people called Quakers.

The subscriber, having purchased him running, will give Fifteen Pounds reward, and reasonable charges, to any person that will secure and bring said Negroe to him, in Albemarle county, or Ten Pounds reward for securing him in any goal, on shortly giving notice thereof to

GEORGE NICHOLAS.

May 24, 1785.

N.B. A letter sent to Richmond, directed for said George Nicholas, living in Charlotte's Vale-Town, Albemarle Court-House, will quickly come to hand.

281. July 13, 1785

Waterford township, Gloucester county, July 12, 1785.
FORTY SHILLINGS Reward.

RAN away from the subscriber, on the 25th of June last, a Negroe woman, named HANNAH, about 35 years of age, pretty likely, about 5 feet 2 or 3 inches high, came from Guinea, has one mark each side of her eye, if examined, and a small lump or scar on the back of her neck; had on, when she went away, a red flannel jacket and petticoat, old blue quilt, with mixed cloth in the fore part, and some patches on the lower part behind, had on a coarse white shift, but expect her dress will be altered. Her husband is a free man, and it is expected he harbours her; his name is Big Bill, formerly belonging to Daniel Cooper, deceased. Whoever apprehends the said Negroe woman, and secures her in any goal in the United States, so that the subscriber may have her again, or delivers her to the subscriber, shall have the above reward, and reasonable charges, paid by   ISAAC HORNER.

282. August 2, 1786

Maryland, Talbot County, July 10th 1786.

RAN away on the 2d day of this instant July, a light coloured MULATTO SLAVE, named JIM, generally went by the name of Jim Byas, he is about 5 feet 10 inches high, thin visaged, rather bow legged, what grows on his head has rather the appearance of hair than wool as it is so long that he frequently tied it behind or queued it though but short, he is a tolerable good shoemaker and carried his shoemaker's tools with him, he is a very humble, submissive fellow, and has that appearance in all his conversation: I have reason to believe that he will make for Kent county on Delaware, or New-Castle county, or perhaps may endeavour to get into the Jersies in the neighbourhood against Reedy island. He is the property of Mrs. Elizabeth Martin, who lives in the Jersies, about 30 miles above Philadelphia, and has been hired out by the subscriber for the benefit of Mrs. Martin for several years; I believe he has nothing in view but freedom, as the man he was hired with and he had no manner of difference. Any person that shall take up the said fellow and secure him in any gaol so that I may get him again, shall have the above reward, and reasonable charges paid if brought to the subscriber, living in the county and state aforesaid.   JOHN STEVENS.

283. September 6, 1786

FORTY DOLLARS Reward.

RAN away, on the 15th of July last, from the subscriber, living in Chester-Town, Maryland, a Negroe man, named Anthony, a slim black fellow, pitted with the small-pox, five feet nine or ten inches high, 28 years of age, but looks older; he is a very artful fellow, has procured a pass, and when examined can tell a very plausible story. He has worked on a farm, in a mill, and blacksmith's shop, is a great gamester, fond of liquor and company, but very seldom gets drunk; it is expected he will pass thro' New-Castle and Wilmington to Philadelphia, and from thence to the Jersies. No person can object to apprehend such an ungrateful rogue; I bought him a slave for life, and since have manumitted him free after a certain term. All persons are forewarned from harbouring or employing said Negroe, or assisting him to get off either by land or water. Whoever secures him in any gaol, where I may get him, and gives notice of the same, shall have Twenty Dollars, or the above reward if brought home.   THOMAS M'CLUER.

284. May 30, 1787

FIVE POUNDS Reward.

RAN away on the 31st of March last, from the subscriber, now living in Middletown township, Chester county, state of Pennsylvania, a MU-LATTO MAN, named Caesar; but some of his associates having formed a pass for him, he has changed his name and calls himself Jacob Holy: to this pass is annexed the subscriber's name and Thomas Levis, Esquire. His clothes cannot well be described, having changes thereof, and in all probability will purchase more, as he was furnished with money, which he procured by disposing of his master's property. He is twenty-five years of age, bout 5 feet 9 inches high, is thick and strong made, walks very streight, with a short quick step, and is very proud. He can read, is a great professor of religion, and has much to say on the subject. Whoever will apprehend said person and secure him, so that the subscriber may get him again, shall receive the above reward.

JAMES ANDERSON.

May 22, 1787.

285. October 31, 1787

WAS left at the house of the subscriber, Inn-keeper, in Nockamixon township, in Bucks county, on the night of the 24th instant, by a certain Negro Woman, who called herself Phillis, a Negro Child about three years old, said wench said she belonged to a French Gentleman near Fleming-town, in New-Jersey, but had some time since purchased her time. The owner or owners of said Child, if any it has, is therefore requested to come, prove property, pay charges, and take it away.

GEORGE SHAW.

Nockamixon, Sept. 29, 1787.

286. April 9, 1788

March 31, 1788.
EIGHT DOLLARS Reward.

RAN away last night from the subscriber, living in Salisbury township, Lancaster county, a Mulattoe Slave named NED, about 21 years of age, about 5 feet 4 or 5 inches high, had on when he went away, a half worn brown coat, an old jacket let out at the sides with brown cloth, tow shirt, old dark corduroy breeches, white yarn stockings, good shoes, with plated buckles, new wool hat cocked up at the sides, has been inoculated last winter for the small pox, and the place may be seen on his left arm. Whoever takes up said slave, and secures him in any goal, so as his master may have him again, shall have the above reward, paid by

ISAAC M'CAMANT.

287. May 14, 1788

Salem, West-Jersey, May 6, 1788.

WAS committed to the gaol of this county on the 31st of March last, TWO NEGROE MEN, on suspicion of being runaways; one by the name of *David Johnson*, but says his name is *David Cornish*, about 5 feet 11 inches high, 25 or 26 years of age, slender built, has a remarkable scar on his left cheek, which extends above his eye, his hair combed back, and middling long; wears a brown cloth coat, red under jacket with sleeves, redish coloured trowsers, white yarn stockings, old shoes and buckles; says he belongs to Henry Waggaman, of Somerset county, on the Eastern-shore, Maryland.

The other by the name of *John Johnson,* but calls himself *Luke Cornish,* about 5 feet 8 or 9 inches high, about 33 years of age, very black, has a high forehead, and hair combed back; had on a brown linen coat, black under jacket, with shirt ruffled at the bosom, corduroy breeches, white yarn stockings, old shoes and buckles; says he belongs to James Sullivan, of Dorset county, Maryland. They are smart bold fellows, very resolute, and seem bent on making their escape, at the risk of their lives, and for their bad conduct are both in irons. Their masters are desired to come, pay charges and take them away, or they will be sold for their charges in five weeks from the above date, by

ZENAS SMITH, Gaoler.

288. *July 23, 1788*

EIGHT DOLLARS Reward.

RAN away last night from the subscriber, living in Salisbury township, Lancaster county, a Mulatto Slave, named NED, about 21 years of age, 5 feet 5 inches high, of a bright colour, well made, broad face, his hair is so long that he can comb it; had on when he went away, an old linen shirt, a pair of striped trowsers, of copperas colour and white, a good wool hat, and calf skin shoes with copper coloured buckles. He was inoculated last winter for the small pox, and the place can be seen on his left arm. He ran away this spring, was put in Easton goal, and sold for his goal fees without my knowledge, to two gentlemen in Bucks county, who gave six dollars to a lawyer to help them to set him free, and had him bound 18 months for the fees. From these circumstances I have reason to suspect he is gone that way, as they were such good friends to him. Whoever takes up said slave and puts him in any goal, so as his master may get him again, shall have the above reward, and reasonable charges, paid by   ISAAC M'CAMANT.
July 13, 1788.

289. *August 20, 1788*

RAN away on Tuesday, the 5th August, instant, from the subscriber, living in Talbot county, Maryland, a likely bright Mulatto Lad, named Damon, 21 years old, about 5 feet 6 inches high, slender and active, and well acquainted with the business of waiting in a house, to which he has been always used; he went off in an Oznabrigs shirt, trowsers and waistcoat, but as he is well supplied with a variety of clothing it is impossible to say how he may be dressed; is extreamly artful, much address must be used in taking, and great care in securing him when taken, otherwise he will certainly make his escape. He has been learning to read, and has succeeded in a small degree; has a scar on one of his legs, but it is not remembered which, occasioned by a scald or a burn. He will very probably change his name, and likely may assume the name of Mat or Matthias, as he was called by that name when a child. He may also have got a pass, as he is capable of any fraud of that sort. He has lately become very fond of strong liquor, and may now possibly indulge himself in it. Whoever will apprehend the said slave, and secure him in such a manner that the subscriber may get him again, shall receive a reward of *One Shilling a Mile* for every mile he may have got from home, and shall be generously rewarded if brought home and delivered to

ROBERT GOLDSBOROUGH, jun.

Maryland, Talbot county, August 12, 1788.

290. *August 20, 1788*

State of New-Jersey, Cumberland county, August 11, 1788.

WAS taken up and committed to the gaol of this county on the 7th instant, a Negroe man, supposed to be a slave, about 5 feet 4 or 5 inches high, and from appearance between 20 and 25 years of age; he is a well made likely fellow, and can speak no English; said negroe landed on the beach, somewhere not far above Egg-island, and is supposed from his dialect to have left some Spanish vessel passing up or down the Delaware. Any person owning said negroe, proving his property and paying charges, may have him again, by applying to the subscriber, within six weeks from the date hereof. Should no claim be made within that time he will be discharged from imprisonment.   JOS. BUCK, Sheriff.

291. *November 19, 1788*

RAN away from the subscriber, on the 28th of August last, a likely mulatto fellow, about 21 years of age, square and well made, with a small scar on his forehead; he had on, when he went away, an old jean coat, new fustian waistcoat, new Oznaburg breeches, shoes and stockings. As he has been bred up altogether as a house servant, he, for a livelyhood, will probably hire himself either in a tavern, or to some private gentleman, his colour being such as to favor his scheme of freedom. Any person, on delivering him to me, on Bull-skin-run, Berkely county, Virginia, shall, if taken out of the state, have a reward of Fifty Dollars, and if in Thirty, besides what the law allows. He has travelled with me to New-York and the West-Indies, and will probably endeavour to get to one of those places. ROBERT BAYLOR.

292. *January 14, 1789*

Cumberland county, state of New-Jersey, Jan. 5, 1789.
SIX POUNDS Reward.

BROKE GAOL in the night of the second instant, a certain man, committed for horse-stealing, by the name of *William Johnson*, but it is supposed his real name is James Sutton, and that he has lately escaped from the wheelbarrow in Philadelphia, as his hair is cut remarkably short. He appears to be a middle aged man, about 5 feet 7 or 8 inches high, well set, short black hair, has been used to the water, and is fond of talking about vessels; had on an old felt hat painted white on the top of the crown, a blue sailor's jacket, the sleeves of which are covered with white canvas, old black sattin vest, a check linen shirt, white linen trowsers, and grey woolen stockings.

Also a Spanish Negroe man, named *John* or *Juan Francisco*, committed about five months ago as a run-away from on board a Spanish vessel then lying in Delaware bay, a short thick but well built fellow, very black and pock-marked, can speak but very little English; had on a round sailor's hat, covered with black oil-cloth, an old grey coatee with yellow carved metal buttons, old white shirt, white woolen trowsers with a blue stripe round each leg near the bottom, blue home-made woolen stockings and old shoes; but it is probable they will change dress with each other.

It is supposed they are gone towards New-York, in order to get on board some vessel; and as two horses were stolen in the neighbourhood the same night, it is also supposed they were taken by these fellows. The above reward will be paid to whoever takes them up and secures them in gaol, so as the subscriber may get them again, or THREE POUNDS for either. JOSEPH BUCK, Sheriff.

293. June 10, 1789

Four Pounds Reward.

RAN away, on the 1st of June instant, two negro men, the one about 5 feet 7 or 8 inches high, about 24 years of age, can speak the German language, being bred amongst the Dutch, speaks broken English, chews tobacco, which makes his teeth blackish, and called himself *Peter Dawson;* had on, when he went away, a felt hat, old light coloured great coat, a brown fustian straight coat, tow shirt and trowsers dyed brown, linsey jacket with broad deep blue stripes, and old shoes; was born in West-Jersey, on the Delaware, and it is likely will try for that place. The other a well made fellow, named *Daniel,* a shoemaker by trade, speaks good English, his cloathing not known. Whoever takes up and secures the above Negroes, so as the owner may have them again, shall have the above reward, or TWO POUNDS for each, and reasonable charges, paid by the subscriber, living near Haverdegrass, Harford County, State of Maryland.   WILLIAM LUCKIE.

294. June 30, 1790

Chester, June 5, 1790.

BROKE out of the goal of Delaware county, four Negroe men, viz. one named HARRY, a stout well made fellow, about five feet eight inches high, not very black, it is likely he will change his cloathing. One other named BILL, about five feet seven inches high, well made, blacker than the other. One other named ABERDEEN, who has lately been sick, about five feet six or seven inches high. One other a lad, supposed about 16 or 17 years of age, a smart active fellow, talks pretty much. Their cloathing it is likely they will change. Any person taking them and bringing them to Chester, and delivering them to my custody, shall receive *Three Pounds* for each of them delivered, paid by me

NICHOLAS FAIRLAMB, Sheriff.

N.B. The two last mentioned Negroes were committed for felony.

295. August 4, 1790

West-Chester, Chester County, August 2, 1790.

WAS committed to the gaol of this county, on the 26th of July last, TWO NEGROE MEN, who call themselves Richard and Harry. Richard is about 5 feet 8 inches high, a stout well made man. Harry is not quite so tall nor so thick built. They are about 30 years old each, and acknowledge themselves slaves to James Amos and Joshua Amos, of Harford county, Maryland. Their Masters are requested to come, pay charges, and take them away, otherwise they will be sold, to discharge the cost, in four weeks from this Date.

CHARLES DILWORTH, Sheriff.

296. September 1, 1790

RAN away, in the night of the 23d of August, from the subscriber, living in Tredyffrin township, Chester county, a Mulatto Girl, named Kate, about 21 years of age; had on, and took with her, an old black bonnet, a long gown striped red, blue and white, two short ditto striped blue, copperas and white, a red petticoat, a lincey ditto striped blue, red and white, a large white shawl, also Russia sheeting for two shirts, one part made up, the other not made.

It is supposed she went off with a black man, named Charles, who served his time with Dr. Vanlear, and stole and took with him a jean coattee, and a pair of overalls and jacket, with small white metal buttons.

Whoever will secure said girl in any gaol, or bring her home to her master, shall have FOUR DOLLARS reward, and reasonable charges, paid by   JOHN WILSON.

297. October 6, 1790

ON Wednesday, the 22d of last month, during the absence of the subscriber from home, his Negroe boy, named JOE, quitted his service. He is about 18 years old, very talkative, of small stature, a yellow complexion, and has his front teeth set wide apart. When he went away, he was dressed in a white linen shirt and trowsers, a sailor's blue jacket, and a flapt hat. He has been in the family from the time he was five years old; can write and read tolerably well; and at the age of 30 will be free, in consequence of a deed of manumission, under hand and seal, *executed by the subscriber soon after* he came into his possession.—Whoever brings him back to his master, shall receive SIX DOLLARS as a reward, and a reasonable allowance for expences and trouble.   JACOB RUSH.

Philadelphia county, Oct. 4, 1790.

N.B. He has been seen sculking in New-Jersey, near Burlington.

298. October 6, 1790

August 14, 1790.

BROKE away last evening from the constable of Kennet, on their way to Westchester gaol, two NEGROE SLAVES, belonging to James and Joshua Amos, of Harford county, in the state of Maryland; the one a stout built fellow, about five feet eight or nine inches high, named RICHARD; the other about five feet six inches high, named HARRY, both very black. Whoever apprehends and secures the abovesaid Negroes, so that they may be had, shall have *Three Pounds* reward for each of them, and reasonable charges, paid by the subscriber, living in Kennet township, Chester county.   ROBERT BARR, Constable.

299. October 13, 1790

EIGHT DOLLARS Reward.

RAN AWAY from the Subscriber, a NEGROE WOMAN, named NANCY, is stout made, about 35 years of age, has a small flesh mole on one side of her nose, is of a black cast, but not the very blackest, is country born, and understands farmers kitchen work very well, was indulged with very good cloaths when she went away, which she took with her about eighteen months ago, is something addicted to spasmodic affections, upon sudden fits of anger or surprize, &c. Whoever secures said Woman so that the owner gets her again, shall have the above Reward, paid by   JAMES ALLEN.

N.B. A letter left at the Crooked Billet, for the Burlington Stage, directed to James Allen, of Monmouth, to the care of Mr. Randolph, Allen-Town, will inform me when she is taken up. October 9, 1790.

300. November 10, 1790

Salem county, and state of New-Jersey, Nov. 2, 1790.

WAS taken up and committed to the gaol of this county, on the 28th of October last, a Negro Man, on suspicion of being a runaway slave, and being closely examined, said that he did belong to John Thompson, near Dover; on his being examined the second time, said that he did belong to Gabriel Kinsbey, in Baltimore; and the third time said that he came from Kent island, in Maryland, and that his master, Gabriel Kinsbey, did live there, and by trade was a shop joiner. After he had been three days in gaol, he then did declare that he belonged to Daniel Heath, near Middletown. The said Negro calls himself JAMES, and says his master bought him of one Charles Masewell, at Newtown, Chester, about four years since. He is five feet six inches high, well set, appears to be about 20 years of age, is very black, laughs but seldom, talks but little, and appears to be very sulky; he had on a coatee and double breasted jacket, both of light coloured cloth, ozenbrig shirt and trowsers, and wool hat, all much worn. His master is desired to come, prove his property, and pay charges, or he will be sold for the same in four weeks from the date of this advertisement, by   JONAS SMITH, Gaoler.

Advertisements for Runaway White Indentured Servants

301. May 19, 1743

RUN away on the 4th of this Instant from Samuel Thompson, of New-Castle-Hundred, an Irish Servant Man, named William Wall, a well set young Fellow of very fair Complexion, has a little of the Brogue on his Tongue, a little sower look'd, he pretends to be a Shoemaker and several other Trades: Had on when he went away a brown slip-over-coat a little too long for him, a brown Jacket, a new linen Shirt, old leather Breeches badly mended, grey yarn Stockings, and half worn Shoes one has a Hole in the Soal, an old Castor Hat, linen Cap made out of an old Shirt, a cotton Handkerchief about his Neck. He has a Scar on his Forhead.

Whoever takes up and secures said Servant so that his Master may have him again, shall have Twenty Shillings Reward, and reasonable Charges, paid by   SAMUEL THOMPSON.

   May 18, 1743.

302. July 21, 1743

THIS Day was committed to the Goal of New-Castle, one by the Name of Richard Homes an Englishman, he is a lusty tall Man of dark Complexion, no Hair, wears a white Cap, good felt Hat, with a black Scarf, good check Shirt, Sailors Trowsers, and blue Jacket with a list of Canvas on the seams, & a brown broad cloth Coat about half worn. About a Week before he was taken up, burnt his Leg with Gun-powder in the

Woods, as he says. His Master if any he has, is desired to appear in 6 Weeks, otherwise he will be set at Liberty, paying his Charges.

Two days before there was one Joshua Bevan, a Servant to one Abraham Ingram, of Somerset County Maryland, taken up and committed to the Goal aforesaid.   SAMUEL BICKLEY, Sheriff.

303. September 12, 1745

RUN away on the 10th Instant from the Subscriber, in New Hanover, Township, Philadelphia County, a Dutch Servant Man, named Caril Witt, a Smith by Trade, between Thirty and Forty Years of Age, middle sized, well set, and fair Complexioned: Had on a bluish coloured Coat, homespun striped Jacket, a fine white Shirt, and Shoes and Stockings. Whoever secures said Servant, so as his Master may have him again, shall have Forty Shillings Reward, and reasonable Charges, paid by

PETER CONRAD.

N. B. He has taken with him a Boy about Fifteen Years of Age.

304. July 10, 1746

Philadelphia, July 24, 1746.

RUN away, about a Fortnight ago, from the Subscriber, in Dover, Kent County, on Delaware, a Servant Man, named David Price, about 24 Years of Age, born in Somerset County, Maryland; he is well set, but very short, fresh colour'd, has short Fingers, brown Hair, lately cut off, talks little, and very low, and is much given to Drinking. Had on when he went away, a Country Cloth grey Jacket, lined with blue and white striped Linsey Woolsey, old Leather Breeches, Oznabrigs Trowsers and Shirt, with brown Linnen Gussets, old Felt Hat, old Shoes, and a Worsted Cap. 'Tis thought he intends to inlist in some of the Companies designed against Canada by some other Name. Whoever brings him back, or secures him, so that he may be had again, shall have Forty Shillings Reward, and reasonable Charges, paid by THOMAS NIXON.

305. May 7, 1747

Philadelphia, May 7, 1747.

RUN away, on the first instant from Edward Wells, of this city, an English servant man, named John Jones, about 25 years of age, 5 feet 6 inches high, pretty well set, round shoulder'd, large nose, and pretty much pitted with the small-pox; he is a bold talkative fellow, and wears his own black short curled hair. Had on when he went away, a butcher's frock, trowsers and shirt, all new oznabrigs, new shoes, and a coarse felt hat. Whoever takes up said runaway, and secures him, so as his master may have him again, shall have if taken within ten miles of this city, Ten-shillings reward, and if twenty, Twenty-shillings, and reasonable charges, paid by   EDWARD WELLS.

306. June 25, 1747

Philadelphia, June 25, 1747.

RUN away from Moses Macilvaine, of Lancaster county, the 16th instant, an Irish servant girl, named Catherine O'Harra, well-set, fair hair, speaks bad English, and is apt to swear; she has been about ten months in the country, and had on, and took with her, a plad gown, and an old striped blue and white one, a yellow petticoat, worsted stockings, silk handkerchief, high heel'd shoes, a hoop, a little black silk bonnet for a child, and several other things not here mentioned. Whoever takes up said servant, and secures her in any goal, so that she may be had again, shall have *Forty Shillings* reward, and reasonable charges, paid by

Moses Macilvaine.

307. August 2, 1750

Run away from the subscriber, living in Pepaek, Somerset county, East-Jersey, a High Dutch servant man, but speaks tolerable good English, named Malachiah, or Melchor Colpen, or Calvin, about 21 years of age, served a certain time in Pennsylvania, and may pretend to be a free-man; he is a short well-set fellow, with black curl'd hair, of a brownish complexion: Had on when he went away, a brownish linsey coat, a blue waist-coat, with white metal buttons, a beaver hat, leather breeches, a pair of light boots, had 4 shirts, 2 pair of blue yarn stockings, and took a great variety of other wearing apparel, besides a sorrel horse, branded VR in one, a bridle and saddle; the horses fore-legs are gauled, by being tied head to foot. Whoever secures the said servant, so that he may be had again, shall have, besides reasonable charges, the sum of FIVE POUNDS reward, paid by me   JACOB OVE.

308. February 20, 1753

Virginia, Lancaster County, Sept. 22, 1752.

RUN away from the subscriber, at the Glebe of the said county, on the 4th of May, A convict servant woman, named Sarah Knox (alias Howard, alias Wilson) of a middle size, brown complexion, short nose, talks broad, and said she was born in Yorkshire, had been in the army for several years, with the camp in Flanders, and at the battle of Colloden, where she lost her husband. She may pretend to be a dancing mistress; will make a great many courtesies, and is a very deceitful, bold, insinuating woman, and a great liar.

In reading of the Virginia Gazette, No. 87, I find an extract of a letter from Chester, in Pennsylvania, July 13, 1752, mentioning a quack Doctor, by the name of Charles Hamilton, pretending to be brought up under Dr. Green, a noted Mountebank in England, who turns out to be a woman in mens cloaths, and now assumes the name of Charlotte Hamilton, and calls herself about 28 years of age, tho' seems to be about 40: Thus much of the letter; and if she talks broad, I have reason to believe that she is the very servant who belongs to me. Whoever apprehends my said servant, and has her convey'd to me, shall have Two Pistoles, besides what the law allows, paid by   DAVID CURRIE.

N. B. This Sarah Knox was imported from Whitehaven, in the Duke of Cumberland, with other convicts, among whom was one William Forrester, who, I have heard her say, was sometime with the above Dr. Green.

309. July 24, 1755

Philadelphia, July 24, 1755.

RUN away from Alexander Hamilton, of the city of Philadelphia, Merchant, on Wednesday morning, the 2d instant, A Dutch servant boy, called Frantz Strother, about 16 years of age, he is a small boy of his age, but very smart, and can speak English very well: Had on when he went away, An old blue coat, with flat metal buttons, coarse white shirt, red shag breeches, which are considerably too large for him, an old black silk neck-cloth, and an old hat, but had neither stockings nor shoes, unless he has got them since; he wears his own pale colour'd hair. Whoever takes up said servant, and either brings him to me, or secures him so as I may have him again, shall have Forty Shillings reward, and reasonable Charges, paid by   ALEXANDER HAMILTON.

N.B. 'Tis believed his father has taken him away with him, as he was seen going out of the town with him in the morning, and is uncertain whether he went for York, in this province, or New-York.

310. August 28, 1755

Norfolk, in Virginia, August 4, 1755.

RUN away from the subscriber, a servant man, named Lewis Miller, by trade a cooper, 5 feet 8 inches high, of a fair complexion, a complaisant fellow, and has a very good countenance; wears a wig: He also carried with him a servant woman, much pockpitted. Whoever apprehends the said man in Maryland or Pennsylvania government, and secures him, so that his master may have him again, shall have Five Pistoles reward, paid by Mr. Reese Meredith, in Philadelphia, or Mr. George [Millakia], at Bohemia, Maryland, on account of   ANDREW SPROWLE.

311. July 31, 1760

Philadelphia, July 28, 1760.

RUN away last Seventh-day Night, from Joseph Richardson, at the Four Lanes Ends, in Middle-Town, Bucks County, a Dutch Servant Girl, named Catharine Burhhart, about 18 or 19 Years of Age, of a middle Stature, light coloured Hair, full fac'd, and has a fresh Look: Her Cloathing uncertain; took nothing with her but what she had on all the Week; and is supposed to be gone towards Philadelphia to her Mother, of the same Name. Said Servant was bought of Abel James and Partner, in November, 1756. Whoever secures the said Servant, so that her said Master may have her again, or takes her to Jacob Duche, in Philadelphia, shall have Twenty Shillings Reward, and reasonable Charges, paid by   JOSEPH RICHARDSON.

312. November 19, 1761

RUN away, on the 27th of October last, from Peter Imlay, Miller, of Upper Freehold, in the County of Monmouth, New-Jersey, a Servant Boy, named Matthias Walker, Country born, about 15 Years of Age, he is slim built; had on, when he went away, a light brown homespun Jacket, a striped under Jacket, a reddish striped holland Pair of Breeches, a Pair of Tow Trowsers, good Stockings and Shoes, and good

felt Hat; it is supposed he is gone to his Father, a School-Master, one John Walker, but where he now keeps is unknown to me. Whoever takes up the said Boy, and secures him, so as his Master may have him again, shall have Twenty Shillings Reward, and reasonable Charges, paid by
PETER IMLAY.

313. *October 14, 1762*
THREE POUNDS Reward.

RUN away from Thomas Gilpin, at the Head of Chester River, Maryland, on or about the First Instant, a Servant Man, named William Stewart, a short well set Fellow, about 25 Years of Age, sandy Complexion, and smiling Countenance, has lost one of his upper Fore-teeth: Had on, and took with him, a blue grey Fearnought Jacket, Leather Breeches, Trowsers, half worn Felt Hat, blue Stockings, and half worn Shoes. He has formerly been in the Provincial Service, under Captain Wells, and it is supposed his Wife is with him, and are probably gone over Sasquehannah, or into the Jerseys. Whoever takes up and secures said Servant, so that his Master may have him again, shall have the above Reward, and reasonable Charges, paid by THOMAS GILPIN.

314. *November 3, 1763*
Philadelphia, October 20, 1763.
FIVE POUNDS Reward.

RUN away, on the 15th Instant from the Subscriber, living in Solebury, Bucks County, Province of Pennsylvania, a Servant Man, named Thomas Kitchin, about 22 Years of Age, 5 Feet 10 or 11 Inches high, has a dark Complexion, down Look, wears his own black Hair tied behind, and is very apt to frequent Taverns, understands Farming, and can make Riddles, born in the Province and County aforesaid: Had on, when he went away, an old Castor Hat, a white Shirt, a red Waistcoat, with a lightish coloured Kersey Ditto over it, a Pair of new Buckskin Breeches, Yarn Stockings, new Pumps, with carved Metal Buckles, and some other Clothes, not known what they are, so it is likely he may change them. Any Person or Persons apprehending said Servant, and securing him in any of His Majesty's Goals, so that he may be had again, or brings him to his said Master, shall have the above Reward, paid by
JOHN CORYELL.

315. August 16, 1764

RUN away, on the 9th of this instant August, from Benjamin Williams, of Nockamixon Township, Bucks County, Pennsylvania, a Servant Man, named John Matthias; he is about 5 Feet 6 Inches high, has a down Look, with short brown curled Hair; had no Clothes with him but a white Flannel Jacket, a Shirt, with new Ozenbrigs at the Wristbands, Tow Trowsers, and Felt Hat. Whoever takes up said Servant, and secures him, so that his Master may have him again, shall have Forty Shillings Reward, and reasonable Charges, paid by

BENJAMIN WILLIAMS.

N.B. He is a West Country Fellow, and talks after that Dialect. All Masters of Vessels are forbid to harbour him, or take him off, at their Peril.

316. August 15, 1765

August 12, 1765.

RUN away last night from the subscribers, living in New-port, New-Castle county, the following persons, viz. Charles Black, an Irishman, about 5 feet 5 or 6 inches high, well set with a down look, and dark brown hair; had on an old hat, old dirty shirt, wide short trowsers of Russia sheeting, with a patch on one leg, a dark brown jacket, above half worn, new pumps, old buckles, one Pinchbeck, and one brass. The other an Irishman, about 5 feet 3 or 4 inches high, speaks very bad English, a tanner by trade; had on, when he went away, a dark grey cloth coat and jacket, a check shirt, pretty much dyed with tan, long trowsers, white thread stockings, old shoes, brass buckles, half worn wool hat, and short brown hair. Whoever takes up and secures said men in any goal, so that their masters may have them again, shall have Five Pounds reward for both, or Fifty Shillings for each, paid by

ALEXANDER MILLER,
ROBERT SLATER.

317. June 23, 1768

RUN away from the subscriber, living at the sign of the Bull's head, in West Nantmil, Chester county, the 11th of June instant, an indented servant man, named John Slye, or Slide, alias Henry Sharp, this country born, about 37 years of age, of a dark complexion, short hair, cut pretty close before, the fore part grey, about 5 feet 6 inches high, has a remarkable halt in his walk, as one thigh is shorter than the other, is very talkative, and apt to swear and lie; had on, when he went away, a tow shirt and trowsers, an old scarlet lapelled jacket, with red mohair buttons, an old home made snuff coloured cloth coat, with clear metal buttons, the pockets in the haunches, a half-worn wool hat, a pair of old shoes, with strings; has with him a counterfeit pass, signed by 3 justices in Loudoun county, Virginia, wherein he passed for John Graham, he has probably made towards the Jerseys. Whoever secures him in any goal, so that I may get him again, shall have Forty Shillings reward, or Three Pounds, if out of the province, and reasonable charges, paid by me JOHN GRAHAM.

318. July 19, 1770

TEN POUNDS Reward.

RUN away from the subscriber, living in Baltimore county, near Charles Ridgely's iron-works, the 9th of July instant, an English servant man, named Thomas Hewitt, by trade a Bookbinder, a lusty well set fellow, about 5 feet 6 inches high, dark brown curled hair, and is about 27 years of age; had on, and took with him, a felt hat, check shirt, blue plush breeches, old shoes, yarn stockings, a blue pea jacket, a striped flannel ditto, ozenbrigs shirt and trowsers; it is supposed he has forged a pass, and changed his name. Whoever takes up and secures the said servant, so that his master may have him again, shall have, if 10 miles from home, Three Pounds; if out of the county, Five Pounds; if 100 miles, Seven Pounds; and if 200 miles, the above reward, and reasonable charges, if brought home, paid by   ROBERT WILLMOTT.

319. October 25, 1770

RUN away from the subscriber, living near the Head of Elk, in Caecil county, Maryland, on the 14th of October instant, an Irish servant man, named PETER HUGHES, about 24 years of age, 5 feet 6 inches high, has short black hair, and a small scar on his forehead; had on, when he went away, a half-worn blue cloth jacket, fore parts deeper blue than the backs, long tow trowsers, old shoes, without buckles, 2 shirts, one check, the other white, and a coarse felt hat, lately come into the country, speaks tolerable good English, this is the second time of his running away, and he pretends to be a weaver, but knows very little about it. Whoever takes up said servant, and secures him, so that his master may get him again, shall have FOUR DOLLARS reward, and reasonable charges, paid by ANDREW FRAZER.

320. March 5, 1772
FIVE POUNDS Reward, Pennsylvania Currency.

RUN away from the subscriber, on the 2d day of January last, near Winchester, in Virginia, a servant Man, named JOHN ROBINSON, came from Ireland, and landed in Philadelphia, and lived in Chester, York, and Cumberland counties, 18 years of age; he is remarkably short and chunky, of a swarthy complexion, and has short black hair; had on two old cloth-coloured jackets, a cloth-coloured great coat, too large for him, leather breeches, blue leggings and stockings; had on an iron collar; he can do something at the miller's business, is fond of driving a waggon, spins on the little wheel, dances, and plays cards, can read, but cannot write; he is impudent and bold, will deny his name, and change his apparel. He took with him a brown waggon horse, and saddle, the horse paces and trots, and is branded on the near buttock G.B. Whoever secures the servant in any goal, so that his master may have him again, shall have Three Pounds reward, and Forty Shillings for the horse, with reasonable charges, paid by me DAVID DAVIS.

321. July 28, 1773

RUN away from the subscriber, living in Reading town, Berks county, Pennsylvania, on the 4th day of July, 1773, a certain indented Irish servant woman, named ELIZABETH WHITE, about 25 years of age, fair complexion, sandy hair, cut before, about 5 feet high, is very talkative, fond of snuff and spiritous liquors; had on, when she went away, two striped lincey petticoats off one piece, homespun shift, and a silk handkerchief; she may change her apparel, as it is supposed she has money with her; she was seen going towards Philadelphia, and has a brother, in or near the city of New-York, named Lee, to which place it is likely she may go. Whoever takes up said servant, and secures her in any goal, so that her master may have her again, shall receive FIFTEEN SHILLINGS reward, and reasonable charges, paid by
MICHAEL BRIGHT.

322. *October 12, 1774*

EIGHT DOLLARS Reward,
To the person or persons who will SECURE

WILLIAM BAILEY, a run-away servant, in any of his Majesty's goals on the continent of America, on their giving notice to any of the following persons, viz. Mr. John Kennedy, merchant, in Baltimore, Maryland, Messrs. Boyle and Glen, merchants, in Philadelphia, or to his master, John Shaw, merchant, in New-York: The above mentioned run-away is about 5 feet 7 inches high, smooth complexion, mild address, knows something of the weaving business, writes a good hand, and has kept a school for some time past, and it is probable may have a forged pass with him. He was seen in Philadelphia in May last: had on a white coat and westcoat, and old fustian breeches. It is supposed he is gone either towards Baltimore or Lancaster: he has behaved in the most ungrateful manner to the subscriber, who will pay, exclusive of the above reward, all reasonable charges, in conveying him to prison, and bringing the account to JOHN SHAW, in New-York.

323. *October 18, 1775*

TEN DOLLARS Reward.

RUN away from the subscriber, the 20th of June last, an Irish servant man, named JOHN M'CAN, a Cabinet-maker by trade, but most accustomed to Chair-making, about 24 years of age, 5 feet 5 or 6 inches high, well made, short black hair, full faced, black eyes and eye-brows, with a scar on either the right or left brow, and a fresh scar on one of his cheeks, a down looking countenance; he is pretty much given to liquor, and has but little talk but when he is in liquor, and pretends to beat the drum; had on, when he went away, a long deep brown duffil surtout coat, almost new, a scarlet jacket, lined with white and blue worsted check, a pair of white corderoy breeches, about half worn, white thread stockings, a pair of new shoes, and an old hat, generally flapped before. Whoever takes up and secures said servant, so that his master may have him again, shall have the above reward, paid by MATTHEW HAND, Cabinet-maker, in Pine-street, Philadelphia.

324. July 7, 1784

TEN DOLLARS Reward,

RAN AWAY from the subscriber, yesterday, an Irish servant WOMAN, named SARAH WELSH, aged about 36 years, says she was bred in Dublin, came to this city a servant in the ship Two Friends, William Cronitch, commander, was only sent out on business and entrusted with cash which she took with her, she is of a swarthy complexion, dark brown hair, mixed with grey, pitted a little with the small-pox, has a reserved dark look, and a remarkable protuberance or lump on her windpipe, and most visible in her when she laughs, she is fond of spirituous liquors, which spot or redden her face, but is not easily intoxicated; had on and took with her a calicoe short gown stamped with red and white lines running through the same, one pea green quilted petticoat, one flannel ditto, white thread stockings, and black everlasting shoes, pinn'd, check apron, and cross barred red and white silk handkerchief, one kenting ditto bordered, several things belonging to her mistress are missing, supposed to have been conveyed away by her previous to her departure; the number and quality of the articles taken by her unknown at present. If taken up in the bounds of the city, Four Dollars reward, if 10 miles distance, Six Dollars, at 30 miles distance, Eight Dollars, any greater distance, Ten Dollars, if secured in any goal, and all reasonable charges, if brought home, will be paid by

WILLIAM ADAMS.

325. June 21, 1786

EIGHT DOLLARS Reward.

RAN away last night, from the subscriber, living in Richland township, Bucks County, a servant Lad, named ROBERT M'MINN, about 5 feet 8 inches high, between 17 and 18 years of age, black curled hair, grey eyes, slow spoken, stammers a little in his speech; had on and took with him, when he went away, a half worn fur hat, bound round the edge, a light coloured napped cloth coattee, almost thread bare, japanned buttons on it, one pair thickset breeches, a pair of striped half worn trowsers, one ozenbrigs shirt, one Irish linen ditto, stained on one side of the skirt with ink, one pair pale blue worsted stockings, with some holes in them, and a pair of shoes almost new. Whoever will apprehend the said servant, and deliver him to his master, shall be entitled to the above reward and reasonable charges, paid by JOSEPH BURR.

N.B. All masters of vessels are forbid to carry him off.

June 19, 1786.

326. September 17, 1788

Eight Month, 30th, 1788.
TWO DOLLARS Reward.

RAN away from the subscriber, living in Concord township, Chester county, on the night of the 28th instant, a Dutch servant boy, named JOHANNES JACOB FREDERICKSON, about 18 years old, near 5 feet high, speaks broken English, is very talkative, chews tobacco, is fond of begging it, had on, when he went away, a walnut coloured linsey coatee, cloth jacket without sleeves, Russia sheeting shirt and trowsers, the latter somewhat patched, new shoes with strings in them, small round hat bound round the edge, but wore ragged. Whoever takes up and secures said servant, so that his master may get him again, shall have the above reward, and reasonable charges, paid by

DANIEL TRIMBLE.

Notes

1. The *Pennsylvania Gazette* (Philadelphia) began publication on December 24, 1728 and continued, with only minor interruptions, until October 11, 1815. Most of its subscribers lived in the Mid-Atlantic region, although the paper regularly circulated from the Carolinas to New England. We reproduced the advertisements from microfilm copies of the newspaper generously supplied to us by Professor Ronald Schultz.

2. A number of studies of eighteenth-century slavery and fugitives have used advertisements for runaways, including Gerald W. Mullin, *Flight and Rebellion: Slave Resistance in Eighteenth-Century Virginia* (New York: Oxford University Press, 1972); Edgar J. McManus, *Black Bondage in the North* (Syracuse, N.Y.: Syracuse University Press, 1973); Daniel E. Meaders, "South Carolina Fugitives as Viewed through Local Colonial Newspapers with Emphasis on Runaway Notices 1732–1801," *Journal of Negro History*, 60 (April 1975): 288–319; Lorenzo J. Greene, "The New England Negro as Seen in Advertisements for Runaway Slaves," *Journal of Negro History*, 29 (April 1944): 125–146; Philip D. Morgan, "Colonial South Carolina Runaways: Their Significance for Slave Culture," *Slavery and Abolition*, Vol. 6, No. 3 (December, 1985), 57–78; and Lathan Algerna Windley, "A Profile of Runaway Slaves in Virginia and South Carolina from 1730 through 1787" (Ph.D. diss., University of Iowa, 1974). Windley also compiled advertisements from southern newspapers in *Runaway Slave Advertisements: A Documentary History from the 1730s to 1790* (Westport, Conn: Greenwood Press, 1983), 4 vols.

3. This idea is taken from Ira Berlin, "Time, Space, and the Evolution of Afro-American Society on British Mainland North America," *American Historical Review*, 85 (1980): 44–78.

4. Among the studies of slavery in eighteenth-century America are McManus, *Bondage in the North*; Allan Kulikoff, *Tobacco and Slaves: The Development of Southern Cultures in the Chesapeake, 1680–1800* (Chapel Hill, N.C.: University of North Carolina Press, 1986); Kulikoff, "The Origins of Afro-American

Society in Tidewater Maryland and Virginia, 1700 to 1790," *William and Mary Quarterly*, 3d ser., 25 (1978): 225–259; Kulikoff, "The Beginnings of the Afro-American Family in Maryland," in *Law, Society, and Politics in Early Maryland*, ed. Aubrey C. Land et al. (Baltimore: Johns Hopkins University Press, 1977), 177–196; Jean Butenhoff Lee, "The Problem of Slave Community in the Eighteenth-Century Chesapeake," *William and Mary Quarterly*, 3d ser., 43 (1986): 333–361; Philip D. Morgan, "Work and Culture: The Task System and the World of Lowcountry Blacks, 1700 to 1880," *William and Mary Quarterly*, 3d ser., 39 (1982): 563–599; Morgan, "Black Life in Eighteenth-Century Charleston," *Perspectives in American History*, n. s., 1 (1984): 187–232; Peter Wood, *Black Majority: Negroes in Colonial South Carolina from 1670 through the Stono Rebellion* (New York: Norton, 1974); and Richard S. Dunn, *Sugar and Slaves: The Rise of the Planter Class in the English West Indies, 1624–1713* (Chapel Hill, N.C.: University of North Carolina Press, 1972).

5. Studies of slavery and black life in the Middle Colonies include McManus, *Bondage in the North;* Jean R. Soderlund, *Quakers and Slavery: A Divided Spirit* (Princeton, N.J.: Princeton University Press, 1985); Soderlund, "Black Importation and Migration into Southeastern Pennsylvania, 1682–1810," *Proceedings of the American Philosophical Society*, forthcoming; Gary B. Nash, *Forging Freedom: The Formation of Philadelphia's Black Community, 1720–1840* (Cambridge, Mass.: Harvard University Press, 1988); Nash, "Slaves and Slaveowners in Colonial Philadelphia," *William and Mary Quarterly*, 3d ser., 30 (April 1973): 223–256; Darold D. Wax, "Quaker Merchants and the Slave Trade in Colonial Pennsylvania," *Pennsylvania Magazine of History and Biography*, 86 (1962): 143–159; Wax, "Negro Imports into Pennsylvania, 1720–1766," *Pennsylvania History*, 32 (1965): 254–287; Wax, "Africans on the Delaware: The Pennsylvania Slave Trade, 1759–1765," *Pennsylvania History*, 50 (1983): 38–49; Wax, "The Demand for Slave Labor in Colonial Pennsylvania," *Pennsylvania History*, 34 (1967): 331–345; Edward Raymond Turner, *The Negro in Pennsylvania: Slavery—Servitude—Freedom 1639–1861* (Washington, D.C.: American Historical Association, 1911); Alan Tully, "Patterns of Slaveholding in Colonial Pennsylvania: Chester and Lancaster Counties, 1729–1758," *Journal of Social History*, 6 (1973): 284–303; Jerome H. Woods, Jr., "The Negro in Early Pennsylvania: The Lancaster Experience, 1730–1790," in *Plantation, Town, and County: Essays on the Local History of American Slave Society*, ed. Elinor Miller and Eugene D. Genovese (Urbana, Ill.: University of Illinois Press, 1974); James G. Lydon, "New York and the Slave Trade, 1700 to 1774," *William and Mary Quarterly*, 3d ser., 35 (1978): 375–394; Joyce D. Goodfriend, "Burghers and Blacks: The Evolution of a Slave Society at New Amsterdam," *New York History*, 59 (1978): 125–144; and Vivienne L. Kruger, "Born to Run: The Slave Family in Early New York, 1626 to 1827" (Ph.D. diss., Columbia University, 1985).

6. Abel appears in advertisements # 182 and # 183. For a discussion of free blacks who were kidnapped or jailed as fugitives and then sold into servitude, see Billy G. Smith and Richard Wojtowicz, "The Precarious Freedom of Blacks:

Excerpts from the *Pennsylvania Gazette, 1728–1776," Pennsylvania Magazine of History and Biography,* forthcoming.

7. Windley's analysis of newspaper advertisements demonstrates that owners in South Carolina generally provided a much less detailed description of their runaways; "Profile of Runaway Slaves."

8. As Peter Wood notes, advertised runaways probably represent "little more than the top of an ill-defined iceberg"; *Black Majority,* 240. See also Betty Wood, *Slavery in Colonial Georgia 1730–1775* (Athens, Ga.: University of Georgia Press, 1984), 170–172.

9. The names and dates of publication of Philadelphia's newspapers are contained in Edward Connery Lathem, comp., *Chronological Tables of American Newspapers 1690–1820* (Barre, Mass.: American Antiquarian, 1972). We found that the great majority of advertisements for runaway blacks in the *Pennsylvania Chronicle* during the 1760s also appeared in the *Pennsylvania Gazette.*

10. Comparing the sample of runaways included in this volume with all of the advertised runaways revealed the following: males comprised 88 percent of the former and 91 percent of the latter; 78 percent of the sample and 77 percent of all fugitives were between twenty and forty years of age; the median height of both groups was 5 feet 8 inches; 20 percent of the sample and 16 percent of all escapees were identified as "Mulatto"; 55 percent of both groups were American-born; 43 percent of the sample and 39 percent of all runaways spoke English fluently, while 17 percent of both groups spoke more than one non-African language; 46 percent of the sample and 47 percent of all fugitives worked as craftsmen; 86 percent of the sample and 92 percent of all runaways escaped from Pennsylvania, New Jersey, Delaware, or Maryland. The variations between the sample and the total number of escapees in all other variables measured were equally small.

11. In 1790 slaves numbered 3,787 in Pennsylvania, 8,887 in Delaware, and 3,748 in Hunterdon, Monmouth, Burlington, Gloucester, Salem, Cumberland, and Cape May counties in New Jersey; see *Return of the Whole Number of Persons within the Several Districts of the United States* (Philadelphia: Childs and Swaine, 1801), 3, 42–44. The northern New Jersey counties contained a greater absolute number and a higher proportion of slaves than the southern counties, but owners in the northern region advertised few runaways in the *Pennsylvania Gazette,* in part because they were much more closely linked to New York City. The figure for slaves in Pennsylvania in 1760 is from the U.S. Bureau of the Census, *Historical Statistics of the United States, Colonial Times to 1970* (Washington, D.C.: Government Publications Office, 1975), Part 2, 1168.

12. The estimates are that blacks comprised roughly 2.4 percent of Pennsylvania's population, 5.4 percent of Delaware's, and 7.5 percent of New Jersey's during the half century preceding the Revolution; U.S. Bureau of the Census, *Historical Statistics,* Part 2, 1168, 1170; and Arthur Zilversmit, *The First Emancipation: The Abolition of Slavery in the North* (Chicago: University of Chicago Press, 1967), 4–6.

13. See the tally of slaves for Maidenhead, Lower-Freehold, and Middle-

town, New Jersey in *Return of the Whole Number of Persons*, 42–43. The best statistics for Philadelphia are calculated by Jean R. Soderlund, "Black Importation and Migration into Southeastern Pennsylvania, 1682–1801," *Proceedings* of the American Philosophical Society, Tables 2 and 3, forthcoming.

14. Berlin, "Evolution of Afro-American Society," 46–47; McManus, *Black Bondage in the North*, 36–54; Soderlund, *Quakers and Slavery*, 72–73; Woods, "Negro in Early Pennsylvania," 447– 448; and Frances D. Pingeon, "Slavery in New Jersey on the Eve of the Revolution," in *New Jersey in the American Revolution*, ed. William C. Wright, rev. ed. (Trenton, N.J.: New Jersey Historical Commission, 1974), 51–52, 57.

15. Nash, "Slaves and Slaveowners," 248–252; Soderlund, *Quakers and Slavery*, 61–65; and Berlin, "Evolution of Afro-American Society," 48–49. Advertisements from the *Pennsylvania Gazette* offering slaves for sale, some of which indicated their occupations, further support this analysis of the jobs performed by bondspeople.

16. Berlin, "Evolution of Afro-American Society," 47–48; Nash, "Slaves and Slaveowners," 247–248; Allan Tully, "Patterns of Slaveholding in Colonial Pennsylvania," 286; McManus, *Black Bondage in the North*, 41–42; Woods, "Negro in Early Pennsylvania," 447–448.

17. Berlin, "Evolution of Afro-American Society," 47–54; Eric Foner, *Tom Paine and Revolutionary America* (London: Oxford University Press, 1976), 48–56; Wax, "Negro Imports into Pennsylvania," 254–287; Wax, "Preferences for Slaves in Colonial America," *Journal of Negro History*, 58 (1973): 374–376, 379– 398; Soderlund, *Quakers and Slavery*, 78–85; Soderlund, "Black Importation and Migration into Southeastern Pennsylvania," forthcoming.

18. Soderlund, "Black Importation and Migration into Southeastern Pennsylvania," Table 3, forthcoming; Gary B. Nash, "Forging Freedom: The Emancipation Experience in the Northern Seaport Cities 1775–1820," in *Slavery and Freedom in the Age of the American Revolution*, ed. Ira Berlin and Ronald Hoffman (Charlottesville, Va.: University Press of Virginia, 1983), 3– 48; and Nash, *Forging Freedom*, 134-171.

19. The following arguments and evidence about the family lives of Philadelphia's slaves are developed more fully in Billy G. Smith, "The Family Lives of Black Philadelphians, 1750–1800," in *Shaping a National Culture: The Philadelphia Experience 1750– 1800*, ed. Catherine Hutchins (New York: Norton, forthcoming). See also Soderlund, *Quakers and Slavery*, 78–85; and Merle G. Brouwer, "Marriage and Family Life among Blacks in Colonial Pennsylvania," *Pennsylvania Magazine of History and Biography*, 99 (1975): 368–372.

20. A few of the advertisements in the *Pennsylvania Gazette* for young children appear in the issues of January 16, February 13, March 19, and December 6, 1750, and November 29 and June 28, 1775. Notices for women appear in the editions of August 4 and October 24, 1765, and February 26 and May 21, 1767. See also Soderlund, *Quakers and Slavery*, 79–80.

21. Soderlund, *Quakers and Slavery*, 78–85; Soderlund, "Black Importation and Migration into Southeastern Pennsylvania," forthcoming; Berlin, "Evolu-

tion of Afro-American Society," 50– 51. Comparative studies of conditions in the Upper and Lower South include Russell R. Menard, "The Maryland Slave Population, 1658 to 1730: A Demographic Profile of Blacks in Four Counties," *William and Mary Quarterly*, 3d ser., 32 (1975): 29–54; Allan Kulikoff, "Beginnings of the Afro-American Family in Maryland"; Lee, "The Problem of Slave Community"; Mullin, *Flight and Rebellion*, 16; Wood, *Black Majority*, 144, 161–164.

22. McManus, *Bondage in the North*, 73–88; Zilversmit, *First Emancipation*, 12–24; Turner, *Negro in Pennsylvania*, 109– 113; and Winthrop D. Jordan, *White over Black: American Attitudes Toward the Negro, 1550–1812* (Baltimore: Penguin, 1968), 103– 110.

23. The quote is from James T. Mitchell and Henry Flanders, comps., *The Statutes at Large of Pennsylvania from 1682–1801*, 18 vols. (Harrisburg: State Printer, 1896–1911), IV, 63. See also Samuel Nevill, comp., *The Acts of the General Assembly of the Province of New Jersey*, 2 vols. (Philadelphia and Woodbridge, N.J.: published by order of the General Assembly and printed by William Bradford, 1752–61), I, 18–19; McManus, *Bondage in the North*, 108–124; Turner, *Negro in Pennsylvania*, 109–113. The decidedly more stringent laws concerning runaways in Virginia and South Carolina are reviewed by Windley, "Profile of Runaway Slaves," 15–62.

24. On some of the dangers posed to the liberty of free blacks, see Billy G. Smith and Richard Wojtowicz, "The Precarious Freedom of Blacks: Excerpts from the *Pennsylvania Gazette*, 1728– 1776," *Pennsylvania Magazine of History and Biography*, forthcoming.

25. The antislavery movement is discussed more fully in Zilversmit, *First Emancipation;* Soderlund, *Quakers and Slavery;* Gary B. Nash and Jean R. Soderlund, *Freedom by Degrees: Emancipation in Eighteenth-Century Pennsylvania* (London: Oxford University Press, forthcoming). See also the recent debate by David Brion Davis, "Reflections on Abolitionism and Ideological Hegemony," *American Historical Review*, 92 (1987): 797–812; and Thomas L. Haskell, "Convention and Hegemonic Interest in the Debate over Antislavery: A Reply to Davis and Ashworth," *American Historical Review*, 92 (1987): 829–878.

26. Mitchell and Flanders, comps., *Statutes at Large of Pennsylvania*, x, 67–73, quote on 67.

27. *Ibid.*, x, 71.

28. *Pennsylvania Packet* (Philadelphia), October 22, 1789.

29. Jordan, *White over Black*, 345–349; Zilversmit, *First Emancipation*, 155.

30. Only 11 percent of 959 runaways advertised in the *Pennsylvania Gazette* between 1728 and 1790 tried to escape during December, January, or February.

31. John Ferdinand Dalziel Smyth, *A Tour in the United States of America*, 2 vols. (New York: *New York Times* and Arno Press, 1968), II, quotes on 306–307 and 403–404. See also the description by *Luigi Castiglioni's Viaggio: Travels in the United States of North America, 1785–87*, trans. and ed. Antonio Pace, Joseph Ewan, and Nesta Ewan (Syracuse, N.Y.: Syracuse University Press, 1973), 265.

32. William Moraley, *The Infortunate: or, the Voyage and Adventures of William Moraley. . . .* (Newcastle, England: J. White, 1743), 31.

33. Moraley, *The Infortunate*, quotes on 20 and 27. See also, Pace et al., trans. and eds., *Travels in the United States*, 246.

34. Moraley, *The Infortunate*, 25.

35. Smythe, *Tour in the United States*, 303; Pace et al., trans. and eds., *Travels in the United States*, 212.

36. Moraley, *The Infortunate*, 27.

37. The data presented in this and the succeeding paragraph are drawn from our statistical analysis of the 1,324 runaways advertised in the *Pennsylvania Gazette* between 1728 and 1790 and, for Virginia and South Carolina, from Windley, "Profile of Runaway Slaves," 63–146. Runaways in the South are also discussed in Wood, *Black Majority*, 239–268; Wood, *Slavery in Colonial Georgia*, 169–187; Meaders, "South Carolina Fugitives"; and Daniel C. Littlefield, *Rice and Slaves: Ethnicity and the Slave Trade in Colonial South Carolina* (Baton Rouge, La.: Louisiana State University Press, 1981), 115–173.

Glossary

Binding: A protective covering for the raw edges of a fabric.

Bodycoat: A dress coat that was worn relatively close to the body.

Brazier: An individual who manufactures and repairs objects in brass.

Brig: A vessel with two masts square-rigged like a ship's fore- and mainmasts, but also carrying a lower fore-and-aft sail with a gaff and boom.

Brigantine: A small craft rigged for sailing and rowing, speedier and more maneuverable than larger vessels.

Broadcloth: A fine, plain-woven black cloth used primarily in men's clothing.

Calicoe, calico: A coarse cotton cloth used in a variety of eighteenth-century clothing.

Camblet, camlet: Originally an attractive, expensive fabric from the Far East, the name later referred to imitations fashioned from different materials. The raw materials for this cloth ranged from camel hair, silk, and velvet to blends of wool and silk.

Castor: The binomial nomenclature for the North American beaver is *Castor canadensis.* Castor referred to a hat made of the fur of this animal or imitating the genuine article. As rabbit fur and other substitutes were employed in hat manufacture, the term *castor* came to be used to distinguish such models from true beaver hats.

Chemise: An undergarment usually made of linen or similar fabric and worn by women.

Clocks: Expensive stockings were embroidered in this manner on the stocking side with silk thread.

The definitions of many of these terms are drawn from Peter F. Copeland, *Working Dress in Colonial and Revolutionary America* (Westport, Conn.: Greenwood Press, 1977); Edwin Tunis, *Colonial Craftsmen and the Beginnings of American Industry* (Cleveland: World Publishing Company, 1965); and the *Oxford English Dictionary* (Oxford: Clarendon Press, 1933).

Cloth coloured: Of a drab color.

Coating: Any material used to make coats.

Cooper: The manufacturer of barrels, tubs, pails, piggins, and other containers.

Crape: A thin, transparent, gauzelike fabric, plain woven, without any twill, of highly twisted raw silk or other staple, and mechanically embossed, so as to have a crisped or minutely wrinkled surface.

Cravat: Apparel worn around the neck, primarily by males.

Cue, queue: An eighteenth-century hair style in which hair hung down behind the head; the hair might be either one's own or a wig.

Dowlas: A coarse sort of hefty linen employed in the fabrication of shirts and smocks.

Drugget: Used primarily in work clothes, this woolen stuff might also consist of wool and silk or wool and linen mixtures.

Duffel, duffels: A coarse woolen cloth having a thick nap or frieze; used to produce jackets and coats.

Duroy: A variety of coarse woolen cloth formerly produced in the west of England—but not synonymous with corduroy.

Everlasting: A sturdy woolen material used in clothing, including ladies' shoes.

Fearnothing: [Obs., rare] *See* fearnought.

Fearnought, dreadnought: A heavy woolen material often used during harsh weather aboard vessels at sea as protective outer wear.

Frize, frieze: A type of coarse woolen cloth with a nap on only one side.

Fustian: An inexpensive, coarse material comprised of cotton and flax.

Gelding: A castrated animal, particularly a horse.

Gilt: Usually specified a metal which covered an object and gave the appearance of gold.

Gingham: A kind of cotton or linen cloth, woven of dyed yarn, often in stripes, checks, and other patterns.

Goal, gaol: Variant spellings of jail.

Great-coat, greatcoat: A topcoat or large, heavy overcoat worn as added protection from the cold.

Grogram: A fabric made of coarse silk, wool, and mohair.

Halfthick: A sort of coarse cloth.

Heckling: The splitting and separating of flax and hemp fibers.

Hempen: Referring to material or cloth made of hemp.

Hodden: The coarse woolen cloth produced by country weavers on hand looms.

Holland: A linen fabric named after the Netherlands' province of Holland from which it originated.

Homespun: Any cloth made of homespun yarn, also including coarse material of loose weave meant to imitate homemade cloth.

Hostler: An individual attending to horses at an inn; a stableman, a groom.

Hundred: A division of a county in the British-American colonies or provinces of Virginia, Maryland, Delaware, and Pennsylvania, still existing in the state of Delaware, e.g. Red Lion Hundred.

Instant: The current calendar month. For example, a notice dated June 24, 1775, that stated that a person ran away on "the 21st of this instant" (often abbreviated "inst.") meant that the individual absconded on the twenty-first of June 1775.

Kersey: A coarse woolen cloth, often ribbed, which originated in Yorkshire, England.

Last: Shoemakers used these wooden or metal forms shaped like a human foot to produce and restore shoes for their clients.

Leggins, leggings: A pair of extra outer coverings (usually of leather or cloth), used as a protection for the legs in inclement weather, and commonly reaching from the ankle to the knee, but sometimes higher.

Lincey: An obsolete variant of linsey or linsey-woolsey.

Linsey-woolsey: A wool-flax blend of textile.

Low Dutch: Referred to the Germans along the sea coast and the northern and northwestern flatlands, including the Netherlands and Flanders.

Match-cloth: A coarsely woven wool often traded by Europeans to native Americans.

Matchcoat: A type of robe prominent among native Americans, initially consisting of fur skins and later of match-cloth.

Molatto, mulatto [various spellings]: The offspring of a Negro and a European. Eighteenth-century Americans freely called any person of mixed blood a mulatto if he or she resembled one.

Nankeen: A sort of cotton material, initially manufactured in Nanking from a yellow variety of cotton.

Nap: Initially describing the projecting fibers found on fabric surfaces, the term subsequently described the purposeful raising of the short fibers on the surface of a textile followed by trimming and smoothing.

Napt: Any surface that has a nap.

Nicanees, niccanee: A kind of piece goods formerly imported from India.

N. B.: The abbreviation for *nota bene,* which means to mark well and pay particular attention to that which follows.

Ozenbrigs, oznabrigs, oznaburg: An inexpensive linen that received its name from Osnabrück or Oznaburg, Germany.

Pea jacket: A stout, short overcoat of coarse woolen cloth, now commonly worn by sailors.

Periwig: An artificial head of hair or part of one; worn formerly by women and then by men as a fashionable headdress.

Pistoles: Spanish gold coins often used in the specie-poor American colonies. One pistole was equal to slightly more than one Pennsylvania pound during the middle decades of the eighteenth century.

Plaited hair: Hair that has been braided.

Plush: A cloth comprised of silk, cotton, wool, or other materials, alone or in some combination, with a nap longer and softer than velvet.

Pock-fretten: "Fret" refers to a wearing away or a decayed spot. Thus, "pock-fretten" described the presence of scars resulting from a bout with smallpox.

Pumps: Thin-soled, light shoes.

Ratteen: A thick, twilled woolen cloth, generally friezed or with a curled nap.

Russet: A reddish-brown color.

Saggathy, sagathy: A woolen stuff.

Sawyer: A worker who cut logs into structural timbers and boards or firewood.

Schooner: A small, sea-going fore-and-aft rigged vessel, originally with only two masts.

Scutching: The beating of flax stalks necessary to separate the straw in preparation for hackling. Hemp, cotton, and silk were treated in a similar fashion.

Scythe: An agricultural implement for mowing grass or other crops, having a long, thin, curving blade fastened at an angle with the handle and wielded with both hands in a long sweeping stroke.

Serge: A durable twilled woolen cloth, sometimes blended with silk.

Shallop, shalloop: 1. A large, heavy boat, fitted with one or more masts and carrying fore-and-aft or lug sails and sometimes furnished with guns; a sloop. 2. A boat propelled by oars or by a sail, for use in shallow waters or as a means of effecting communication between, or landings from, vessels of a large size; a dinghy.

Sheeting: A heavy fabric comprised of cotton or linen, such as is used for bed linen.

Shift: Underclothing made of cotton, linen, or other fabric.

Sloop: 1a. A small, one-masted, fore-and-aft rigged vessel, differing from a cutter in having a jib-stay and standing bowsprit. 1b. A relatively small ship-of-war, carrying guns on the upper deck only. 2. [*obs.*] A large open boat; a long boat.

Snuff colour: The color of snuff, that is, a brownish color.

Sorrel: Of a bright chestnut color; reddish-brown.

Stuff: Woven material, especially wool, used to manufacture clothing.

Surtout: A man's greatcoat or large overcoat.

Swanskin: A fine, thick, fleecelike fabric; a kind of flannel.

Thickset: A material possessing a close-grained nap.

Ticklenburg, ticklenburgs: For Tecklenburg, from a town and county of this name in Westphalia, noted for its manufacture of linen; a kind of coarse linen cloth.

Tow: The short fibers of flax or hemp which are separated from the longer ones through heckling.

Ultimo: The last or previous month. Thus, an ad dated June 4, 1748, that described someone as running away "on the 3rd ultimo" (often abbreviated as "ult.") meant that the person escaped on the third of May 1748.

Waistcoat: An underjacket or a vest.

Waiting-man: One who waited or attended on an employer or official; a personal servant.

Watch-coat: A stout coat or cloak worn in inclement weather.

Wen: A lump or protuberance of the body; a knot, bunch, wart.

Wherry: 1. A light rowing boat used chiefly on rivers to carry passengers and goods. 2. A large boat of the barge kind.

Wilton: A type of cloth named after a town in southern England.

Wollen: A variant spelling of woolen.

Worsted: A woolen fabric first produced in Worstead, England; it was manufactured from well-twisted yarn spun from long-staple wool with combed parallel fibers.

Subject Index

Name Index

Note: The number following each name refers to the case number preceding each advertisement.

Abel, 102, 182, 183, 262
Aberdeen, 294
Abraham, 4, 109, 110, 117, 139
Adam, 12
Adams, Daniel I., 271
Adams, James, 274
Adams, William, 324
Alexander, Robert, 204, 213
Allen, James, 299
Allen, William, 273
Allison, 273
Allison, Captain William, 196
Amos, James, 295, 298
Amos, Joshua, 295, 298
Anderson, James, 248, 284
Andrew, William, 260
Anne, 61
Anthony, 199, 283
Antrim, Isaac, 159
Applegate, Ebenezer, 125, 126
Armstrong, Col. William, Esq., 50
Atcheson, Captain, 215
Aten, Derrick, 45
Attmore, Isaac, 198

Bachman, Jacob, 156
Bail, Robert, 220
Bailey, Mr., 36

Bailey, William, 322
Baily, John, 2
Balding, Caleb, 213
Balvaird, Jannet, 24
Bard, Mr., 137
Barnard, Thomas, 98
Barr, Robert, 298
Bartholomew, Thomas, 49
Bartholomew, Thomas, Jr., 83
Batuer, Henry, 56
Bauchman, Jacob, 101
Baylor, Robert, 291
Bean, William, 187, 193
Beatho, George, 194
Beaver, 141
Beck, 24
Bedford, Ganning, 271
Beech, Thomas, 153
Begill, 131
Bell, Pompey, 273
Ben, 52, 82, 165, 168, 219, 256
B[enat], Doctor, 273
Betsy, 273
Betty, 9, 87
Bevan, Joshua, 302
Bevis, 141
Bickley, Samuel, 302
Bill, 70, 257, 294

Index of All Advertisements for Runaway Blacks

Each advertisement for a runaway black which appeared in the *Pennsylvania Gazette* between 1728 and 1790 is indicated in this index, although only 300 of these notices are reprinted in this volume. If the newspaper carried an advertisement for a specific runaway attempt for more than one edition, only the first appearance of the notice is recorded (unless a subsequent advertisement carried considerably more information about the fugitive). The index is structured by the date of the edition followed by the name or names of the escapee. The names after the slash identify the master and any other whites (except escaped indentured servants) contained in the advertisement. The lack of a slash separating names indicates that the fugitive was not identified by name.

March 18: Jeffery/Peter Prall
April 15: Cato, Toby/Richard
  Stillwell
June 10: Jack, Tom/Darby
  Shawhorne, John Wallis
June 24: Jacob, Pompey/John
  Anderson, John Bullen, Benedict
  Calvert
July 1: Bess/Peter Ganthony,
  Humphrey Jones, John Springer
August 5: Ming/James Black, John
  Calley, John Thomson
August 12: Harry/Thomas
  Bartholomew, John Clark, George
  Johnson, John Lindsay, Cookson
September 9: James/Joseph Bell,
  Joseph Chambers
September 9: John Clark, John
  Rodman
September 9: James Hoburn/Col.
  William Armstrong, Esq., Godfrey
  Brown, David Bush, Esq.,
  Richard M'William, Esq., Mary
  Reel, Henry Rennalds, John
  Thompson
September 16: Sam/Joshua Emlen,
  Thomas James
September 16: Hagar/William
  Bransen, John Jones
October 21: Ned/Valentine Dushane
October 21: Judith/John Thompson
November 11: Ben, James,
  Jem/Captain Samuel Blunt, Rhody
  Neil, Spencer Smith, John
  Thompson
November 18: Tom/Samuel Miller
December 2: John Pennington,
  James Wells

1757

March 17: Timothy Jeffries/Thomas
  James, Gideon Pierce
March 31: Timothy Jeffreys/George
  Wells, Thomas Wells
April 7: Charles Leeper,
  Monday/Robert Boyle
April 14: Jerry/John Thompson

June 9: Dick/Samuel Jones, Samuel
  Smith
June 16: Christmas/Thomas Riche
August 11: Cato/Richard Stillwell
September 1: Peter, Tom/Mr.
  Andrews, Mr. Pollien, John
  Thompson
September 8: Charles/Brian
  Wilkinson
September 8: Cy/David M'Cullough
September 8: Will/John Duyer
October 13: Tom/Henry Batuer,
  James Bleake, Anne Milton
November 3: Pomp/George Ely,
  Moses Standley
November 17: Peter/Andrew Doz
November 17: Scipio/Marcus Kuhl,
  Joseph Nicholson
November 24: Chloe/James Craig,
  Capt. Hubbard
December 1: Dick/James Whitehead
December 15: Abraham Vandegrift
December 15: John Jufee/John
  Reid, Jr.
December 15: Dick/Edward
  Shippen, John Thompson
December 29: Hercules Coutts

1758

January 5: Jack/Joseph Burr
March 30: Sam/Stephen Green
April 6: Joe Leek/Robert
  Cummings, George Rock, Story,
  Wharton
April 20: Will/James Hunt
June 22: Harry, Peter/William
  Hopkins, Abraham Kinsey
June 22: Hercules/James Hockley,
  John Potts
July 27: Thomas Ashby, John Burk,
  Capt. Massey, John Thompson
September 14: Frederick/John
  Cheshey, James Seager
October 5: Plymouth, Sue/Charles
  Edgar, Henry Forst, Joseph Hart,
  Joseph Leech, Joseph Thornton,
  Stephen Williams

October 26: Anne, Frank/Alexander
    Collay, Robert Wakely
November 23: Jacob Glover,
    Jacob/John Hall
December 21: Harry Pratt/Philip
    Price

1759

March 29: Festus/Sarah Brown,
    Isaac Snowden
June 14: Cyrus/John Lloyd, Richard
    Smith
June 14: Dick/Allan MacRae
June 21: Bood, Bristol, Jack,
    Tom/Joseph Golder, John Hart,
    William Hunt
June 28: Cuff/James Anderson
July 5: Jemmy/Richard Britton
July 12: Jane/Henry Brooks, John
    Hughes, Catherine M'Claughlin
August 2: Hercules/William Bird,
    John Potts, Esq.
August 2: Thomas Williams/John
    Bordley
August 2: Peter/Paul Pierce
August 23: Foode/Samuel Coles
September 6: Davy/G. W. Fairfax
September 20: Caesar/Sarah Massey
December 13: Abraham/Caleb Luff
December 20: Peter Stelle

1760

January 10: Sharper/Robert
    M'Lonen
February 7: Jim/William Morris
March 13: George/William Patterson
March 13: Jack/Joseph Burr
March 20: Dick/Richard James
May 8: Joe/John Sayre, Sr.
May 29: Hercules/William Bird,
    Esq., Jacob Kern
June 26: Abraham/John Cox
July 17: Dick, Richard
    Jenkins/Wood Jones
July 24: Bill/Dennis Hicks, Moses
    Foot
July 31: Nancy/Michael Graham

August 14: Nathaniel Norris/John
    Blackistone
August 21: Friday/Benjamin Jackson
August 28: Cate, Sue, Tony/Thomas
    Parke, Thomas Caten
August 28: Edward Kello,
    Ned/William Eaton, Richard
    Hanson, Robert Jones, Jr., Col.
    Theodorick Bland
September 4: Joe Lane/John
    M'Michael, Reverend Joseph Tate
September 18: John Harper, Hugh
    Vance
September 25: John Weiser
October 2: John Miller/Henry
    Hainey
October 9: Sharper/Robert M'Lonan
October 9: Toppen, Will/Captain
    Charles Ratcliffe, Joseph
    Shankland
October 23: James Start,
    Jacob/Gilbert Smith
November 13: Cuff/John Leacock
November 13: Sam/William
    Weathers, Edward Pryce Wilmer,
    William Wittet
November 20: Jack, John
    Johnson/Joseph Burr
November 27: Jacob/James Mather,
    James Sharp
December 18: Parkgate/Thomas
    Gilbert

1761

March 5: Jack/Samuel Rains
March 26: Black Joe/John Bell,
    Nathan Hayes
May 29: Ephraim Phillips
May 21: Charles/David Elder, Ann
    Holly
May 28: Shadwell/Thomas Cockey
July 2: James Starett
July 9: Peter/Gen. Gage, James
    Henry, John Manby, Esq.,
    Abraham Mitchell
July 16: Sampson/George Smith
August 6: Grigg/John Wilcocks
August 27: Isaac Webster

August 27: Sam/Nathaniel Giles
September 10: Peter/John Wood
September 17: Felix Donnaly,
George Weidner
October 1: William Wilson/Swen
Colsberry
October 22: Peter/Hugh Thompson
October 22: Cyrus/John Lloyd,
Richard Smith
October 29: Robert/Andrew Hunter
November 12: William Wilson/Swen
Colesbury
November 19: Robert Broady
November 26: Joe/Derrick Wilkeron

1762

January 7: John Lucken
January 28: Francis Miller/Thomas
Perke
February 18: John, Louis/Jonas
Seely
February 18: Rodman's James,
York/John Comes, Justice Hall,
Lewis Jones, Justice Rodgers
March 25: York/Swen Colesberry,
John Comes
April 1: Pompey/John Blacksher
April 22: Moses, George Keen
April 29: Charles, Charles Roberts,
German/John Holt
May 13: Thomas M'Kee
May 27: James Anderson, Jr.,
Alexander Harvey
June 24: John/George Craghead
July 1: James Stuart/Henry Hayes
July 8: Shadwell/Thomas Cockey
July 8: Harry/Jeremiah Smith,
Commander Thomas Smith
July 8: Harry/Moore Furman,
Robert Lettis Hooper, Jr.
July 15: Sam/Samuel Raine, James
Say
July 22: Ben, Jack/Emanuel Josiah,
George Lusher, William Poppell,
Esq., Capt. Richard Todd
August 26: Paris/Thomas Maybury,
William Maybury

August 26: Joseph Boudron,
Joe/Thomas Bartholomew
August 26: John/Hugh Bowes,
Denny
August 26: Joe/Teter Welker, James
Whitehead
August 26: Mike/Peter Carroll
September 2: Joe/William Callender
September 2: George/Archibald
Gardner, William Patterson
September 2: Betty/Jo[hn] Newton
September 2: Friday/Jackson
September 9: Jack, John
Johnson/Joseph Biddle, James
Smith
September 16: John Mullan
September 16: George/William
Patterson
September 23: Cuffy/Col. Byrd,
David Franks, Michael Moses
October 7: Spencer Lake/John
Jennings
October 14: Venus/John Allen,
Samuel Stout, Jr.
October 14: Bob/William Campbell,
Alexander Harvey
November 4: Isaac Webster
December 23: Peter/William Craig
December 23: Caesar/John Hall
December 23: Caesar/John Hall,
Esq., Alexander Harvey
December 30: Moses/Standish Ford,
George Keen, Samuel Parr
December 30: Peter/Josiah Godfrey,
Alexander Lunan

1763

January 20: Tom/Alexander Harvey,
Thomas Riche
January 20: Martin Cronmiller,
Henry Wolfe
February 7: Stephen Carpenter
April 7: Tom/Archibald Cary, Isaac
Webster
April 28: Spencer Lake/Jacob
Bachman, Col. Palmer, John
Pennel
April 28: Jack Cornish/John Turner

July 10: Cato/Joseph Johnston, Sr.
July 17: Ephraim Logue, Joseph Thomas
July 17: Jemmy/John Hillier
July 24: Theophilus Elmer, William Goosey
August 7: Prince/Thomas Plumsted
August 28: Moll/Robert Anderson, John Fullerton
August 28: Joe Lane/Reverend Joseph Teat
September 11: John Johnston/Abia Brown, Joseph Clayton
September 18: Samuel Carruther, Alexander Harvey, Jonathan Vaughan
September 18: Thomas Bishop, Alexander Harvey
October 2: Samuel Logan
October 16: Jem/Mr. Salmon, John Sealy, Joseph Thomas
November 6: Hagar/William Payne
November 6: Jack/Peter Wentz
November 13: Jack/Ephraim Phillips, Peter Wentz
November 13: Ibbe, Sabrah Johnson/Arnold Elzey, Captain George Noarth
December 4: Cato/Samuel Jones
December 11: Cato/Thomas Beech, Samuel Jones, Thomas Pusey
December 18: Charles/Richard Keene

1767

January 1: Sam/Abraham Cunningham, William Denny, Daniel Turner, Ubey
January 8: Glasgow/Alexander Moore, Stephen Reeves
January 8: Charles Cornish/Richard Keene, Ephraim Phillips
January 29: John Lyndsay/Jacob Bachman, John Postlewait
February 5: Gallinda/Laton Albro
February 12: Daniel Edwards/Henry Cunningham, Stephen Mendenhall

March 19: Phill/Thomas Jones, Sr.
March 26: Joe/Robert Duncan, John Strawbridge
April 2: Tom/Andrew Bryan
April 9: Jerry/Henry Elliot, Andrew Lawrenson, Joshua Vanzant
May 7: Tony/Anthony Teate
May 21: London/Gizebert Lane
May 28: Ben/Matthias Bugh, James Campbell
June 25: Dick, Richard/Robert Field
July 2: London/William Gardner, Joseph Thomas
July 16: Charles/Samuel Harker
July 23: Jack, Swacamockhum/George Brown
July 30: Charles/Samuel Harker, Samuel Sharp, Michael Stites, Joseph Thomas
August 6: Charles/Richard James
September 10: Tony/Anthony Teate
September 17: James, Will/Hamilton, Hammil, Daniel Hughes, James Whitehead
October 1: Harry/Levin Crapper, Nicholas Veight, Charles Wharton
October 22: Dick/Jacob Kern
December 3: Cornelius Gollahon/William Hugg
December 10: Jack Hamman/William Coursey, Ephraim Philips
December 17: Dan, Mose/Thomas Ogle

1768

April 28: Jack Hammand/Joseph Haight
May 12: William Sutton/Isaac Antrim, Joseph Thomas
May 26: Peter, Will/Isaac Antrim, Ephraim Seely
June 9: Benn/William Currer
June 9: Jacob/William Cooper
June 23: Isaac/Persifor Frazer
July 7: Esther/John Jackson, Samuel Kennedy, William Kennedy
July 14: Sharper/Alexander Porter

1770

January 11: Cuff/Captain Burn,
John Doyle, Jacob Philimon,
Thomas Pusey, Jonathan Smith
January 11: Jack/Peter Wentz
January 18: Cuff, James Pemberton,
Pen/Thomas Savin
February 1: Joe, John
Mitchell/William Rowan, Esq.,
Phillip Wetheall, James
Whitehead
February 8: Samuel Kennedy,
Samuel Martin
February 8: Jupiter/William
Buchanan
April 12: George Duffee/Joseph
Meredith
April 12: Pedro/Robert Powell
May 10: Dick, John Linch/David
Evans
May 17: Moses Grimes/Henry
Davis, Thomas Minshall
May 24: Dick/Melchior Stecher
May 24: Frank/William Webb
June 7: Harry/John Corrie
June 14: Prince/Joseph Allen
June 21: David/Benjamin Sylvester
June 21: Jack/Joshua M'Dowell
June 28: Mingo, Fanny/Caleb
Hewes, Captain Samuel Hewes
June 28: Lewis/Bright, Pechin,
Jeremiah Poulton
June 28: Philip, Sharper/Timothy
Carroll, Thomas Lennon, Robert
M'Lonan, Samuel Shoemaker, Esq.
July 5: Ben/Daniel Badger, James
MacCubbin, Thomas Renshaw
July 19: Charles Hamilton/Joseph
Garrison, John Spearing
August 2: Tom/Mark Cook, John
Elton, Ann Reardon, Parson
Sturgeon
August 16: William Weathers
August 30: Abel/Thomas Butler
September 13: Jack/Captain James
Potter, Joseph Thomas
September 13: Abel/Thomas Butler,
Joseph Thomas

September 27: Samuel Lefever,
David Watson
October 4: Jack/John Morgan
October 11: Jacob,
Wetheridge/Thomas May
October 11: Will/Daniel Cooper
October 18: Jack/Dorinton Boyle
October 25: Jack/James Potter
November 1: Thomas Bucher/John
Starrett
November 1: Hannah/Nicholas
Cooper
November 8: Paul/John Patrick
November 22: Jack, John
Richison/William Bean
November 29: Toney/Samuel
Paynter
December 13: Bristor/Joseph
Burroughs
December 20: Joe/Henry Stevens

1771

January 3: Moses/Thomas Ogle
January 10: Joe, Prince
Orange/Doctor Sluyter Bouchell,
Mr. Witherspoon
February 7: William Chipley
February 21: London/George Black
March 7: Sam/Stafford Lightburn,
Jr., Charles Yates
March 28: Harman Blake,
Spencer/William Holland
March 28: Brit/Elias Desbrosses,
Esq., Nathaniel Salmon, Jecamiah
Smith
April 18: Jack, Jack, Prudence,
Tom/Widow Bayard, Duncan
Caudon, James Cronhelion,
Thomas Davis, Francis Holland,
Robert Mack, Daniel Turner
May 16: James/Charles Green
June 6: Stanhope/Robert Erwin
June 6: Anthony Sernetor/Casper
Singer
June 13: Jack/William Allen
July 4: Violet/Edward Bonnel,
Philip Kearney, James Lock,
Thomas M'Kean, Esq.

April 17: Toney/James Hinchman,
Joseph Sharp, James Talman
May 1: Ned Levy, Ned/Blathwaite
Jones
May 15: John Brown/Thomas
Dewees, Joseph Milburin
May 22: John, Sally/Mr. Bogle,
Michael Graybill, Samuel Moore,
Joseph Samons, John Tremble
June 12: Limerick/Robert Shewell
June 19: Ben/John Taylor
June 19: Frank/Dominick Joyce,
John Telles
July 3: Ishmael/William Thomas
July 10: Harry/Alexander M'Callum
July 10: Ben/Dr. Seal, James Black,
Charles Heath
July 17: Greg/Mr. Starr, Mr.
Crookshank, Jacob Winey
July 17: Newry, Cuffe/John Jones
July 17: Cuff Dix/Mark Bird
July 24: Ben/John Taylor, [Just
Willis]
July 24: Violet/Anthony Hall,
Christopher Pechin
July 24: Jack, Jacob Kelly/Hugh
Whiteford, William Whiteford
July 31: Moses Graves/Henry
Stevens
July 31: Ned, Ben/Samuel Moore,
Peter Ealer
July 31: Bill, Jerry/Jacob Shoemaker
July 31: Isaac/Robert An[drews],
John Mitchell
August 7: Maria (slave)
August 21: Jacob Johnston/Michael
Graybill, Thomas Kirkly, Lee
Masters, John Miller, Joseph
Miller, Dorcus Perkins, William
Read, Dr. Ridgley
September 4: Cuff/William Read
September 18: Peter/David Franks,
Samuel [Pulvianos]
September 25: Moses/Charles Read
October 2: Alexander Lawson
October 9: Bet/Michael Clark
October 9: Charles Case/Joseph
Pemberton
October 9: William/John C[ox]ros,

Amos Grubbs, Thomas Owings,
Peter Riblet
October 16: Cuff Dix/Mark Bird,
Thomas Clark
October 16: Joe/John Lesher, Jacob
Morgan
October 30: Charles,
Ma[xaline]/John Neveu, Paul
Fooks
October 30: James/William Bryan,
Samuel Morgan
November 6: Tone, Ned/William
Wikoff
November 13: Dick/Rebecca
Turner, Peter Turner
November 20: Jack, George/Felix
Doyle, John Gillis, Samuel
Postlethwait, Samuel Willick
November 27: Caesar/Samuel
Jackson
November 27: Girshon/Joseph Park
November 27: Dick/Alexander Tod

1777

February 5: Jack Jones/Captain
Jones, Elisha Price
March 5: Nancy/Martha Wallace
March 12: Cuff Dicks/Mark Bird,
Thomas Clark
March 19: Tom, Cuff Dicks/John
Clark
May 28: Modo/Thomas A[ud]y,
John Jackson
June 4: Cuff/Henry Burr, Sr.
June 18: James Ellot/John Young
June 25: Greg/Daniel Utrel, Jacob
Winey
July 9: Dick/Robert Robeson,
William Graham
July 9: Ben/Thomas Scott
July 9: S. Thompson
July 30: Jess/Enoch Edwards
July 30: York, Roger/Matthias
Slough
July 30: Nell/John Le Telier,
Thomas Hogelet
August 6: Hannah/Isaac Horner
August 13: Caesar, Tone, Anthony